ROUTLEDGE LIBRARY EDITIONS:
HOUSING POLICY AND HOME OWNERSHIP

Volume 3

RURAL HOUSING: COMPETITION AND CHOICE

RURAL HOUSING: COMPETITION AND CHOICE

MICHAEL DUNN, MARILYN RAWSON AND
ALAN ROGERS

Routledge
Taylor & Francis Group

LONDON AND NEW YORK

First published in 1981 by George Allen & Unwin Ltd

This edition first published in 2021
by Routledge
2 Park Square, Milton Park, Abingdon, Oxon OX14 4RN

and by Routledge
52 Vanderbilt Avenue, New York, NY 10017

Routledge is an imprint of the Taylor & Francis Group, an informa business

British Library Cataloguing in Publication Data
A catalogue record for this book is available from the British Library

ISBN: 978-0-367-64519-9 (Set)
ISBN: 978-1-00-313856-3 (Set) (ebk)
ISBN: 978-0-367-67814-2 (Volume 3) (hbk)
ISBN: 978-0-367-67818-0 (pbk)
ISBN: 978-1-00-313295-0 (Volume 3) (ebk)

Publisher's Note
The publisher has gone to great lengths to ensure the quality of this reprint but
points out that some imperfections in the original copies may be apparent.

Disclaimer
The publisher has made every effort to trace copyright holders and would welcome
correspondence from those they have been unable to trace.

Rural Housing:
Competition and Choice

MICHAEL DUNN
MARILYN RAWSON
ALAN ROGERS

London
GEORGE ALLEN & UNWIN
Boston   Sydney

GEORGE ALLEN & UNWIN LTD
40 Museum Street, London WC1A 1LU

© Michael Dunn, Marilyn Rawson and Alan Rogers, 1981

British Library Cataloguing in Publication Data

Dunn, Michael
   Rural Housing. – (Urban regional studies;
   no. 9).
1. Housing, Rural – England
   2. Housing policy – England
   I. Title II. Rawson, Marilyn
   III. Rogers, Alan, *1945-*
   IV. Series
   363.5'0942   HD7289.G8   80–41944

   ISBN 0–04–309105–9

Set in 10 on 11 point Times by Computacomp (U.K.) Ltd, Fort William, Scotland,
and printed in Great Britain by A. Wheaton & Co, Exeter

Preface

Housing has always featured as a matter of concern for those with an interest in rural social policy. Historically, that concern centred on housing quality and rural living conditions. Today, while poor living conditions can still be found in rural areas (particularly in parts of upland Britain), the focus is rather on inequality of opportunity and the unfair effects of competition for a limited supply of houses in the countryside. In recent years the complaints against the commuter, the second home owner and the retirement migrant have grown steadily, and there has been more and more attention given to the lot of the poorer, locally born or locally employed family.

This study began at a time when many of these issues were of interest only to those professionally involved. It set out to describe the broad structure of housing in rural England and to trace the influence of population migration through the housing stock. The Social Science Research Council had awarded a joint research grant to the Centre for Urban and Regional Studies at the University of Birmingham and the Countryside Planning Unit (now the Department of Environmental Studies and Countryside Planning) at Wye College, University of London, to carry out research in this area of rural policy. This book is a product of that collaboration. The idea for a joint project, bringing together the expertise available at both centres and linking the two areas of research, was essentially that of Gordon Cherry, who has maintained a continuing interest in this study since its inception.

During the period of the study rural housing policy has featured increasingly in public debate and comment. While growing public awareness of an issue may be an encouragement for those involved with research, it brings with it inevitable problems of topicality when policies and views are changing rapidly. The book was completed at a time when a Housing Bill was proceeding through Parliament and undergoing significant modification at the committee stage, which was of great concern to rural areas. By the time it is published, it is certain that there will have been further developments in this crucial area of countryside planning. The book remains, therefore, a statement at one point in time and as such tries to put forward the main issues which are at the heart of a changing situation.

Any piece of research such as this inevitably involves a large number of people. This study has been no exception, and we are very conscious that many people have given freely of their time to help us with our inquiries. Any errors that remain are, of course, our responsibility alone. Equally any views or opinions contained in this report are personal to the authors and do not reflect the position of any outside authority, in particular the

Department of the Environment and the Welsh Office for whom two of the authors now work.

It is impossible to list all those who have helped and with whom we have corresponded and discussed issues surrounding rural housing problems, but particular mention should be made of some.

First, of course, the Social Science Research Council for its generous funding and its willingness to adjust its administrative procedures to the rather odd situation where research was being carried out in two centres.

Colleagues in the Centre for Urban and Regional Studies at Birmingham and the Department of Environmental Studies and Countryside Planning at Wye. Gordon Cherry has already been mentioned, and in addition we are particularly grateful to Gerald Wibberley, not only for his advice, but also for the generous financial help with the production of maps and diagrams for this report. Paul Kentish of the Statistical Unit, Wye College, deserves a special mention for his help with statistical and computing matters.

The officers of Cotswold and South Oxfordshire District Councils, particularly members of the housing departments and especially Mr M. K. Barnett (Cotswold District) and Mr P. Benny (South Oxfordshire District) who willingly answered questions and replied to inquiries throughout.

The many respondents to our household surveys in the two rural areas and representatives of estate agents and building societies.

The twenty-three students of Wye College who enthusiastically and capably carried out the door-to-door household survey in July 1977: Penny Brown, Tim Brown, Chris Butterworth, Colin Cameron, Sarah Clarkson, Nick Collin, Stephen Day, Judith Green, Pip Hayes, Frank Hopkinson, Oriel Kenny, Graham Lacey, Jonathan Leyland, Robert Miller, Tim Mills, Pat Monteath, Jeremy Peters, David Ray, Janet Ridge, Sue Ryder, Sue Stebbing, Hilary Thomas and Toby Veall.

Ken Wass, chief cartographer in the Department of Geography, University College London, who produced the maps and diagrams.

Sam Edwards (formerly Department of the Environment) and Ian Gordon (University of Kent) who allowed us to use data from their joint project on local indicators, without which our national analyses would have been very much the poorer.

Alan O'Dell (Building Research Establishment) for his help in providing data from the DoE House Condition Survey, 1976.

Finally to the secretaries in the Centre for Urban and Regional Studies and in the Department of Environmental Studies and Countryside Planning for their typing and secretarial skills. Special mention must be made of Sue Briant who not only acted as secretary for the entire period of the research, but typed virtually the whole book in its final version.

MICHAEL DUNN
MARILYN RAWSON
ALAN ROGERS

Contents

Part One

Introduction

Chapter 1

Postwar Change in Rural Communities

DIMENSIONS OF CHANGE: FROM SCOTT REPORT TO COUNTRYSIDE REVIEW COMMITTEE

The difficulties caused by the rapid pace of postwar social and economic change in the countryside, especially for the long-standing rural dweller as opposed to the more recent in-migrant from an urban background, have frequently been the subject of a rather ill-defined concern. Yet the essence of the rural problem, despite its changing nature since 1945, can readily be appreciated: conflict arising from competing demands for the use of land and houses in the more accessible areas; concern for the protection of the rural heritage in areas subject to rapid and far-reaching physical change; recognition of the need to maintain employment and the viability of communities in less accessible rural areas with a declining population; and, overall, the emergence in clearer focus of a pattern of advantage and disadvantage among particular groups in the countryside.

It is with the competition between these discrete groups of rural dwellers that this study is primarily concerned. It seeks to examine imbalances between groups in the distribution of financial and other power in the sphere of activity which is central to rural living by analysing the operation of rural housing markets, with particular attention paid to the dynamic and competitive element of the market, namely, household movement.

Competition for rural housing is inevitably at its height in those areas of the accessible countryside which have proved particularly attractive to an increasingly mobile middle class, seduced by the apparent advantages of rural living. Such groups have had the financial ability to establish themselves within rural communities, but such has been their domination of local housing markets that they have created disadvantage for the local population. In particular the young, who are denied the chance of owner-occupation in villages because of vastly increased house prices, inflated to a level well beyond the reach of those in traditional rural employment, and the elderly and poor, virtually trapped in rural areas because they lack financial power, physical mobility and the potential for economic advance, and at the same time have few of the resources which are increasingly necessary for comfortable life in the countryside.

Some of these changes in the social and economic structure of rural areas were foreseen in the work of the Committee on Land Utilisation in Rural Areas (Scott Report, 1942); nevertheless, more than thirty years passed before a further comprehensive examination of the social, economic and environmental problems of the countryside was set in motion in 1974 (Countryside Review Committee, 1976, 1977), and the final output from that review has been disappointing. Research and the development of policy-making impinging upon rural problems have been comparatively scarce in the intervening period, with an emphasis upon fragmentary and unstructured responses to extreme pressures which have manifested themselves in the postwar period, rather than upon sustained and coherent research and policy formulation.

Successive waves of concern, and hence research effort, can be detected in this post-Scott period, beginning with a general concern for the survival of the traditional rural way of life (for example, W. M. Williams, 1956; Littlejohn, 1964; summarised in Frankenberg, 1966). There has followed a recognition of the major problems resulting from the considerable and continuing losses of population in isolated upland areas (H. R. Jones, 1965; Johnston, 1966), conflicts consequent upon the urbanisation of the accessible countryside around London (Pahl, 1965), and second home development in, and retirement migration to, coastal or other attractive rural areas (Bielckus, Rogers and Wibberley, 1972; Downing and Dower, 1973; Karn, 1977). More recently, attention has been focused upon agricultural tied cottages (Gasson, 1975), the difficulties of satisfying local housing need and the problem of poor housing conditions, whether in established settlements or in mobile homes in the urban fringe (Larkin, 1978a).

It is not necessary to review such research in detail here, given the existence of a number of studies dealing with the general field of countryside planning and social change in rural England (for example, Cherry, 1976; Davidson and Wibberley, 1977; Gilg, 1978; Newby, 1979). Moreover the emergence in recent years of a debate on rural deprivation has led to a plethora of reports and position statements rehearsing the arguments in favour of new rural policies and greater financial provision to deal with the problems of rural areas (for example, Hereford and Worcester County Council, 1978; Association of District Councils, 1978; Shaw, 1979). Previous research of particular relevance is in any case comprehensively reviewed in Part Two of the present study.

HOUSING AND HOUSEHOLD MOVEMENT: KEY AREAS OF CHANGE

The overwhelming impression from the list of problems upon which attention has been focused is that pressure upon the housing stock, and in particular the twin themes of access to housing and the movement of households through the housing stock, lies at the heart of many current rural problems. Two examples can be used to illustrate this general point. The issue of local housing need has gained currency with the use of the term, often in a vague and emotive way, in many structure plans, and with the advent of restrictive policies in areas such as the Lake District where the housing stock is limited and under severe pressure for use as second homes. The Lake District planning board solution has been to try to impose agreements under section 52 of the Town and Country Planning Act 1971 which would limit the use of new houses to local people. A number of other local authorities have made similar proposals. But there are many problems to be surmounted in implementing such local need policies, in particular how to define 'local' (living there? working there? a strong local association?) and how to prevent resale to outsiders of housing originally allocated to local people. This whole question of local need has been placed in even sharper focus by proposals for the sale of council houses – proposals which have led to fears that another section of the rural housing stock will pass out of the reach of many rural people.

A second issue, that of worsening housing conditions in established settlements, has been highlighted by publicity given to two particular villages, each of considerable architectural merit and set in an attractive rural area. The villages of Great Barrington in the Cotswolds (one of the two fieldwork areas of the present study) and Great Tew in north Oxfordshire have seen progressive dereliction following from a policy of inaction on the part of private landlords. The owner of Great Barrington village 'does not choose to let or sell his houses' and as a result it is 'quietly dying' (O'Donovan, 1977). Virtually all of the houses which are still lived in are occupied rent-free by retired estate workers, and the implication is that the village will eventually wither away. As Forester (1976) said, 'good houses are going to waste in Great Barrington, and the life of a village is stifled'. In Great Tew the landlord has been concerned to prevent weekenders and speculators from gaining a foothold, but as a result the fabric of the village has been allowed to decay and 'now it is dying ... what has been allowed to happen to Great Tew has made a mockery of the very idea of conservation' (Rocca, 1978). Of the thirty-five houses in the village twenty-two are now unfit for habitation and even the village pub has had to close.

The degree and variety of housing problems in the countryside is therefore considerable, and their solution requires positive and flexible policies tailored to suit the wide range of circumstances of different rural areas. The primary objective of this study, therefore, has been to assist the formulation of appropriate policies by investigating in some detail two previously neglected aspects of changing rural circumstances, namely, the movements of people into, out from, or within the rural area, and the housing environments to which they are attracted or in which they are obliged to remain.

Two complementary approaches are used: desk studies of the national situation and case studies of two particular district council areas, with questionnaire surveys relating to housing and household characteristics and migration behaviour. The desk studies of the national situation include reviews of the literature and appraisals of current thinking. They deal, first, with population change and movement and its influence upon settlement planning (Chapter 2) and, secondly, with the historical development of policies dealing with rural housing (Chapter 3) and more recently the treatment of rural housing as a key issue in those structure plans with a substantial rural component (Rawson and Rogers, 1976; further developed as part of Chapter 10). But the major innovative analysis at the national level involves the development of a classification of English rural districts defined specifically in terms of housing and household characteristics and using data from the 1971 Census in conjunction with data supplied by the Department of the Environment Local Indicators Project (Edwards and Pender, 1976). This work parallels similar studies at the local level and allows an insight into the varying spatial importance of particular factors within the rural housing system (Dunn, Rawson and Rogers, 1980b; see also Chapter 4).

Much of the book, however, concentrates upon two study areas where the compound influences at work in lowland England can be seen. The choice of lowland areas, rather than the upland and marginal hill lands of Wales and Scotland, is justified on a number of counts. These latter have been very well studied in the past, whereas lowland rural areas have been relatively neglected. More important, the Scottish and Welsh uplands show the classic symptoms of rural depopulation and the rundown of an ailing local economy as young people leave, whereas in lowland England the concern applies equally to seemingly prosperous rural areas where local populations are subject to incoming pressures rather than outward attractions.

Two broad complexes of such incoming pressures are recognised and the study areas defined accordingly. First, there are those areas of high landscape quality which are accessible to an urban population and where retirement migrants are also significant. The combination of recreational uses and retired populations produces a vocal and often powerful lobby which is concerned to protect its investment despite the consequences for less powerful groups in the area. The new Cotswold District (formerly North Cotswold, Northleach, Cirencester and Tetbury Rural Districts) was selected. It includes the area which Jackson (1968) took for her study of population in the countryside, and the present study provides an opportunity to update and extend some of her findings. Secondly, there are areas where metropolitan influences are strong, especially from the viewpoint of a commuting population. Although these influences are present in the first area, they are better seen in parts of the home counties; South Oxfordshire District (formerly Henley, Bullingdon and Wallingford Rural Districts) was chosen.

Not only do the case study areas meet criteria related to the size and direction of population change, types of housing, tenure characteristics, and so on, but they also include examples of particular issues which merit closer investigation. The issues considered important by Cotswold inhabitants are conveniently summarised in the survey of public attitudes carried out for Gloucestershire County Council prior to the preparation of the county structure plan (Freeman Fox & Associates, 1976). Among local authority elected representatives housing was identified as the area presenting most problems; the most serious problem was considered to be a shortage of local authority housing, and the other major problems a shortage of privately rented accommodation and lack of suitable private housing. The general public recorded a degree of satisfaction with general housing conditions but considerable concern for some local housing issues, especially the standard of housing in the Northleach area and the cost of private housing around Cirencester. The most important individual issue recognised by the general public, however, was an improvement in the local employment market, with concern over the lack of jobs, the lack of variety of jobs, difficulties faced by school-leavers, and the frequent necessity for long-distance commuting.

Several specific issues arise from the above, including the problems of older privately rented accommodation, especially in the estate villages (as with Great Barrington), and local need problems in a high-price area. Others include the characteristics of the population, and consequent demands upon services, in settlements favoured by retirement migrants, such as Stow-on-the-Wold and Chipping Campden; problems of accommodating institutional populations, including the armed forces (Miller, 1973); and the general problems associated with tied accommodation. In South Oxfordshire other issues such as social tensions in commuter villages, mobile homes and their attendant problems in urban fringe locations in and around the Thames Valley (Department of the Environment, 1977), and environmental problems consequent upon suburban sprawl in the Chilterns (Brett, 1965) assume greater importance, though the concern with local housing problems is equally apparent (Joint Oxfordshire County and Districts General Committee, 1975).

While the case studies make use of census material, the basic source for Part Three of this book is a questionnaire survey of 1,150 households conducted in July 1977 in the Cotswold and South Oxfordshire Districts. Details of this survey can be found in Appendix I. This case study material

is, however, no more than a detailed examination of certain general themes
running through the study as a whole. To recap, Part Two considers rural
population change and movement and rural housing, leading towards an
investigation of the main competitors for rural housing and the
development of the concept of rural housing profiles at the national level.
Part Three consists of a detailed exposition of the results of the case studies,
including an analysis of housing structure at the local level (through the
technique of developing local housing profiles) and a consideration of links
between rural housing and rural households. Evidence for deprivation and
advantage in rural housing based on differing housing opportunities is
assessed and there follows investigation of migration into and out from the
study areas, with emphasis upon motivation and differences between
movers and stayers and between in-migrants and out-migrants. Part Four
takes a view of policies – rural planning and housing policies at the national
level and, in contrast, settlement planning and housing management in local
areas. A final chapter brings together the main findings and policy
implications of the study.

Part Two

Housing and People in the Countryside

Chapter 2

Patterns of Rural Population Change and Movement

The close interrelationship between rural housing and rural population movement, two of the crucial variables in any analysis of social and economic change in the contemporary countryside, has been emphasised in the previous chapter. The intention of the present chapter is to set the discussion in perspective, first, by considering the recent spatial variation in the operation of the dynamic element in the housing process – household movement – and, secondly, by examining possible explanations for movement, both at the level of the individual household and in aggregate, as expressions of regional variations in opportunities and constraints.

Any investigation of historical trends in the volume and direction of rural household movement is inevitably based upon the slenderest of evidence. It can be suggested, however, that movement was intensely local in character and, at least until the growth of large industrial towns in the nineteenth century, consisted largely of a regrouping of the rural population rather than a significant element of rural-urban migration. Certainly the inference to be drawn from early census returns is that any net out-migration from rural areas was at least balanced by a comparatively high level of natural increase, since the total rural population increased slightly during the first half of the nineteenth century.

By the time Ravenstein was listing his laws of migration in 1885 the direction of population change in the countryside had been reversed, with an increasing displacement of the rural workforce from agriculture, brought about by a combination of the after-effects of enclosure and the improvement of agricultural land, and compounded by the drastically reduced demand for labour as a result of increasing mechanisation. This displacement from agriculture, together with a natural drift to the towns in search of higher wages and greater welfare, explained the 'currents of migration' which operated to channel movement 'in the direction of the great centres of commerce and industry which absorb the migrants' (Ravenstein, 1885). In many areas, typically (but not exclusively) those dominated by marginal farming, the pattern of steady rural depopulation continued until the 1920s, although the problem was perhaps not as extensive or as pronounced as was suggested at the time by Masterman (1909): 'rural England, beyond the radius of certain favoured neighbourhoods ... is everywhere hastening to decay. No one stays there who can possibly find employment elsewhere.'

Two new factors conspired to reverse the process of depopulation in at least some rural areas in the period after the First World War. The first of these factors, gradual in its initial effect, was the encroachment of expanding towns upon the most accessible surrounding countryside, a process of suburbanisation which had its origins in the late nineteenth century but which accelerated as a direct consequence of the increase in personal mobility of the burgeoning middle class after 1918. The growth of this new, adventitious rural population was a major influence on the gradual blurring of distinctions between town and country, and an erosion of the character of many rural areas, which were becoming increasingly less recognisable as countryside with each urban-inspired, urban-styled housing development. The second factor, the economic crisis centred on 1929, had a more immediate but equally far-reaching effect in turning urban areas which had hitherto attracted rural migrants because of their greater employment opportunities into depressed areas with high unemployment. As a result of these two new influences there was an apparent reduction in the rate of population loss from the countryside, although this overall reduction masked the enormous variation within rural areas from peri-urban, rapidly expanding, rural districts to isolated and steadily declining rural districts in more remote locations.

CONTRASTING PATTERNS OF CONTEMPORARY POPULATION CHANGE

While there naturally exists a spectrum of recent population change within which it is inappropriate to specify only the extreme situations outlined above, it is nevertheless useful to analyse initially the basic dichotomy between the characteristic patterns of population change in remoter rural areas and in the accessible countryside closer to population pressures emanating from urban areas (House, 1965). In the remoter areas – which, in the British context, can be taken to include most of upland Britain: the Highlands and Islands of Scotland, mid-Wales, much of the Pennines and the Welsh Borders, and parts of Devon and Cornwall, together with less obviously remote areas which are relatively inaccessible, such as parts of East Anglia – the pattern has been one of steady depopulation, often largely as a result of contracting employment opportunities in agriculture. The incidence of such depopulation is to some extent reflected in census returns, which indicate a concentration of population losses in the upland areas described above, characterised by difficult terrain, poor accessibility and marginal hill-farming. Many such areas have recorded intercensal losses of 10 to 20 per cent or more of their population in the twentieth century, with even greater losses among younger elements of the population and higher social classes.

The greatest share of attention has understandably been focused upon marginal areas beset by problems of depopulation and the contraction of the traditional rural economy; not enough, perhaps, has been devoted to the processes and effects of population change in apparently prosperous rural areas which are subject to incoming population pressures rather than to the consequences of outward movements. The composition of these incoming pressures varies with the location and characteristics of the areas concerned, but two specific sets of circumstances can be discerned: first, in areas where metropolitan influences are prevalent and the socio-economic patterns of nominally rural areas may be distorted by the presence of a large commuting population, and secondly, in areas of considerable scenic attractiveness, where recreation and tourist pressures (including pressures for second home development) coincide with pressures for retirement in-migration. In either case one result may be to create a vocal and powerful sectional interest group, composed largely of recent in-migrants, which is concerned to protect its housing and environmental investment, often at the expense of less organised groups in the area. Rural areas which are both attractive and accessible may be doubly assailed by the effects of decanted housing and recreational pressures from adjacent urban concentrations.

This twofold division into depopulation in remote areas and expansion in the accessible countryside is simplistic in a number of ways, and its limitations are especially apparent at local level. Just as there is no such thing as one rural England (R. Williams, 1973), there is little uniformity even among adjacent villages in respect of population trends or socio-economic structure. Among the many factors which tend to induce this extreme diversity are landownership (parishes within commuting range of towns may see little or no development if the land is in single ownership and there is no intention to sell), together with differences in infrastructure provision, local-authority housing policy and planning restrictions, including green belts, national parks and designated areas of outstanding natural beauty.

Simple analysis of trends in total population has further disadvantages since it pays scant attention to the question of motivation of migrant (and, equally important, non-migrant) households, or to the planning response to the problems resulting from different types of population change.

The analysis of population change and movement in remoter and accessible areas, the reasons for household movement and the planning problems which ensue, all of which are discussed in this chapter, are therefore complemented in Part Four by a consideration of settlement planning policies and the way in which they relate to, or attempt to influence, fluctuations in the levels of population in rural areas.

POPULATION DECLINE IN REMOTER RURAL AREAS

Population losses in the British countryside are by no means a new phenomenon: the Black Death in the mid-fourteenth century, the mediaeval enclosure of arable land for sheepwalks and the eighteenth-century creation of parkland all produced shrunken or totally deserted villages (Beresford, 1954; Hoskins, 1955) and less dramatic but more extensive depopulation has been consistently characteristic of disadvantaged rural areas. Census indications of population decline together with the physical manifestations of depopulation, such as decaying cottages and boarded-up schools, have stimulated considerable interest and research in the peripheral rural regions, although emphasis upon the severity of rural deprivation is of surprisingly recent origin, with concern for the rural environment only now paralleled by interest in the social and economic fabric of the countryside.

THE EXTENT OF DECLINE

The incidence of population decline is seen at its most considerable and sustained level in the marginal regions of Scotland and Wales, although the population characteristics of those areas and the implications of population decline for the provision of services and facilities for the residual population are also applicable in large measure to the declining rural regions of England. Consistently high population losses in mid-Wales, illustrated in Table 2.1, have been matched, somewhat unusually, by the political will to reverse the prevailing demographic trend, and thus the area is of particular interest in the present context. The statistics present an overwhelmingly bleak picture, with a decrease of 19·6 per cent between 1901 and 1971; more significantly, however, the distribution of this decrease has been uneven, both spatially and in terms of losses of particular age- and sex-groups, with especially heavy losses of the younger working population in general and females aged 15 to 24 years in particular. The census data confirm the conclusions of the Welsh Office report on depopulation in mid-Wales, that the crucial problem is the loss of the young, especially those 'possessing ambition and initiative, and more particularly those who have attained a high level of education' (Welsh Office, 1964).

Spatial variations in the pattern of recent population losses in central Wales can be ascribed to a number of factors, including the growing popularity of Aberystwyth and the Cardigan coast for holiday and retirement homes, with possibly the first fruits of the growth towns policy, especially around Newtown, contributing to a reduction in the rate of population loss in Montgomery. These improved figures contrast, however, with continuing heavy losses in the more isolated areas which, until the establishment of the Development Board for Rural Wales in 1976, received little or no benefit from the promotional activities associated with the growth towns policy. Furthermore, the statistics in Table 2.1 underestimate the severity of population decline in the rural areas of central Wales because they include figures both for the rural districts and for urban areas where much of the growth (if any) was concentrated.

Table 2.1 *Population changes in mid-Wales, 1901–71* *

Former county	1901	1911	1921	1931	1951	1961	1971
Cardiganshire	61,078	59,879	60,881	55,184	53,278	53,648	54,882
	—	(−1·97)	(1·67)	(−9·36)	(−3·46)	(0·69)	(2·30)
Merioneth	48,852	45,565	45,087	43,201	41,465	38,310	35,330
	—	(−6·73)	(−1·05)	(−4·19)	(−4·02)	(−7·61)	(−7·78)
Montgomery	54,901	53,146	51,263	48,473	45,990	44,165	43,119
	—	(−3·20)	(−3·55)	(−5·45)	(−5·13)	(−3·97)	(−2·37)
North Brecknock†	29,165	27,362	27,634	25,822	25,003	23,952	22,994
	—	(−6·19)	(0·99)	(−6·56)	(−3·18)	(−4·21)	(−4·00)
Radnorshire	23,281	22,590	23,517	21,323	19,993	18,471	18,279
	—	(−2·97)	(4·10)	(−9·33)	(−6·24)	(−7·62)	(−1·04)
TOTAL	217,277	208,542	208,382	194,003	185,729	178,546	174,604
	—	(−4·03)	(−0·08)	(−6·91)	(−4·27)	(−3·87)	(−2·21)

* Figures in parentheses refer to percentage change during the previous decade.
† Defined as Brecknock MB, Builth Wells UD, Hay UD, Llanwrty Wells UD, Brecknock RD, Builth RD, Hay RD.

H. R. Jones (1965), in a study of migration in part of mid-Wales, was able to extend the analysis of causes and effects of population change in remote areas by supplementing census data with information derived from electoral registers and subsequent interviews with key members of the communities studied. He was therefore able to construct not only a statistical impression of change and movement but also an outline of the socio-economic and behavioural characteristics of the migrants involved. The starting point, as with many studies, was an attempt to assess the accuracy of Ravenstein's propositions in respect of migration: primarily that most population movement takes place over short distances, but also that females are more migratory than males, and that currents of migration exist which channel migrants by stages towards the cities (Ravenstein, 1885). But the methods employed allowed a much more complete examination of factors such as the age of migrants, distance moved and motivation, and it is this analysis which is of most interest.

Significant differences were found to exist between out-migrants and in-migrants, thus confirming an impression which still remains valid, namely, that the volume of net migration is only a very limited guide to total migration trends and to the demographic health of an area. Out-migration from the study area was dominated by younger age-groups (62 per cent of out-migrants were aged 39 or under; indeed, 38 per cent were under 25), and out-migration over long distances was even more closely correlated with younger age-groups. Middle age-groups accounted for most of the movement to other places locally, while out-migration by the elderly was specifically directed at local towns, either to hospitals, old people's homes or to be nearer to essential services.

The characteristics of in-migrants, on the other hand, were quite different. The average age of in-migrants was substantially greater, mainly because of the very high incidence of return migration, and a much higher proportion of migrants were of local origin, with two-thirds moving only from adjacent rural districts. The net result was a significant ageing of the population, undermining the delicate demographic balance in the area: thus between 1951 and 1961 the rate of natural increase in mid-Wales was 0·4 per cent, compared with 4·5 per cent for Wales as a whole. This is not to say that the problems of rural Wales are unique. Rees (1978) catalogues a similar range of characteristics for the South Wales valleys, including 'the decline in employment opportunities consequent upon the reorganisation of the coal and steel industries; population decline as a result of both the decline in birth rate and net out-migration; the disproportionate net out-migration of the economically active age groups, leaving behind an ageing population.'

What differentiates rural population decline from its urban counterparts, especially the inner cities and decaying industrial areas, is a combination of its areal extent, the lack of possible employment or other palliatives, and its hidden nature, so that real concentrations of decline and poverty are superficially diluted by the apparently small number affected in any one locality. This is nowhere more true than in the Highlands and Islands of Scotland. In the Scottish Islands alone the population declined from 113,000 in 1951 to just over 93,000 in 1971, a decrease of 17·6 per cent in twenty years. The rate of decline was reduced in the second half of the period, but this was largely attributable to the success of a number of the small towns in stabilising their population, and in the country areas the prevailing trend of steady depopulation remained typical. Despite a number of recent developments, including an increase in tourism and developments related to the North Sea oil industry, together with the creation of the Highlands and Islands Development Board (Grieve, 1972), net out-migration, especially by the young and the able, remains widespread. This demonstrates the substance and the intransigence of the problems of such areas, including the declining demand for agricultural labour, the failure of a number of attempts to introduce small industrial enterprises, the lack of support for new fishing developments and, most of all, the intractable consequences of sheer isolation (Caird, 1972).

Many peripheral areas in England have been just as severely affected by sustained depopulation and its consequences, although the severity of the problem has been recognised and publicised only comparatively recently (see, for example, the Association of District Councils, 1978). The extent of depopulation and underemployment in the north Pennines, for instance, led to the establishment of the North Pennines Rural Development Board in 1969, but despite its apparent success in sustaining agriculture in the area this board was a victim of political change and was wound up two years later (Childs and Minay, 1977).

The former county of Herefordshire has always been conscious of its fringe location within the West Midlands region, a relative location which has led to its almost total neglect by planners preoccupied with the problems of the West Midland conurbation. Indeed its demographic structure has more in common with mid-Wales than with the English midlands. Table 2.2 indicates the extent of the decline in numbers of the rural population, and emphasises in particular the heavy losses characteristic of the more isolated rural districts in the west of the county (Dore and Bredwardine, Kington, and Leominster and Wigmore). When Hereford Rural District, which has undergone considerable growth through the expansion of the built-up area of Hereford city on to greenfield sites outside the former Hereford Municipal Borough, is excluded from the rural district figures the total population of rural Herefordshire can be seen to have fallen by 6,450 between 1951 and 1971, and when the effect of natural increase is extracted, the estimated net out-migration becomes 13,400, roughly 21 per cent of the 1951 population – perhaps the highest rate of depopulation in England during this period (Hereford and Worcester County Council, 1978).

So far the accent has been on population losses in the remoter parts of Britain, including peripheral areas in England (and the northern Pennines,

Table 2.2 *Population change in Herefordshire rural districts, 1951–71*

Former rural district	1951	Change 1951–61 (%)	1961	Change 1961–71 (%)	1971	Change 1951–71 (%)
Bromyard	8,903	− 4·47	8,505	0·68	8,563	− 3·82
Dore and Bredwardine	8,760	− 11·43	7,759	− 6·55	7,251	− 17·23
Hereford	17,489	0·49	17,575	9·52	19,248	10·06
Kington	4,949	− 9·96	4,456	− 11·58	3,940	− 20·39
Ledbury	12,174	− 5·58	11,495	− 2·71	11,184	− 8·13
Leominster and Wigmore	10,506	− 8·60	9,602	− 3·01	9,313	−11·36
Ross and Whitchurch	12,013	− 3·20	11,628	− 2·22	11,370	− 5·35
Weobley	6,450	− 12·62	5,636	0·46	5,662	− 12·22
RD TOTAL	81,244	− 5·62	76,676	− 0·18	76,536	− 5·79
RDs EXCL. HEREFORD	63,755	− 7·30	59,101	− 3·07	57,288	− 10·14

Source: Dunn (1973).

or parts of Devon and Cornwall, would also serve to illustrate this point). But the process of depopulation is also in evidence, with perhaps equally devastating results, in less obviously remote areas which are nevertheless relatively inaccessible to potential rural dwellers. For example, the north Cotswolds (an area considered in detail in Part Three) have been severely affected by the decline of the traditional employment base of agriculture without a concurrent rise in alternative employment or an influx of commuters, since regional centres and good communications are too far away (Jackson, 1968). Sustained and substantial net out-migration has been characteristic of the high, undulating sheep-farming country of the central Cotswolds, and the evidence suggests that this emigration has been mainly of young people.

The incidence of depopulation in an apparently prosperous region has been examined further by Drudy (1978). Taking the example of North Norfolk, he demonstrates the advances in farming techniques characteristic of a prosperous agricultural region, and the resultant rapid decline in employment prospects, with widespread redundancy in agriculture and insufficient alternative employment to absorb the surplus released from farming. During the 1960s, 32 per cent of all workers leaving a sample of farms did so because they had been made redundant, principally because of the substitution of capital for labour on the larger farms. Depopulation was therefore widespread between 1951 and 1971, with smaller communities affected most severely, and the rate of decline actually increased during the latter half of this period.

EXPLANATIONS FOR POPULATION DECLINE

The census data outline the extent of the problem, but are unable, except indirectly, to suggest who the migrants were in terms of age, sex, socio-economic status, and so on, and are completely unable to shed light on one crucial aspect of population movement: reasons for migration. Local surveys, though less comprehensive, are clearly needed to supplement the bare numerical representation of movement in the census. In the case of Herefordshire, a questionnaire survey in twenty-four parishes confirmed intuitive impressions of many characteristics of the migrants, but was also able to demonstrate the complex nature of migrant decision-making (Dunn, 1979). There was a substantial loss of younger households (48 per cent of out-migrants were aged under 45, compared with 41 per cent of in-migrants) and a significant negative correlation between age of head of household and distance moved. The classic symptoms of rural decline – a tendency for the population to become increasingly male-dominated as a result of lack of employment opportunities for women and the net out-migration of women on marriage, together with an ageing population – were very much in evidence.

A summary of the primary causes of household movement is given in

Table 2.3; the comparison between out- and in-migrants is particularly instructive. Any interpretation of reasons for movement is, however, subject to the cautionary note that such decision-making is often complex, usually influenced by multiple factors, and occasionally incapable of rational explanation. Employment and housing reasons may therefore be regarded purely as convenient generic labels concealing a considerable variety of detailed motives, and the interplay of different reasons may render general classification of limited value in explaining individual choices. Accepting the limitations, however, a number of tentative inferences can be drawn from Table 2.3, to be refined by reference to individual responses.

Table 2.3   *Primary reasons for movement in Herefordshire, 1966–71*

Reason	Out-migrants (%)	In-migrants (%)	In-migrants as % of out-migrants
Employment	33·7	32·0	95·0
Housing	27·7	32·9	118·5
Marriage	11·7	8·7	74·3
Retirement	8·8	10·0	113·6
Relatives/friends	11·2	12·2	108·8
Education	0·2	0·2	100·0
Other	6·6	4·0	60·6

Source: Dunn (1979).

The proportion of moves attributable to employment reasons is surprisingly low; House (1965) found that 72 per cent of his sample in north-east England were motivated by employment factors. However, the inclusion in the Herefordshire survey of migration over very short distances tended to emphasise the importance of house availability and underlined the contrast between long-distance, job-oriented out-migration among younger households and housing-related movement over much shorter distances by more established households. The net gain of households motivated by housing reasons is attributable to the process of regrouping inherent in an area where housing opportunities were limited (that is to say, where particular types and sizes of house, and particular tenures, were locally in short supply) and local authority allocation and new-build policies were geared to concentration in a small number of settlements. Employment reasons were, however, rather more common in triggering household movement, reflecting the lack of job opportunities in a relatively remote area which was subject to contracting demand for agricultural labour and unassisted by central government regional policy. Net out-migration upon marriage re-emphasised the lack of variety of jobs (and housing), and the gain of moves upon retirement and by elderly households to friends, relatives or old people's homes re-emphasised the progressive ageing of Herefordshire's population.

Two insistent causes of out-migration, dissatisfaction with employment opportunities and with the availability of housing, may well provide the primary motivation for people to move from remoter areas, but a further crucial factor which may underlie a significant proportion of moves is the low, and still contracting, level of provision of many basic services in more isolated areas (Standing Conference of Rural Community Councils, 1978). House (1965) found that among potential migrants from north-east England the desire for better transport services and shopping, educational and social facilities was a significant reason behind the decision to consider household movement. This perception of disadvantage is the inevitable consequence of the reduction of many rural services, a process that has occurred sometimes as a result of conscious planning and sometimes as a response to economic forces. But the concentration of services into a few settlements often has the effect of accelerating the rate of loss from other settlements in the area, since in these communities 'the provision of services to the residual population becomes increasingly unsatisfactory and a further cause of rural discontent' (House and Knight, 1965). Corroboration of this last point was provided by Lee (1960), who found that the rate of out-migration from a village increased shortly after the closure of the school in that village.

It could therefore be concluded that there are three major factors which explain flows of population out of, into, and within remoter rural areas: employment, housing and social provision. Employment-related reasons include the diminishing demand for agricultural labour, the lack of sufficient and suitable alternative sources of employment and the dearth of jobs for women in rural areas. Housing factors are centred around availability, with house condition, tenure (a particular problem concerning tied cottages, where Cowie and Giles, 1957, found 'an element of fear and insecurity' among older tenants) and location of prime importance. The low level of social provision and especially the withdrawal of existing services and facilities is the third important influence upon levels of out-migration.

To conclude that these three sets of factors are all-important, however, would be to assign too much weight to the environment in which rural households operate, and would emphasise external factors at the expense of equally significant social and individual factors affecting the household's propensity to move. This second set of internal individual characteristics includes age, sex, marital status, presence or absence of dependents, occupation and income, and perhaps may best be integrated into a cohesive explanatory framework for household movement through a consideration of the relationships between migration, household structure and the stages of the family life-cycle.

Family life-cycle theory has provided a popular approach for researchers interested in the differential use of the housing stock and has been used particularly to hypothesise about the moves which households make between different types of housing. Most life-cycle models have been developed in an urban context. A good summary of the general picture is provided by the simple five-stage sequence suggested by Donnison (1967):

1   For about the first twenty years children live with their parents.
2   An increasing proportion spend a brief period living alone or sharing accommodation with friends after leaving the parental home for study or employment. The first few years of marriage is a continuation of this phase. The household is small and mobile and with both partners out working the home is not the centre of their lives.
3   When the first child is born the household's need for space and other facilities increases during this expanding phase.
4   The phase when all or most of the children leave home results in a small remaining household unless increased by elderly relatives. Although households are now less dependent on the local community and its services because they are well established in their home and the area movement is less likely than in phase 2.
5   In old age households become smaller, less mobile, and more dependent on local services and the support of relatives and friends.

This simple outline of life-cycle models has been elaborated in a number of ways. It has been agreed that older households tend to be less mobile than younger households (Cullingworth, 1968) and that in consequence the final movement stage noted above may not take place (Needleman, 1965). Equally, surveys have shown that whereas households may move to increase housing space as families grow they tend often not to move to economise on housing space as families contract (Nationwide Building Society, 1970). Older households, therefore, display an inertia with regard to housing resources which leads inevitably to underoccupation (Golant, 1972). Certainly the evidence in the following chapter, which links older households in rural areas with underoccupation, would seem to confirm this view. Another view of housing movement has been put forward by Doling (1976), who has argued that moves must be seen in the context of capability and access to housing and that changes in housing, particularly for owner-occupiers, are to be related to the accumulation of wealth as the family cycle moves on. Changes in family structure may precipitate a desire to move, but this can only be realised if the financial resources are available.

Few researchers have explicitly considered the role of rural areas in any model of housing and life-cycle theory. Clearly one aspect would be the tendency among middle-class urbanites to move from city locations out into the countryside rather than the suburbs. Another would be the trend for older households which had lived in the city to retire to the countryside once the children had left home and employment had ceased. But there are contrary flows as well, particularly of indigenous young rural couples who fail to gain access to the various sectors of rural housing and who, perhaps in consequence, migrate to the towns in search of wider opportunities.

Although the life-cycle approach is of limited general applicability because of its reliance upon housing motivations, it is of particular value in understanding migration because it identifies the situations in which the likelihood of migration is comparatively high. If information detailing the propensity to migrate of particular households at particular times is integrated with more general factors relating to job opportunities, house availability and social provision, it should prove possible to consider migration as a household's attempt to optimise its social and environmental satisfaction (Simmie, 1972) by trading off its values and aspirations against economic and locational realities. Inevitably such optimisation is constrained by financial limitations, familial links and other restrictions, and to a large extent only the 'migratory elite' (Musgrove, 1963) is in a position to take this course of action, leaving lower-income households, who are financially unable to move despite the incentive to do so, stranded in declining rural areas.

The underlying cause of dissatisfaction for many out-migrants from remoter rural areas is undoubtedly the widening gap between urban and rural levels of living: an amalgamation of differentials in, for example, employment prospects, social life, available facilities and relative prosperity. Where such urban/rural differentials are at their greatest, the rate of depopulation is also likely to be highest; further, it is most likely to be at its most selective, with dissatisfaction and the decision to move away varying according to factors such as age, sex, level of education, marital status, social class. The probability of out-migration is greatest among the single, educated, young and higher-income groups with weak familial links. To a great extent these form the mobile element of the population identified by Dickinson (1958), who suggested that settlements 'contain a stable element of varying size, and that the high migration rates derive, to a large extent, from the continued turnover of population among a mobile element; migrating population frequently staying in a village for only a short while'.

This notion of a division between movers and stayers in any community is by no means novel (Blumen, Kogan and McCarthy, 1955) but has an engaging simplicity and has been demonstrated in a number of empirical studies. It has been found that the propensity to migrate out of a settlement is highest in smaller settlements, those furthest from towns, and those in which a declining agricultural base is still prevalent (Dunn, 1979). Johnston (1967) was able to classify the population in his study area in terms of their length of residence in Nidderdale. Fifty-two per cent of the population had lived at the same address in Nidderdale for ten years or more despite high rates of population turnover. The impression was one of very considerable movement among the mobile element of the population, with population change related as much to the settlement pattern and the process of suburbanisation as to employment problems.

The different characteristics of movers and stayers, and the relative size of the two groups in the population, are of crucial importance in explaining patterns of movement (C. Jones *et al.*, 1976) and the case studies in Part Three are therefore designed to incorporate this point. The interaction between housing and employment aspirations, satisfaction with present environment and life-cycle variables affecting the probability of movement is different for each household, and produces a decision to move or not to move which is perhaps most easily understood in terms of its effect than its genesis. In remoter communities the effect is more often than not to generate a group of stayers which contains higher than average proportions of low-income groups, lower social classes and older age-groups, and which has a greater need for community services but a declining ability to support them. A self-perpetuating vicious circle of decline may therefore become characteristic of the depopulating remoter areas (Myrdal, 1957) unless policies are evolved to counter the causes and effects of decline.

THE ACCESSIBLE COUNTRYSIDE: PRESSURES FOR GROWTH

Rapid population growth was characteristic of the major industrial cities in the late nineteenth and early twentieth centuries. After the First World War, congestion and the shortage of building land in the urban areas, allied to the preferences of the newly mobile middle class for more space and a supposedly rural way of life, resulted in a population explosion at the suburban edge of cities and in the accessible countryside. Uncontrolled development in the countryside was by the 1930s using up some 60,000 acres of farmland each year, much of it of high quality. This unprecedented land-take (unsurpassed in the post-Second World War growth period), coupled with the effects of urban sprawl and associated traffic congestion and environmental pressure, brought demands for local government reform and a co-ordinated planning framework. But it also underlined the fundamental trends of the interwar and early postwar periods: 'population moving *into* the great urban regions, and simultaneously *out* of their congested inner areas and *into* their suburban fringes' (Hall *et al.*, 1973).

The extent of the suburban fringe, the area accessible to those retaining their employment, shopping and possibly recreational links with the city but deciding to occupy housing in its hinterland, has grown as personal mobility has increased, as the pressure on the most accessible areas has inflated house prices, and especially as planning restrictions on the suburban fringe have intensified. This is notably true of those urban areas now encircled by green belts, first encouraged in 1955 and much criticised for their purely negative function (White and Dunn, 1975). In keeping towns apart and preventing further peripheral development from encroaching into the countryside, green belts have been distinctly successful

– the protection of the countryside between Birmingham and Redditch, despite the repeated attempts of Birmingham City Council to build at Wythall (Long, 1962) is a notable instance. They have had the effect, however, not of dissipating the demand for rural housing but merely of transplanting it, with developers and house purchasers able and willing to move outside the green belt and build even further from the cities.

All this leads to the conclusion that the 'accessible countryside', an elegant concept but one whose definition and spatial demarcation is, like 'rural England', surprisingly elusive, does in fact extend over virtually the whole of lowland rural England, with some differentiation in the pressures exerted and in their effects, largely as a result of variations in their accessibility to nearby urban areas. Location relative to motorways and the primary route network is therefore crucial in determining the extent and type of pressures for growth, although other secondary influences include attractiveness for recreational use.

The accessible countryside, with its attendant problems of population growth and competition for a limited stock of rural housing, therefore includes the commuting hinterlands of the major cities (and, in the case of London, this encompasses most of rural south-east England, including the greater part of Kent, Surrey, East Hampshire, Berkshire, South Oxfordshire and much of Buckinghamshire, Hertfordshire and Essex), with additional areas along main rail or road corridors. It also includes some areas of particular attraction to retirement migrants, notably the suburbanised fringes of many south coast resorts.

During the 1950s and 1960s the conurbations, notably Greater London and Greater Manchester, were steadily losing population at a time when the population of their suburbanising hinterlands was increasing more rapidly than anywhere else in the United Kingdom. The 1961 Census confirmed that the population of the rural districts of England and Wales had increased from 8,420,000 to 10,770,000, an increase of 35·8 per cent, in the preceding ten years. In the rural parts of the home counties the growth amounted to 800,000 – a third of the total increase in Britain. By 1971 the major change in south-east England was that the areas where the greatest increase was recorded were 40 miles or more from the centre of London; yet, despite the 1947 planning system, this population growth had been accommodated not in new towns but in privately built suburban developments within and, more commonly, outside the green belt. Throughout wide areas of southern, midland and north-west England population gains of 20 per cent or more were commonplace in the period 1961–71: much of Sussex, Berkshire and other London commuter counties, Worcestershire and Warwickshire in the West Midlands, and Cheshire and Lancashire in the North West followed this pattern.

The population of Cheshire, for example, grew by 175,000 between 1961 and 1974 to a total of 905,000 in 1974, largely as a result of planned overspill into the new town of Runcorn and town expansion schemes at

Winsford (which alone grew from 13,000 to 27,000 in this period), Widnes, Ellesmere Port, Crewe and elsewhere. There was, however, a parallel move into low-density, high-quality private housing in the rural areas of Cheshire, particularly around Macclesfield, Chester and Ellesmere Port. The original development plan for the county recognised the potential demand for sites for speculative house-building and hence included large residential land allocations in these areas. The need to decant population from the crowded inner cities took priority over the protection of both countryside and communities in the urban fringe.

Lower birth rates and a new emphasis on urban regeneration in the strategies for the conurbations (Merseyside County Council, 1979, for example) have allowed a re-examination of the effects of previous policies, a number of which are now felt to have resulted in an unbalanced population structure and high house prices (Cheshire County Council, 1977), to the detriment of the original rural population. Since the expectation both in the short and the medium term is for levels of population growth far lower than those experienced in 1966–74, when net in-migration alone averaged 8,000 a year (one-third from Merseyside), the opportunity exists to reduce residential land allocations and consider the implementation of a local needs housing policy or some other mechanism to safeguard the interests of the indigenous population – if indeed this is a legitimate objective.

While there are aggregate data available with which to implement a crude analysis of the scale of suburbanisation of the English countryside, it remains true to say that 'there is an obvious and desperate need for studies of rural areas in England and Wales which are experiencing acute pressures as a result of population growth and economic prosperity' (Edwards, 1973). The early investigations of W. T. Martin (1957), who concluded that the influence of an urban area declined evenly from the centre to the edge of its hinterland, and Wissink (1962), who recognised in the rural-urban fringe an area of heterogeneity lacking such consistent gradients of influence and development, should have been followed by detailed examinations of the mentally urbanised, but physically rural, parts of the countryside (Constandse, 1962); but more than a decade after the pioneer studies of the accessible countryside in south-east England there is little other than incidental evidence of the process and effects of the urbanisation of these rural areas.

First among these initial case studies was the one carried out by Pahl (1965) in Hertfordshire. He selected two green-belt villages, located in the metropolitan fringe some 25 miles north of central London, which had experienced considerable recent population increase. The context for the study was the massive, and to some extent planned, decentralisation of London from its congested core into the rural-urban fringe and particularly into what Pahl termed the 'inner country ring', which recorded a population increase of 585,000 between 1951 and 1961 – a proportionate increase of 46·5 per cent. Little more than half of this increase was accounted for by planned dispersal into the eight new towns in the area, so that existing towns and villages in the suburbanising countryside accepted a largely unplanned influx of about 240,000 people in ten years.

The implications of population pressures of this scale range beyond traditional morphological and functional changes to pose a fundamental challenge to the social and community structures of settlements whose small size renders them particularly vulnerable to dramatic change. These changes were made all the more pressing as a result of the policy adopted by Hertfordshire County Council which aimed to stabilise the population of the county at around one million. The consequence of this action, which was founded on a restrictive attitude to development proposals in and around the green belt, included the distortion of the housing market in the green belt with high and rapidly increasing house prices; the diversion of development pressures to accessible areas immediately outside the green belt; and a population explosion in certain villages in nominally rural areas, despite apparently rigid development control. This phenomenon has been repeated in national parks and other areas which either have a high landscape value or, because of their location, are vulnerable to pressures for development (Gregory, 1972).

Pahl was able to illustrate significant differences between newcomers and the established population in his rapidly developing Hertfordshire villages; the differences related to background, occupation, lifestyle and aspirations. This dichotomy between newcomers and established residents was brought into sharpest focus, however, in respect of social class differences, with an influx of professional, middle-class households competing with the skilled or unskilled manual workers who formed the indigenous population. It became clear that in-migration into the urban fringe was increasingly the prerogative of the middle class, who had the financial ability to pay not only the extra cost of housing but also the extra costs of travel to work. The vast majority of commuters were drawn from the middle-class newcomers, many of whom had previously lived in London and still worked there. Increasingly, therefore, 'rural-urban fringe parishes are attracting mobile middle-class commuters who live and work in distinct and separate social and economic worlds from the established populations'.

Not only was there little evidence of an integrated community structure in these areas of suburbanised countryside, either in terms of micro-spatial coexistence or social groupings, but there was also a clear indication of a balance of disadvantage for the indigenous population as a result of recent change. The proposition thus emerged (Pahl, 1966) that the working class was economically constrained as a result of remaining in the countryside, largely because it was unable to compete successfully with incoming middle-class households. The cutting edge of disadvantage was the gradual reduction in housing choice for lower social groups, purely as a result of house price inflation caused by the in-migration of an affluent, mobile middle class into accessible areas.

The survey *Village Life in Hampshire*, carried out by Mass Observation (1966) at about the same time as Pahl was investigating the metropolitan fringe in Hertfordshire, was able to confirm a number of his conclusions although the extent of urban influence was considerably less because of the greater distance from London. No typical pattern of rural life could be discerned, and indeed there were more similarities than differences between town and village life, and variations *within* villages in respect of, for example, occupational groups, place of work, reasons for living in the village and social activities were greater than variations *between* villages. This is not to say that rural life is indistinguishable from urban life, but that 'their coincidences over-ride their contrasts to a much greater extent than popular or professional sentiment is prepared to allow' (I. Martin, 1976). In the Hampshire study only the higher social groups referred to the distinctive qualities of rural life as a reason for moving into a village, and these supposed qualities had motivated only 27 per cent of these groups; other reasons for movement were markedly more prosaic. The inference is that it is a fundamental error to represent the village as an idealised average, since its inhabitants in no sense form a cohesive, homogeneous group.

This impression of villages in the accessible countryside as heterogeneous, almost amorphous, collections of households whose coexistence is fortuitous is less evident from other studies, notably that of Stratfield Mortimer in Berkshire (Crichton, 1964). Specifically designed to assess the degree of integration of newcomers into the life of a village which was fast becoming a dormitory settlement for Reading and London commuters, this study also sought to stress the better features of village life whose existence might be threatened by rapid and large-scale suburbanisation. This stance pre-empted discussion of the utility or distinctive nature of rural community life but nevertheless a number of significant trends emerged.

The central conclusion was that newcomers did indeed acquire a sense of identity with the village and valued their association with specific aspects of community activities. Such assimilation, however, was a slow process and confirmed the impression that integration into the community varied directly with length of residence. Conversely, the newcomers were the group of residents most implacably opposed to any further housing development, presumably on the grounds that any further expansion would dilute the rurality which they had sought in moving to Stratfield Mortimer. It was suggested that the present population of around 2,000 was optimal in that it was sufficient to ensure the survival of facilities such as shops and public transport, yet was small enough to enable traditional rural values to survive. Less emphasis was laid upon the dramatically changed context in which those traditional rural elements now existed and the fundamental changes in the rural economy which had already occurred in order to accommodate the influx of newcomers. Crichton was convinced, however, that if expansion was controlled and gradual 'there [was] no reason to expect the commuter to be less well integrated than the local worker'. Even so, uninspired local planning had created a physical separation between private and council housing, and between newcomers and established – classic conditions in which the class segregation identified in Hertfordshire could operate.

An example of the sheer distance over which urban-generated housing demand, constrained by green belt restrictions and conurbation land shortages, was able to exert its influence is provided by an analysis of housing pressures in villages in Worcestershire in the 1960s (Radford, 1970). Diverted beyond the green belt, developers reacted by providing housing for a considerable distance beyond its outer edge on any site with reasonable services and accessibility. Kempsey, one of the villages studied by Radford, had seen the construction of two large housing estates in the early 1960s and had become, functionally as well as morphologically, a distant suburb of Worcester. The other village, Martley, had seen comparatively little development, with a much higher proportion of its population employed in agriculture and the remnants of traditional village form and life still extant.

Surprising similarities between the two communities were discovered: in-migration to both villages was motivated by house availability over short distances and by employment reasons for those moving from further afield, especially from the West Midland conurbation. Radford concluded that differences were largely those of scale, and that the two settlements represented different stages in the process of suburbanisation: Martley was a dormitory for some urban households but retained its essentially rural functions and outlook, while Kempsey functioned more as a suburb of Worcester despite the retention of some rural attributes. In both cases the integration of newcomers into the life of the village was considered to have been comparatively successful, perhaps partly because of the local origins of many in-migrants.

Thorns (1968) recognised the accelerating pace of change in a village which was transformed into a reluctant suburb of Nottingham when its comparatively slow rate of population increase in the immediate postwar years was followed by a doubling of the population between 1951 and 1961. He reported that 'this migration from the city was once more predominantly middle-class and its advent led to the creation of separate groups of newcomers and established'. The activities and attitudes of the new in-migrants were still oriented towards the city, while the established population viewed the village very differently as a community. The result was conflict and separation rather than the cherished ideal of integration, begging the question as to what extent the pace of change rather than change itself was responsible for the disintegration of village social life which appears to have occurred in many of the settlements examined.

It becomes clear that the process of urban decentralisation, complex though it is, has several key parameters which influence the relationship between the forces responsible for the suburbanisation of the accessible countryside and the effects of such suburbanisation. Crucial factors include the pace of change, the consequent distortion of the housing market, the extent of pressures from potential second home owners, the prevalence of commuting and the operation of planning policies, particularly in areas where these policies, by their restrictive nature, exacerbate the effects of other factors. The problems of the indigenous population, and hence their reactions to incoming pressures, hinge upon these primary factors.

Local reaction against housing pressures probably reaches its most intense level in those areas where demand for second homes is highest. In the Lake District Bennett (1976) found that 10 per cent of the dwelling stock had been acquired by second home owners, and the proportion rose to one-third in certain attractive, accessible parishes. In the Lleyn peninsula in north-west Wales the overall proportion rose to 17 per cent in Dwyfor District and 46 per cent in the parish of Llanengan (Gwynedd County Council, 1978). In this latter case further grounds for differentiation between newcomers and established are added, with particular problems caused by distinctions of language, culture and religious observance (Lewis, 1967). Infiltration by newcomers into social and community life is not universally welcome, although some protection is afforded by the practice (unique in Wales) of Dwyfor District Council, which adopts Welsh as its official language for all internal business. These are extreme examples in the locational sense, but the impact of second home owners can be even more severe where they are competing for houses in areas where commuters and the indigenous population are already in the market. The Peak District affords one example, and this theme will be considered further in subsequent chapters.

Clearly the growth of second homes can pose a threat to the continued existence of some places as permanent settlements, with a seasonal extension of suburbia destroying the foundations of community. In this context recent estate developments consisting purely of second homes, as at Port Dinorwic in Gwynedd, can be a useful means of diverting pressure from the general housing market. The more fundamental expression of the decentralisation of the city, however, is the vast quantity of permanent outward migration which has had such far-reaching social and physical consequences for the English countryside.

The physical consequences of suburbanisation have been moderated by the rigid application of policies restricting scattered development (Ministry of Housing and Local Government, 1969), in direct contrast to, for example, the Irish policy of favouring new housing in the open countryside. This has resulted in a strengthening of the pattern of nucleated villages in lowland England – again an environmental achievement of some merit compared with, for instance, the bungalow-and-glasshouse landscape which is so characteristic of inland Guernsey. There is less merit, perhaps, in the consequence of this type of policy in that it divides up the built rural environment into quite distinct areas of old-established village nucleus, peripheral local authority estate and peripheral or freestanding private housing estate, all inhabited by people with different characteristics and outlook.

The foregoing analysis rather overemphasises the inbuilt forces for change in the countryside, since one of the fundamental conclusions to be drawn must be the remarkable variety of recent patterns of change, with adjacent villages experiencing completely different pressures, often purely as a result of the historical accident of a particular form of landownership. Jennings (1968), for example, recognises that 'some villages are almost untouched, some have new commuter communities, some are almost swallowed up by neighbouring towns', observing that while there tends to be a nucleus of old-established residents in many villages in the accessible countryside the numbers and influence of this nucleus are usually on the decline, and the inevitable result of increased affluence and mobility is the demise of the village as a closed, stable community.

The weight of numbers involved in this colonisation of the countryside near towns is almost impossible to assess, given the inadequacy of recent census statistics, tied as they were to increasingly irrelevant administrative areas. It is certainly possible to overstate the case; in one view, 'it is by now clear that the greatest part of the inhabitants of British rural areas are either ex-urbanites, with households from which one or more travel every day to work in towns, or else they are retired folk who lived and worked in towns before coming to the rural areas where they are now rapidly buying up property vacated by people who formerly worked on the land' (Radford, 1970). Nevertheless there are crucial problems caused by the imbalance of needs and demands resulting from the extra pressure on the housing stock in certain areas: the problems faced by the children of established residents, who find it increasingly difficult to compete for rural housing and may tacitly accept the situation and move to the town, are representative. In this case the twin consequences are extra out-migration of younger people and a further encroachment of the commuting middle class.

Not only is there a displacement of population on an age-selective basis, but there is also a parallel relocation or cessation of many traditional rural activities. Particularly hard hit are local shopkeepers, whose trade suffers as the proportion of residents who are accustomed to shopping in larger outlets in town increases; but there are similar repercussions for public transport operators in rural areas where the level of car-ownership is rising, and for suppliers of specialist services, many of them dependent upon a dwindling agricultural trade. The newly-arrived ex-urban rural dwellers, attracted by peace and quiet, space and especially by their idealised conception of traditional country pursuits and the associated social life, may find to their chagrin that their arrival precipitates the destruction of precisely those elements of rural life which they were seeking.

In summary, therefore, the encroachment of urban pressures for growth upon wide areas of the accessible countryside has had a number of far-reaching consequences, with rapid population increases leading to suburbanisation and loss of identity and rural character for many previously distinct settlements. Frequently growth has been insensitively managed, with the plantation of middle-class commuter communities in developments alien to their surroundings within or adjacent to existing villages, which has resulted in difficulties of integration between established residents and newcomers. These difficulties are aggravated where there is a displacement of disadvantaged sections of the established population as a result of the pressures on a limited housing stock. The use of planning controls in these areas of pressure is a further element in creating problems for certain sections of the population, and even where restrictive green belt or landscape policies apply, they are effective only in creating privilege within certain specified areas and in redistributing the problems of pressures for growth in an intensified form to other accessible but unprotected rural areas.

In direct contrast to the problems of pressure and growth in the countryside around the major urban areas are the difficulties faced by the remoter areas, as indicated earlier in this chapter. In these areas the problem is caused by age-selective migration activated in many cases by a perception of widening urban/rural differentials, with the recognition that the more isolated areas of countryside will become progressively more disadvantaged. Expressions of this cumulative decline include the withdrawal of public transport, the concentration of facilities and public utilities in a very restricted number of settlements and the problems faced by residual retail and other services. This economic retreat from less favoured rural areas will inevitably result in depopulation, augmented by discontent with the lack of employment opportunities and weighted towards younger, educated, single and middle- or higher-income residents whose links with the area are comparatively weak. A period of sustained and selective out-migration may therefore produce a residual population dominated by the elderly and the poor, with greater need for community services and less ability to contribute towards their provision.

Without intervention to prevent a continuing polarisation there would appear to be a real prospect of the emergence of two totally distinct types of countryside, differentiated purely in terms of the consequences of relative location. The accessible countryside would be subject to unprecedented and ineluctable population pressure, without adequate control mechanisms to prevent development; the remoter areas, shorn of younger and skilled workers, variety of employment and provision of services, would be trapped in a vicious circle of decline.

Chapter 3

Rural Housing: a General View

A HISTORICAL INTRODUCTION

The impact on the accessible countryside of a migratory urban population which was outlined in the previous chapter is a relatively recent phenomenon in any historical perspective upon rural housing. Until perhaps the last two decades problems of rural housing were conventionally equated with issues of housing quality. The absence of physical amenities such as piped water or proper sewerage systems, the squalor of dampness and mould and gross overcrowding with children sharing parents' rooms were the focus of concern for rural reformers until at least the late 1940s, often coupled with a related concern for moral standards (Aronson, 1913). Indeed it is fair to argue that the increasing involvement of both local and national government in rural housing affairs particularly since the end of the First World War was a direct recognition of these physical problems. It is only in more recent times that such concern has tended to move away from physical conditions towards an involvement with the differential access to housing of particular social groups and the attempt to meet housing needs in a situation of what some would regard as unfair competition.

The appalling state of much rural housing at the start of the twentieth century contrasted with the idealised picture which many people had of country living. Then, as now, rural life was glorified both for its simplicity and its gentle rusticity. This view is still with us and is of course a major explanation for the postwar exodus from our towns. The idea of the countryside as an attractive antidote to the horrors of urban living is basic also to some strategies of urban planning, notably the idea of decentralisation and the new town philosophy. Although Ebenezer Howard fully recognised that some of the problems of rural housing rivalled urban slums his remedy centred upon a version of rural living with people attracted by the 'country magnet' to the 'natural healthfulness of the countryside' (Howard, 1902).

A preoccupation with housing quality and an idealised view of rural living were two themes in the general attitude to rural housing at the start of the present century. A third theme was the presumption that the provision of housing in rural areas was entirely the province of the private landowner. Since for the majority of the working population rural living was naturally equated with rural employment, it followed that housing was generally provided by the private landlord. The involvement of public authorities was unknown except in the limited and degrading context of the parish poorhouse.

PUBLIC HOUSING, 1919–30

Just as concern over housing quality has been superseded by concern for social equity and for countryside protection, so has the notion of rural housing as a private good tenanted to a working population been overtaken by the idea of owner-occupation for a burgeoning rural middle class on the one hand and public provision of rented property on the other. The second of these changes, the involvement of national and local government in the construction and control of rural housing, was the first influence to be felt. Although some houses had been built by local authorities under the Housing Act of 1890, it was the Housing and Town Planning, etc., Act of 1919, popularly known as the Addison Act, which first encouraged local authorities to build houses for the working population.

The Addison Act was generally responsible for about 34,000 houses built by local government in the designated rural districts of England and Wales (Central Housing Advisory Committee, 1944) and it set a trend for the period between the wars. It is reckoned that some 160,000 houses were built by the rural districts during this period. This was perhaps only one-fifth of all houses constructed in the period 1919–39 but it can be argued that this number had an influence out of all proportion to its size. For the first time public housing was introduced into the countryside in significant numbers in many areas and often only the smallest villages failed to get their quota. Council houses, frequently grouped in a little estate or strung out along a main road, became a common sight and one which was distinct both architecturally and socially from the rest of the village.

A further 64,000 houses were built by the designated rural districts under the provisions of the Housing Act 1924, the so-called Wheatley Act. The 1924 Act made a distinction between agricultural houses and houses for general needs, and the former attracted a larger subsidy from the Treasury. None the less it is doubtful whether this distinction made a significant impact upon the problem of housing the agricultural worker. Many rural districts were still reluctant to build houses and in many rural authorities no building at all was carried out during this period (Marshall, 1968). Rural building costs were certainly high but probably a more important factor was the reluctance of local councils (which just as today were frequently controlled by local landowners) to create an extra charge upon the rates. Moreover the low level of agricultural wages meant that farmworkers could not easily afford the rents charged for the new council houses.

As well as providing for the construction of new houses the interwar legislation also tried to tackle the major problems of overcrowding and poor housing conditions. The Addison Act had contained some provisions to encourage reconditioning but the first real attempt in this direction was the Housing (Rural Workers) Act of 1926. This allowed a grant of up to two-thirds of the cost of improvement, subject to a ceiling of £100. Its effect was, however, mitigated by further provisions in the Act which restricted the rent charged on the improved property to agricultural levels. Although this was an understandable attempt to ensure that the benefit accrued to the working population rather than city migrants, it resulted in fewer landlords taking up the grants than had been hoped.

The Housing Act of 1935 was particularly concerned with the relief of overcrowding. A survey following this Act reported more than 40,000 overcrowded properties in England and Wales. Paradoxically public authority houses were recorded as generally being more overcrowded than private houses, a situation that still persists today though on a much reduced scale. Special subsidies were made available to rural districts to build cottages for farmworkers in order to relieve overcrowding and in the period until the outbreak of war over 8,000 houses were built.

Official reports on the working of interwar legislation to improve housing were frequently critical of the overall level of success. Then, as now, there were some rural districts which failed to respond at all to any of the newly improved statutory duties. Many authorities built no houses and many more fell down on their responsibilities to inspect properties. In part this was perhaps because of the reluctance of many rural district councillors to view housing provision as a legitimate area of public investment. Housing for a working population was still regarded by many as the responsibility of employers and the inevitable cost upon the rates of council houses was resented.

It should also be added that local authorities were often ill equipped to carry out their new tasks. Housing departments were either non-existent or were poorly staffed. The inspection of properties, particularly in remote rural areas, was a time-consuming process and it was perhaps understandable that by the outbreak of the Second World War many rural areas were little influenced by the trend towards public involvement in housing matters.

It has been argued that the introduction of council housing into many areas of rural England in the interwar period was a matter of major significance. As will be seen when the involvement of today's local authorities in rural housing is considered, the patterns then established remain. There still are enthusiastic rural authorities which have built large numbers of houses and others which have been noticeably reluctant.

Equally, the emerging professionalism within housing departments is more evident in some authorities than in others. Finally, there can be seen the influence of local councillors, often antagonistic to the very concept of council housing in rural areas and therefore reluctant to interfere with the operation of the private market and to vote substantial sums of money in that area.

PRIVATE HOUSING BETWEEN THE WARS

While government involvement after 1919 introduced a major social and political element into housing in rural areas private housing was numerically dominant. More than four-fifths of all new houses in the rural areas of England and Wales were built by private builders for the private market – a proportion which has generally been maintained ever since. Some of these private houses were built under the subsidy provisions of the housing legislation already referred to. This only accounted for perhaps 135,000 houses out of a private enterprise total of over 700,000 for the period, but it should be noted that this was only 25,000 houses fewer than the number built by the designated rural districts.

The interwar period saw a massive exodus of urban dwellers to the countryside. Land was cheap and relatively unfettered by planning regulations. Speculative building was particularly characteristic of the urban fringe where an economically weak agriculture looked a poor alternative to house-building. Not surprisingly this period recorded the greatest average annual loss of farmland to urban development ever seen (Best, 1976). The vast majority of private houses were built in the newly emerging suburbs on the urban fringe. As such they were often only nominally in the countryside, despite the attempts of enthusiastic developers to stress the rurality of parts of the home counties or Cheshire. In the postwar period many of these areas have been subsumed within the administrative boundaries of the towns.

The effect on the existing problem of housing in the rural areas was slight. It did nothing to improve conditions for the average rural family. New houses were built for new residents in the accessible countryside around the major cities and to a lesser extent in the small towns and larger villages which were blessed by a railway station with a service to town. In the more isolated areas the influence of the private builder was even less important and it was not until the greater mobility of the postwar period that these areas of countryside were to be similarly affected.

A secondary influence of rural house-building in this period was the introduction of what would now be regarded as distinctly alien house designs which clashed with the vernacular architecture of those small towns and villages that did expand. Though the styles of the 1930s, mock-Tudor and debased forms of 'art and craft rurality', have their enthusiasts, many people would argue that they were intrusive and unacceptable forms for the countryside. The relatively strict controls upon house design that were subsequently introduced, particularly in areas of great scenic value, can be seen as a direct result of the *laissez-faire* approach between the wars, just as at a more general level the strict control of rural development maintained by planning legislation since 1947 reflected a general concern for farmland loss and urban sprawl.

POSTWAR DEVELOPMENTS

By the middle of the Second World War over 870,000 new houses had been built in the designated rural districts. Nearly 30,000 houses had been demolished since 1919 and another 22,000 had been reconditioned under the 1926 Housing Act.

And yet as the nation turned its mind to postwar reconstruction, the state of housing in rural areas was still viewed with alarm. Moreover the concern was still centred around housing conditions and the quality of rural life. The Scott Report expressed its concern for the thousands of houses which were still without piped water or electricity. Accommodation was cramped with much overcrowding, particularly in sleeping arrangements. Many cottages still had only one or perhaps two rooms downstairs with at most a wooden partition to separate off the living area from the kitchen and scullery. Food storage facilities were often non-existent and toilet arrangements were a rudimentary earth closet in the garden.

These complaints were echoed by others at the time. In a series of reports produced in the late 1940s, the National Federation of Women's Institutes reported on the reactions of their members to poor housing conditions as well as issues such as bad roads, poor sewerage facilities and no streetlighting. One of the most illuminating accounts came from the agricultural economist C. S. Orwin. Writing in 1944 he reported on a study of an area of north Oxfordshire which considered housing as part of a wide-ranging survey of social and economic conditions (Oxford Agricultural Economic Research Institute, 1944). He was appreciative of the work done by some rural districts acting under the housing legislation between the wars, but he was forthright in drawing attention to the remaining problems of rural housing.

Two years later the Central Office of Information took Orwin's report as the basis of a film setting out the nation's task for rural reconstruction. Anyone looking at that film today would have difficulty in recognising the area. To those born since, say, 1950 the housing conditions portrayed seem as remote as those of the nineteenth century. Cottages were substantially built but they frequently remained in the structural condition in which their original builders in the sixteenth and seventeenth centuries had left them. Families of six shared two small bedrooms which were difficult to clean because they had no ceilings and were poorly lit. Downstairs, cooking was done on a paraffin stove or an antiquated range separated from living quarters by a thin partition. The front door led from the living room straight into the unpaved road. There was no running water, no bathroom and often not even a sink. All hot water had to be heated on the stove and in some places drinking water from polluted wells and springs had first to be boiled; slops had to be emptied in the garden.

Only a generation later a restudy of the area recorded a total transformation in the housing conditions of the population (Bates and Cudmore, 1975). With few exceptions, all the houses were in a condition which compared favourably with urban areas. Concerns for housing quality had been replaced with the modern worries of commuters and second home owners: the destruction of the community spirit and the housing access problems of young couples.

The paradox behind this transformation lies in the fact that virtually none of the changes in the intervening thirty years can be accounted for by government legislation aimed specifically at the housing problems of rural areas. While the various interwar Housing Acts often singled out rural areas for special treatment, there were only a few cases after 1945, such as tied cottages in agriculture, and then only in relatively recent times.

The explanation for the changes in rural housing conditions is basically twofold. First, of course, legislation passed to deal with problems in housing as a whole, and not just in rural areas, has benefited the countryside. Legal requirements to improve housing have at least in part been matched by the financial resources to do so and by the growing professionalism of housing managers. Planning, which as will be seen later may have had adverse effects in restricting housing development, has certainly had a beneficial influence in preventing sprawl and in maintaining standards of design. Many rural authorities still have a very bad record in building houses and the national ratio of public to private house-building remains at about the prewar level of 1:5. Yet the houses that have been built since 1945 have frequently been of a higher standard, owing to Parker-Morris guidelines, than many private houses.

But the second part of the explanation for the improvements since the Second World War has to do with private investment. Expectations as to acceptable levels of housing quality have risen in the last thirty years just as have the incomes needed to translate ideals into reality. The population of rural areas in England and Wales increased by two and a half million people in the period 1951–71, and a high proportion of this increase was accounted for by a migratory urban middle class, eager to invest its money in rural property. Moreover, local authorities have been able to help this desire by the provision of improvement grants, even if there are doubts about the extent to which such aid has been a major force in initiating the improvement in the quality of the housing stock and about the distribution of such benefits among different social groups.

This historical background to housing in rural England has necessarily stressed inadequate housing conditions as being the most important issue until quite recently. As the next section of this chapter records, there were still about a quarter of a million houses in rural England and Wales which were judged as unfit in 1976 (DoE, 1978). Notwithstanding criticisms of the unfitness standard adopted, there is powerful evidence of a massive improvement in rural housing standards, fuelled largely by private investment, since the end of the Second World War. Though housing quality necessarily remains a focus of some concern, the basic question behind much of what follows is: a massive improvement – but for whom?

THE NATURE OF RURAL HOUSING

The increases in population in many rural areas which were mentioned above and which provided a major theme for Chapter 2 have naturally had a more elementary influence than the improvement of housing standards. A population increase in English rural districts of 30 per cent (2·3 million people) between 1951 and 1971 has been reflected in an even greater rate of increase in the number of rural dwellings as headship rates have increased and more households have been formed.

This increase in the housing stock has been in large part accounted for by private development. For each local authority house built in rural areas over this period some five or six houses have been built for the private sector. Immediately, then, any attempt to understand the structure of rural housing comes up against a basic dichotomy in the tenurial status of housing. The discussion must therefore start with an understanding of rural housing tenure.

RURAL HOUSING TENURE

Three broad sectors characterise the British housing system – owner-occupation, local authority renting and private renting. In common with the country as a whole, rural areas have seen a marked increase in the first group which has been paralleled by a decline in the last group. Council tenancies, as was seen in the previous section, are a more recent phenomenon, dating in general only from the interwar period. In 1971 rather more than one in five houses in rural England belonged to the local authority (Table 3.1) and the proportion has probably changed little since that time. This figure is noticeably lower than for the nation as a whole where the larger municipal housing stocks of urban authorities, particularly in Scotland, increase the local authority element to about one in three.

Privately rented housing has always been of great importance in the English countryside. In Scotland and Wales, where farms have generally been smaller and based essentially on the family, owner-occupation has been more significant in backing up the rural economy. By contrast in England, where farm businesses have traditionally employed more labour,

Table 3.1 *Housing tenure in English rural districts, 1971 (%)*

Tenure	English rural districts	England*		Great Britain
Owner-occupied	54·5	50·0	(54·4)	48·3
Local authority	21·1	28·0	(29·8)	30·4
Private rented (unfurnished)	20·9	17·1	(10·9)	16·7
Private rented (furnished)	3·3	4·7	(3·5)	4·5
Not stated or other	0·2	0·2	(1·3)	0·1

* 1977 figures in parentheses.
Source: Census, 1971; 1977 figures from Department of the Environment (1979a) *National Dwelling and Housing Survey.*

particularly in the more prosperous lands of the south and east, the privately rented cottage has been an essential component of the agricultural economy. The massive decline in agricultural labour during the present century has reduced this important link, but rural areas still show a higher proportion of privately rented houses than do urban areas, and in 1971 the numbers of privately rented houses were in excess of the local authority element in the total housing stock. The absence of a 1976 census means that any decline in the proportions of privately rented housing since 1971 cannot accurately be gauged. However, sample data from the 1977 *National Dwelling and Housing Survey* (Department of the Environment, 1979a) for England as a whole are shown in parentheses in Table 3.1, and suggest, along with other evidence, that a substantial reduction has occurred.

Figure 3.1 shows the pattern of dominant tenures in English rural districts as it was in 1971. It records all those districts where the proportions of houses in the four main tenure groups were at their highest, that is, districts which were in the upper quintile division of the frequency distribution for each tenure group. Owner-occupation was concentrated especially in the accessible countryside, particularly around the north-west conurbations and to the south and east of London. Similarly, local authority housing was more common around the major urban centres, notably north of London, south of Manchester and in South Yorkshire, and around Tyneside. Districts around the Wash also scored highly in this regard. Elsewhere local authority housing was often related to development on the edge of expanding towns (for example, Ashford, Kent; Swindon, Wiltshire) and was far less common in the more remote rural areas.

The continued importance of privately rented property in rural areas, which was referred to above, is also emphasised in Figure 3.1. Large areas of the north of England, together with concentrations in Herefordshire and other rural counties like Dorset, Suffolk and the counties of the South West, had high proportions of unfurnished lettings, often tied to local employment

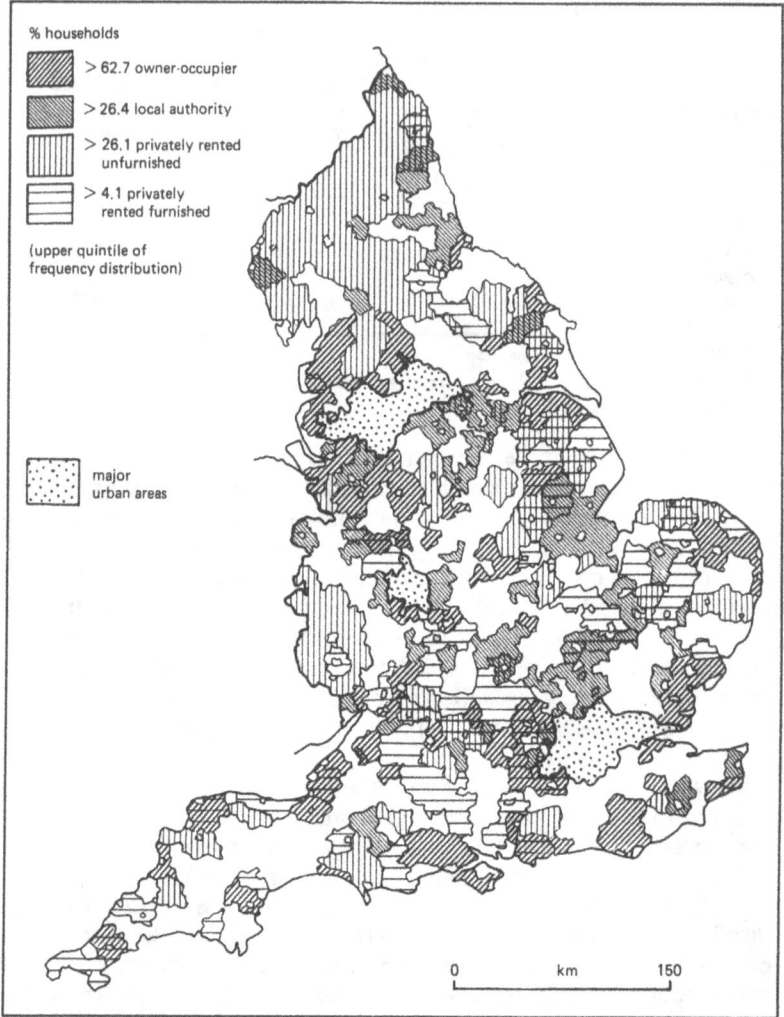

Figure 3.1   *The dominant pattern of rural housing tenure, England, 1971*

in agriculture. Furnished lettings were less common in rural areas than in towns and cities, but some districts recorded a substantial proportion of their housing stock in this sector: for example, Barnack RD (now Cambridgeshire), 38·4 per cent; Oakham RD (Rutland), 26·4 per cent; Amesbury RD (Wiltshire), 28·4 per cent; and Richmond RD (Yorkshire NR), 33·4 per cent. Invariably the high proportions in these districts relate to houses rented by armed service personnel living on or near important army or air force camps. The distribution of this sector around Salisbury

Plain, in Lincolnshire and in North Yorkshire illustrates this point. Elsewhere smaller concentrations of privately rented furnished property, where perhaps 10 per cent of the housing stock was involved, may well relate to private second homes and holiday homes available for summer letting, particularly in Devon and Cornwall.

THE QUALITY OF RURAL HOUSING

The early part of this chapter emphasised the historical importance of rural housing quality and the tremendous improvement in rural living standards during the last thirty years. It was argued that this improvement reflected both the effects of private investment in rural property and the influence of government legislation to improve housing standards, especially through local authority activity. The end result is that rural housing standards as a whole are now significantly better than those in urban areas and the countryside compares favourably with the nation as a whole (Table 3.2).

Table 3.2 *Housing quality in English rural districts, 1971 (%)*

Quality	English rural districts	England		Great Britain
Households lacking exclusive use of one or more basic amenities*	13·8	17·6	(5·8)†	17·5
Non-permanent buildings	1·3	0·5		0·4

* Basic amenities = hot water, fixed bath or shower, inside toilet.
† 1977 figure in parentheses.
Source: Census, 1971; 1977 figure from Department of the Environment (1979a) *National Dwelling and Housing Survey.*

Yet some rural areas fare much worse than the average suggested by Table 3.2. Judged, for example, by the rather crude index of households lacking one or more of the basic housing amenities, there were still areas in 1971 where up to a third of the housing stock was deficient: for example, Sedgefield RD (Co. Durham), 30·1 per cent; Dore and Bredwardine RD (Herefordshire), 28·8 per cent; Ashby de la Zouche RD (Leicestershire), 27·0 per cent; and Hepton RD (West Yorkshire), 29·6 per cent. Significantly, those areas which have lagged behind the general trend towards improvement are to be found in the remote countryside – in Cornwall, Devon, Herefordshire, Shropshire, Norfolk, Derbyshire and parts of northern England (Figure 3.2). It is clear that housing quality is still poor where the old rural economy remains, where newcomers from the town have been relatively few in number and where local authorities, for one reason or another, have been less able to enforce higher standards. Something of an exception to this general rule relates to those areas often close to towns where there are substantial concentrations of mobile homes,

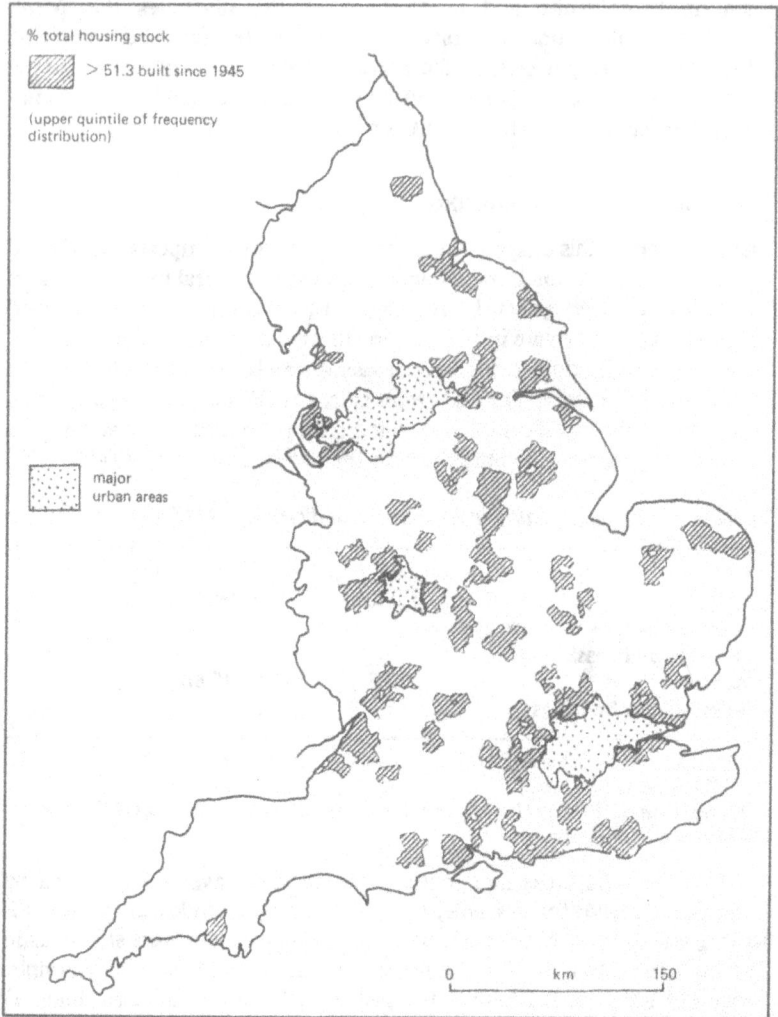

Figure 3.2   *Rural housing quality – housing lacking basic amenities, 1971*

notably in counties such as Lancashire, Bedfordshire, Berkshire and Oxfordshire. Rural England has a significantly higher proportion of these non-permanent dwellings (Table 3.2) which, though they can have high housing standards, tend also to contain notable examples of very bad conditions.

It is certain that housing conditions have continued to improve since the 1971 Census. The English national figure for 1977 given in Table 3.2 certainly confirms this view. It is likely, however, that while there has been some improvement, it has been at a much slower rate than during the 1960s. Moreover it is clear from other sources that certain areas of poor housing still remain. The particular concentration of poorer housing covering much of the (former) county of Herefordshire in 1971, for example, has been subsequently highlighted by a report on the Rural Community Development Project (Hereford and Worcester County Council, 1978). The report recognises housing as one of eight areas of need which relate to an assessment of rural deprivation within the county. Two district councils in Herefordshire have carried out sample surveys of housing in their districts which certainly suggest that standards are still very poor in some areas. In 1975 South Herefordshire District Council found out that 15 per cent of their sample were unfit and a further 12 per cent lacked one or more basic amenities, and these figures were regarded as probable underestimates of the problem. Similarly, Leominster District Council reviewed thirteen parishes around Kington in 1975 and found that 19·4 per cent of houses were unfit.

More recent data on housing quality can be found in the *English House Condition Survey, 1976* (Department of the Environment, 1978). This is based on a sample of some 9,000 dwellings in 215 local authorities and the survey recognises 'rural areas' as settlements of up to 1,000 houses and isolated dwellings.

Unfit dwellings are defined by the survey according to the Housing Act 1969 (section 71) where it is stated that an unfit house is one deemed to be so far defective in one or more of the matters specified as not to be reasonably suitable for occupation. These specified matters are repair, stability, freedom from damp, internal arrangement, natural lighting, ventilation, water supply, drainage and sanitary conveniences, facilities for the preparation and cooking of food and for the disposal of waste.

Nearly one-third (28·2 per cent) of all unfit dwellings in England were to be found in rural areas and 5·6 per cent of the total rural housing stock was found to be unfit (Table 3.3). Indeed in contrast to previous surveys where rural areas had generally shown up better than urban areas, the 1976 survey suggested that a higher proportion of rural houses were deficient than in towns and cities. Since the previous survey in 1971 the number of unfit houses in rural England was estimated to have declined by 12 per cent, a less substantial decline than in the previous period when, between 1967 and 1971, the reduction had been no less than 46 per cent. While it must be borne in mind that these figures are only based on a sample, they do suggest that rural housing improvement has slowed down noticeably since the 1960s. Between 1971 and 1976 both public and private purses were hit hard by inflation. While housing certainly remained a safe repository for private investment, owners were inevitably less willing to spend large sums in renovating old properties. Equally, rural housing authorities felt the financial squeeze, particularly after 1974 with the changes in the Rate Support Grant (see Chapter 10).

Table 3.3   *Rural housing – some quality comparisons, 1976 (thousands)**

Quality	Conurbations	Other urban areas	Rural areas	England
Fitness standards				
Unfit dwellings	315 (4·8)	255 (3·9)	224 (5·6)	794 (4·6)
All dwellings	6,598 (100·0)	6,534 (100·0)	3,983 (100·0)	17,115 (100·0)
Lack of amenities				
Inside WC	456 (6·9)	397 (6·1)	230 (5·8)	1,083 (6·3)
Fixed bath in bathroom	347 (5·3)	273 (4·2)	180 (4·5)	800 (4·7)
Wash basin	455 (6·9)	345 (5·3)	191 (4·8)	991 (5·8)
Sink	6 (0·1)	13 (0·2)	24 (0·6)	43 (0·3)
Hot and cold water at 3 points	525 (8·0)	417 (6·4)	231 (5·8)	1,173 (6·9)
One or more of the basic amenities	677 (10·3)	529 (8·1)	287 (7·2)	1,493 (8·7)
All dwellings with or without amenities	6,598 (100·0)	6,534 (100·0)	3,893 (100·0)	17,115 (100·0)

* Figures in parentheses are % of all dwellings in the area.
Source: Department of the Environment (1978), *English House Condition Survey, 1976.*

This point is illustrated in another way by Table 3.4 which gives details of estimated repair costs, again from the *English House Condition Survey, 1976.* Whereas only 11 per cent of dwellings in urban areas had estimated repair costs of £1,000 or more, the corresponding figure for rural areas was 16 per cent. The explanation lies partly in the age of the housing stock, which is significantly greater in rural areas. This in turn often means that major reconstruction is needed to improve housing conditions, especially if houses have to be re-roofed or ceilings raised to conform to present-day standards. These estimates of housing quality and repair costs will be returned to later in this chapter when the relationship between rural houses and rural households is considered.

The age of the housing stock in itself can thus be a crude indicator of housing quality and of the problems of rehabilitation. Surveys conducted by the planning authority in Norfolk, for example, showed that half the rural housing stock was built before 1900 (Green and Ayton, 1967) and the regional estimates made in 1964 by Stone (1970) recorded similar figures for predominantly rural regions. The corollary of this point can be seen in Figure 3.3 which uses data from the DoE Local Indicators Project to record those rural districts which have particularly benefited from housing construction since 1945. With relatively few exceptions the rural areas which have gained are in the accessible countryside, in particular around the conurbations and large towns. Elsewhere housing investment has been at a lower rate and the average age of the dwelling stock remains high.

Table 3.4 Estimated housing repair costs, 1976

Estimated repair costs	Rural areas			Conurbations			Other urban areas			England		
	No.	%	% dwellings in each row	No.	%	% dwellings in each row	No.	%	% dwellings in each row	No.	%	% dwellings in each row
<£250	2,478	62·2	22·0	4,186	63·4	37·2	4,586	70·2	40·8	11,250	65·7	100·0
£250–£499	767	19·3	24·5	1,293	19·6	41·2	1,076	16·5	34·3	3,136	18·3	100·0
£500–£999	93	2·3	18·9	249	3·8	50·5	151	2·3	30·6	493	2·9	100·0
£1,000–£1,999	254	6·4	22·4	522	7·9	46·1	357	5·5	31·5	1,133	6·6	100·0
£2,000–£2,999	148	3·7	32·1	154	2·3	33·4	159	2·4	34·5	461	2·7	100·0
£3,000–£3,999	74	1·9	27·4	79	1·2	29·3	117	1·8	43·3	270	1·6	100·0
£4,000 +	169	4·2	45·4	115	1·7	30·9	88	1·3	23·7	372	2·2	100·0
ALL DWELLINGS	3,983	100·0	23·3	6,598	100·0	38·6	6,534	100·0	38·2	17,115	100·0	100·0

Source: Department of the Environment (1978), English House Condition Survey, 1976.

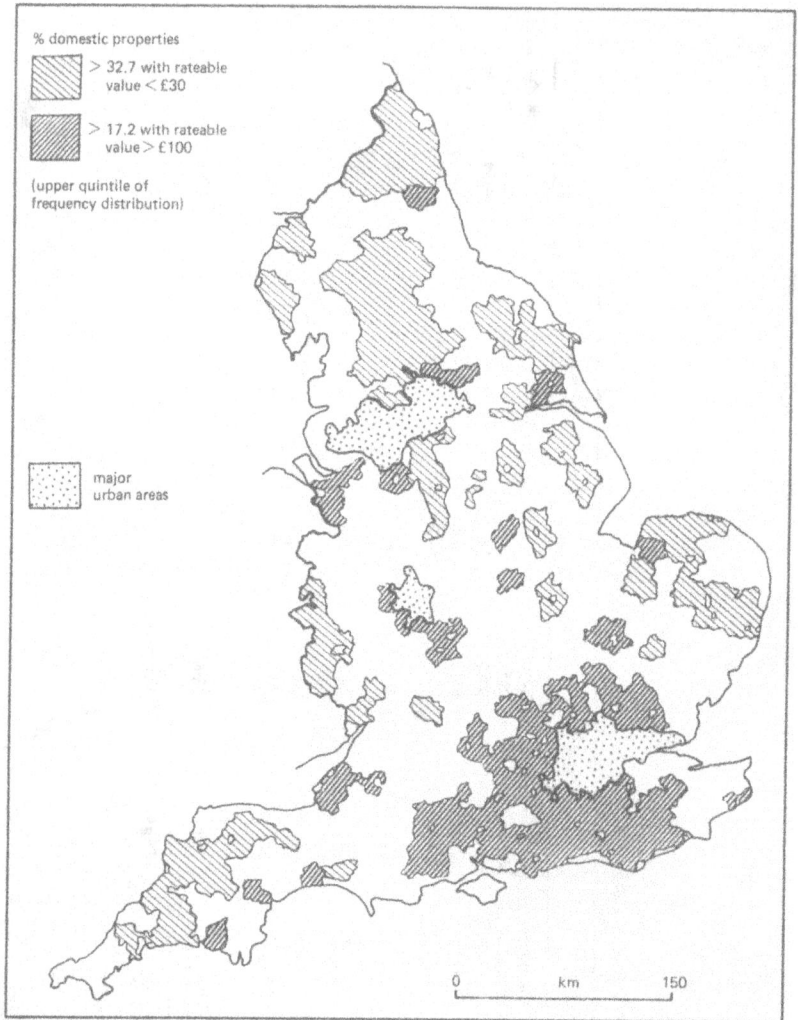

Figure 3.3   *Major areas of post-1945 housing development*

A final indication of housing quality can be gained from a study of domestic rateable values. The link between quality and rateable value is somewhat tenuous but it provides a useful guide nonetheless. Rateable value broadly reflects a local assessment of housing in relation to a theoretical rent which the property could be expected to produce, bearing in mind its size, condition, amenities etc. Again using data from the DoE Local Indicators Project, Figure 3.4 illustrates the extremes which existed in 1971, recording areas of high rateable value (> £100 in 1971) and those of low rateable value

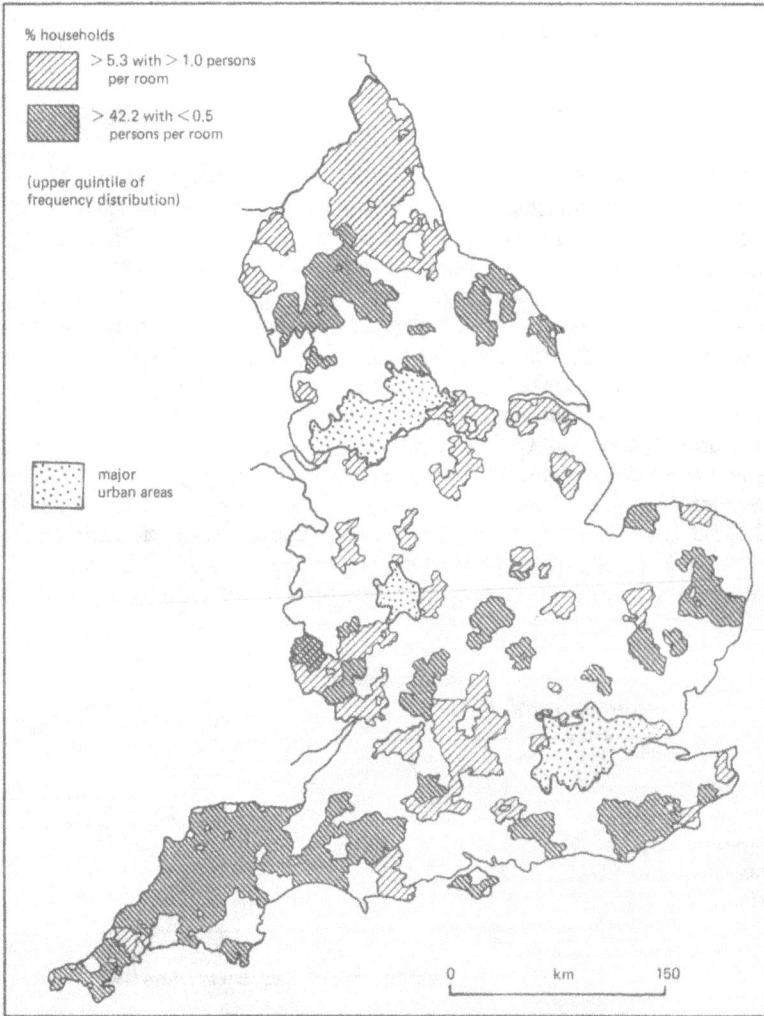

Figure 3.4 *Rateable value of rural housing, 1971*

(<£30 in 1971). The outer metropolitan region and more prosperous rural areas of Hampshire, Cheshire and south of Birmingham contrasted strongly with the remoter areas of the north Pennines, North Yorkshire, and large parts of East Anglia, the Welsh Borders and Devon and Cornwall. Over and above any indication which this contrast may give of relative housing quality it also emphasises the problem faced by many rural areas of a low return from domestic rates. The significance of this point in relation to low budgets for housing and other sources and consequent dependence upon financial support from central government to make up the deficit will be made clear as this study progresses.

RURAL HOUSING AND RURAL HOUSEHOLDS

This discussion of the nature of the rural housing stock has so far largely ignored the relationship between housing and the households which occupy it. In its simplest form this relates the numbers of people in a household to the available rooms. Conventionally, occupancy rates in excess of 1·0 persons per room are regarded as indicating a level of overcrowding, and conversely rates below 0·5 persons per room imply underoccupancy and relatively inefficient use of the housing stock. The limited data available from the census suggest that rural areas suffer less from the problems of overcrowding and sharing facilities which are a particular problem in inner city areas (Table 3.5). On the other hand underoccupancy is a problem in some rural areas, especially when elderly people occupy unsuitably large accommodation which is expensive to maintain. None the less, as Figure 3.5 indicates, overcrowding is an issue in some areas, particularly in the north of England, though in 1971 only two rural districts (Whiston RD and Morpeth RD, Lancashire) recorded proportions of overcrowded households of 10 per cent or more.

Table 3.5   *Occupancy rates and households sharing facilities in English*
            rural districts, 1971 (%)

Occupancy rate and sharing	English rural districts	England*	Great Britain
Overcrowding (>1.0 p.p.r.)	4·4	6·0 (3·1)	7·2
Underoccupancy (<0.5 p.p.r.)	37·9	33·9 (39·6)	32·7
Households sharing facilities	0·5	4·4	3·6

* 1977 Figures in parentheses.
    Source: Census, 1971, 1977 figures from Department of the Environment (1979a) *National Dwelling and Housing Survey.*

Underoccupancy is much more characteristic of the rural housing stock, a large number of areas having between 40 and 50 per cent of their households living at densities of less than 0·5 persons per room. The elderly populations of the South West of England, the southern Lake District, North Yorkshire, Herefordshire and parts of the South East and East Anglia include a high proportion of one- and two-person households, often occupying relatively large houses.

It is argued elsewhere that tenure status is perhaps the most significant characteristic of households. An illustration of its importance can be seen

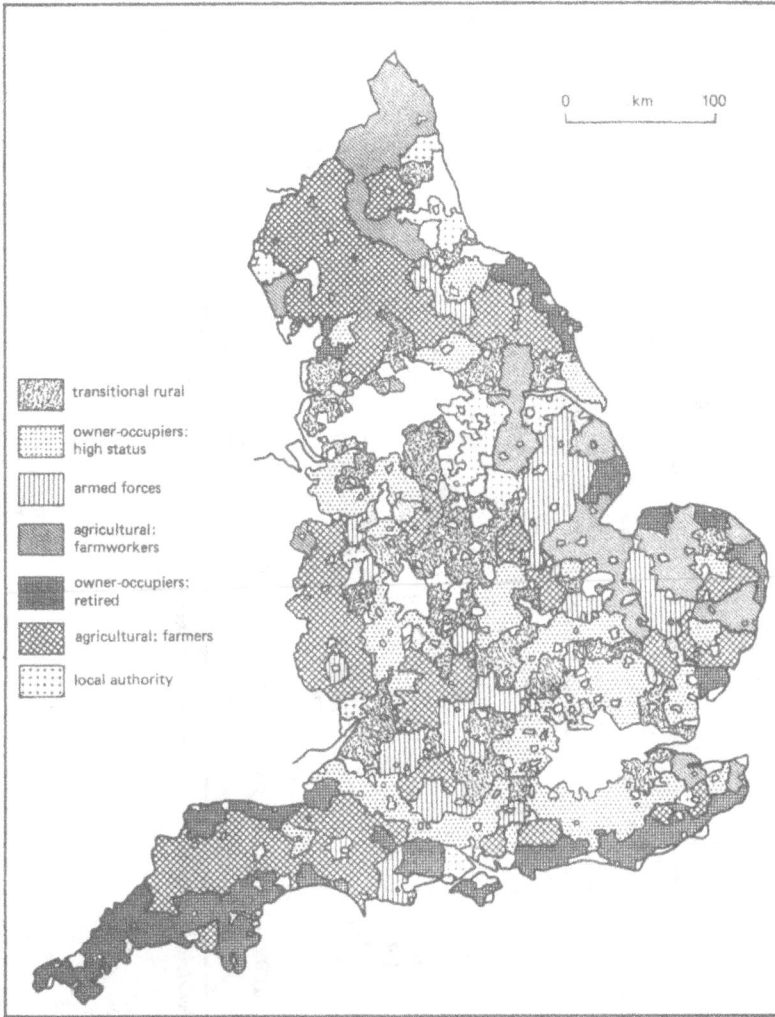

Figure 3.5 *Overcrowding and underoccupancy in rural areas, 1971*

from an examination of housing quality and its relationship with the type of rural household. Using data from the *English House Condition Survey* Tables 3.6 and 3.7 allow an assessment of the links between tenure status and poor-quality housing.

In some contrast to the situation in towns and cities, a high proportion of rural owner-occupiers were judged to be living in unfit houses or to be lacking housing amenities. Equally the proportion of households living in substandard rent-free properties in rural areas greatly exceeded that in the

Table 3.6 *Housing quality in England – by tenure characteristics of occupants, 1976 (%)*

Tenure	Unfit houses				Houses with less than 3 amenities			
	Rural areas	Towns	Conur-bations	England	Rural areas	Towns	Conur-bations	England
Own outright	36·7	31·8	21·2	29·3	36·5	29·2	14·4	23·7
Buying	12·5	11·4	10·2	11·7	11·2	4·8	10·5	8·7
Renting – local authority/ new town	5·4	9·9	9·8	8·1	10·7	17·9	26·4	20·6
Renting – housing association/trust	2·6	—	—	0·8	1·1	—	3·2	1·6
Private rented furnished	1·4	7·0	9·2	6·0	—	3·3	3·3	2·7
Private rented unfurnished	31·0	34·8	42·4	36·2	25·6	41·8	34·3	35·3
Rent free/relative	10·3	4·1	—	4·5	12·2	1·2	2·4	3·7
Rented – no detail	—	1·2	7·2	3·2	2·7	1·8	5·6	3·7
TOTAL	100·0	100·0	100·0	100·0	100·0	100·0	100·0	100·0
TOTAL NUMBER	78	76	95	249	87	171	227	485

Source: Calculated from *English House Condition Survey* data (Building Research Establishment, 1978).

Table 3.7 *Estimated repair costs – by tenure characteristics of occupants, 1976 (%)*

Tenure	<£1,000				>£1,000			
	Rural areas	Towns	Conurbations	England	Rural areas	Towns	Conurbations	England
Own outright	28·8	23·9	18·2	22·8	35·3	30·5	22·9	28·7
Buying	37·1	33·6	31·7	33·6	13·0	16·2	15·0	14·9
Renting – local authority/ new town	21·0	32·6	37·6	32·0	7·2	14·7	16·1	13·2
Renting – housing association/trust	0·2	1·2	1·5	1·1	1·9	0·2	0·3	0·6
Private rented furnished	1·8	1·8	2·8	2·1	2·9	5·3	9·1	6·2
Private rented unfurnished	6·4	5·4	6·1	5·9	25·3	30·3	31·4	29·4
Rent free/relative	4·2	1·2	1·5	2·0	12·0	1·5	1·0	4·2
Rented – no detail	0·6	0·3	0·5	0·5	2·3	1·5	4·2	2·8
TOTAL	100·0	100·0	100·0	100·0	100·0	100·0	100·0	100·0
TOTAL NUMBER	1,290	2,305	2,281	5,876	236	277	349	862

Source: Calculated from *English House Condition Survey* data (Building Research Establishment, 1978).

towns, probably because this group includes tied cottages. In contrast, local authority housing was generally in rather better condition as was the limited amount of privately rented furnished accommodation. Since much of this last category relates to housing supplied for the armed forces, it is hardly surprising that it is in general found to have a uniformly adequate standard.

As mentioned previously, the age of much of the rural housing stock is an important factor in this respect. The major, large-scale redevelopments which have characterised towns and cities since 1945 have been absent from the countryside with the result that housing conditions and amenities in the private sector are often poor. This point is re-emphasised in Table 3.7 which disaggregates estimated repair costs by tenure status. In general more rural houses need repairs in the privately owned sectors (owner-occupiers and private furnished tenancies) than their urban equivalents, though urban unfurnished rented property and local authority housing were generally poorer, particularly in the conurbations.

The links between housing and households can be explored further by simple statistical analysis looking at correlations between housing and related social and economic variables for English rural areas. Table 3.8 considers the four main tenure groups reviewed earlier, on the basis of significant correlations. The data are from the 1971 Census and from the DoE Local Indicators Project (see Appendix II).

Each tenure group is seen to reflect a different character. Owner-occupation relates strongly to professional and non-manual groups while council housing is more the province of manual workers. Overcrowding is also related to council housing, a correlation which will appear again when the two case study areas are considered in more detail.

Rented unfurnished accommodation is placed firmly within the agricultural sector both in terms of occupation and rateable value, since many such properties would be rated at the lower agricultural level. The negative correlations here are particularly interesting. That with population size suggests that this tenure is more common in more remote areas where population concentrations are lower, and this would seem to be linked with low levels of building since 1945. This tenure group also correlates negatively with female employment, suggesting again the domination of the agricultural economy and relatively fewer job opportunities for women. The correlations for the rented furnished category link this tenure with younger households which are at an early stage in household formation and particularly dependent upon furnished lettings.

Some of the simple measures of housing quality which were reviewed above are considered again in Table 3.9. Broadly speaking the four variables here identify the extremes of housing quality. Thus low-rated housing and housing lacking amenities are linked with the agricultural economy, with pensioners and, in the case of low-rated housing, with privately rented property. Conversely higher quality housing correlates strongly with

Table 3.8 *Correlation analysis: rural housing tenure*

Variable	*Positive correlation*	*Negative correlation*
Owner-occupiers	non-manual workers (0·5373) professional workers (0·5079)	overcrowding (− 0·5221) household without cars (− 0·4637) unskilled manual workers (− 0·4411)
Local authority tenants	unskilled manual workers (0·4994) households lacking cars (0·4850) overcrowding (0·4463) skilled manual workers (0·4312)	underoccupancy (− 0·4444)
Tenants in rented unfurnished accommodation	low rateable values (0·6162) agricultural workers (0·5701) farmers (0·5411)	postwar housing (− 0·6879) non-manual workers (− 0·6568) no. of households in rural districts (− 0·5064) working wives (− 0·4800) married females aged 30–44 (− 0·4745) accessibility (− 0·4720) economically active females (− 0·4063)
Tenants in rented furnished accommodation	armed forces (0·9091) married females aged 16–29 (0·4288) children (0·4034)	married females aged 45–59 (− 0·4485)

Note: Correlations greater than ± 0·4: significant at 0·001.

Table 3.9 *Correlation analysis: rural housing quality*

Variable	Positive correlation	Negative correlation
Households lacking exclusive use of basic amenities	low rateable values (0·6976) farmers (0·4468)	non-manual workers (−0·5782) postwar housing (−0·5542) high rateable values (−0·5085) professional workers (−0·4773) population with higher education (−0·4528)
Domestic properties with low rateable values (<£30)	households lacking amenities (0·6976) farmers (0·6425) rented unfurnished accommodation (0·6162) agricultural workers (0·4532) pensioners (0·4115)	non-manual workers (−0·7360) postwar housing (−0·7334) high rateable values (−0·6214) no. of households in rural district (−0·5479) professional workers (−0·5418) married females aged 30–44 (−0·5191) working wives (−0·4734) economically active females (−0·4697) accessibility (−0·4661) population with higher education (−0·4447) children (−0·4291)

Domestic properties with high rateable
values (> £100)

professional (0·7578)
population with higher education (0·6206)
2-car families (0·5796)
non-manual (0·5753)

households lacking basic amenities
(−0·5085)
households lacking car (−0·4230)

Postwar housing

non-manual workers (0·6988)
married females aged 30–44 (0·6401)
accessibility (0·5668)
no. of households in rural district (0·5528)
working wives (0·5374)
children (0·5302)
economically active females (0·5106)
married females aged 16–29 (0·5082)
average no. of persons per household
(0·4446)
population of working age (0·4240)

low rateable values (−0·7334)
rented unfurnished accommodation
(−0·6879)
farmers (−0·6689)
underoccupancy (−0·5904)
pensioners (−0·5729)
lack of household amenities (−0·5542)
agricultural workers (−0·4616)

Note: Correlations greater than ± 0·4: significant at 0·001.

Table 3.10 *Regression analysis: rural housing tenure and housing quality*

Dependent variable	Independent variables significant at 1% level	Code name
% owner-occupiers (OWNOCC)	% households with head in SEG 5, 6	NONMAN
	% households with <0·5 p.p.r.	<0·5 p.p.r.
	% households with head in SEG 7, 10, 11	MANWORK
	% households lacking exclusive amenities	LAKEXAMEN
	% households with head in SEG 15	AGRICWORK

$$\text{OWNOCC} = 0.244 + 0.92\ \text{NONMAN} + 24.00\ {<}0.5\ \text{p.p.r.} - 0.76\ \text{MANWORK} - 0.26\ \text{LAKEXAMEN} - 0.25\ \text{AGRICWORK}$$
$$(0.12)\ (0.09) \qquad\qquad (3.58) \qquad\qquad (0.09) \qquad\qquad (0.06) \qquad\qquad (0.05)$$

$$R^2 = 0.535$$

% local authority tenants (LARENT)	% households with head in SEG 7, 10, 11	MANWORK
	% households with no car	NOCAR
	% postwar housing	NEWHSE
	% population of working age	WORKPOP

$$\text{LARENT} = -1.11 + 0.63\ \text{MANWORK} + 0.47\ \text{NOCAR} + 2.32\ \text{NEWHSE} + 1.00\ \text{WORKPOP}$$
$$(0.17)\ (0.09) \qquad\qquad (0.06) \qquad\qquad (0.46) \qquad\qquad (0.21)$$

$$R^2 = 0.443$$

Table 3.10 (continued)

Dependent variable	*Independent variables significant at 1% level*	*Code name*
% households renting private unfurnished accommodation (RENTUNF)	% postwar housing % households with head in SEG 15 % households with no car % males unemployed	NEWHSE AGRICWORK NOCAR UNEMP (M)

$$\text{RENTUNF} = 0.51 - 4.28\ \text{NEWHSE} + 0.45\ \text{AGRICWORK} + 0.33\ \text{NOCAR} - 0.45\ \text{UNEMP (M)}$$
$$(0.04)\ (0.32) \qquad\qquad (0.04) \qquad\qquad\quad (0.04) \qquad\qquad (0.09)$$

$$R^2 = 0.642$$

% households renting private furnished accommodation (RENTFUR)	% households with head in SEG 16 % households with head in SEG 8, 9, 12	FORCES SKILWORK

$$\text{RENTFUR} = 0.20 + 0.56\ \text{FORCES} - 2.0\ \text{SKILWORK}$$
$$(0.01)\ (0.02) \qquad\qquad (0.03)$$

$$R^2 = 0.794$$

% households lacking exclusive use of one or more basic amenities (LAKEXAMEN)	% domestic properties with rateable value <£30 % households with head in SEG 8, 9, 12 % households in non-permanent buildings % households sharing dwellings % households with head in SEG 15	LOWRATES SKILWORK NONPERM SHARE AGRICWORK

$$\text{LAKEXAMEN} = - 0.06 + 0.34\ \text{LOWRATES} + 0.35\ \text{SKILWORK} + 0.24\ \text{NONPERM} + 0.54\ \text{SHARE} + 0.16\ \text{AGRICWORK}$$
$$(0.03)\ (0.02) \qquad\qquad (0.04) \qquad\qquad (0.05) \qquad\qquad (0.10) \qquad\qquad (0.04)$$

$$R^2 = 0.616$$

professional and non-manual employment and with such status elements as two-car families and higher education.

The final variable in this analysis, postwar housing, is only indirectly related to housing quality. It can be taken as a rough measure of housing investment since the Second World War and as such gives an insight into those groups and those parts of the countryside which have gained and lost in this crucial area of public investment and social policy. Again the picture is clear. Housing investment, both public and private, has favoured accessible areas where population totals are higher than average and, within such areas, has benefited younger rather than older families in non-manual employment. The correlation with children confirms the view that these areas are likely to be in those parts of rural England which are gaining rather than losing population.

On the other hand, housing investment would seem not to have helped the areas of older population still dependent upon agriculture. Perhaps because of this absence, housing stock in these low-growth areas remains poor, lacking basic amenities and of low rateable value. Rented accommodation, often the tied cottage, remains a common feature – important either because of the absence of other forms of housing or perhaps the indirect cause of this absence because housing demand has been frustrated by a poorly paid rural population trapped within a particular tenure.

These attempts to explain the links which exist between rural housing and rural households can be continued on from the correlations noted above by using multiple regression, a technique which can conveniently illustrate the relative strength of the relationships between housing variables and indicators of social and economic structure. Using data from the same sources as for the correlation analyses (the variables are listed in Appendix II) a stepwise regression was performed using consecutively as the dependent variable the four main tenure categories and a measure of housing quality. To conform with the necessary assumptions of linearity an arcsine transformation was applied to the variables, and obviously reciprocal variables, together with one variable from any pair of very highly correlated variables, were excluded to reduce autocorrelation. The results are given in Table 3.10.

The regression analyses detailed in Table 3.10 confirm all the relationships which have so far been discussed. In the case of owner-occupiers, the variables of non-manual workers and underoccupancy were clearly of greatest significance, accounting for a level of explanation of 42·6 per cent. Negative correlations with manual workers, agricultural workers and housing lacking amenities raised the explanatory power to 53·5 per cent.

The most significant variables in the case of local authority housing were skilled manual employment and households lacking a car. Two further significant variables, postwar housing and population of working age, gave a final R^2 of 0·443. The analysis thus suggests a simple if somewhat stylised picture of a council tenant, employed in the skilled manual trades, lacking a car and living in a rural growth area.

In contrast the view of the typical private tenant of unfurnished property suggests a farmworker living in a rural area which has probably not seen much new housing, public or private, since 1945. Indeed this simple picture is remarkably strong and these two variables alone account for 59·1 per cent of the relationship. With the addition of variables relating to low car-ownership and male unemployment, the latter confirming the idea of limited employment opportunities, the R^2 is raised to 0·642.

The final tenure group, rented furnished accommodation, records only two significant variables, and yet their explanatory power is the highest by far for all the four tenure groups. The importance of this sector for housing the armed forces is confirmed, suggesting that outside the armed services there is relatively little rented furnished accommodation accessible to households seeking this tenure, while the negative link with the skilled manual trades implies an absence of alternative employment in the areas.

A final regression analysis involves using the proportion of households lacking at least one basic amenity as a dependent variable in an attempt to explain poor housing in rural areas. The link with low rateable values is to be expected and is in some senses an inevitable correlation. Interestingly none of the four main tenure variables was significant in this regression, though the presence of variables relating to skilled manual and agricultural employment is suggestive of links with local authority and tied property. The poor level of housing amenities sometimes found in the mobile home sector inevitably brings in the variable recording households in non-permanent dwellings. Together with a link with households sharing amenities, the final level of explanation is 61·6 per cent.

Simple correlations and multiple regression analysis have been used to elaborate on the structure of rural housing which started with a straightforward split between four tenure groups. It is already clear that each sector is characterised by clearly defined types of household and, moreover, there is already emerging some idea of the relative strengths and weaknesses of each group. Before these relative positions are explored further, a dynamic element should be introduced, linking rural housing not just with social class and material circumstances but with the varying use made of the housing stock through time as households form, change and disappear. The next section of this chapter attempts such a dynamic view by tracing links between housing and the family life-cycle.

HOUSING AND THE FAMILY LIFE-CYCLE

Links between rural housing and the different characteristics of households which occupy it lead on naturally to a consideration of the varying roles which housing plays through time as households change their size and structure and their perceived need for housing.

The general development of family life-cycle theory in the context of household movement has been introduced in Chapter 2 and in this chapter it is only possible to consider what is essentially a static picture by relating successive stages of the family life-cycle to the broad housing circumstances in which they seem to exist. The view is national and looks at a series of 'snapshots' taken at particular points in the formation and development of households. The techniques used are once again simple correlation and regression analysis and this section represents a continuation of the descriptive analyses considered earlier.

A major problem arises in attempting to match up the idealised stages of the family cycle with suitable data. All that can be done is to make use of variables which approximate to the various stages since the published census does not allow easy definition of household types in rural areas. Largely based on data from the DoE Local Indicators Project (see Appendix II for the list of variables), it is possible to delineate four stages in the family

Table 3.11   *Rural housing and the family life-cycle: Stage 1*

Positive correlations	Negative correlations
Population aged 0–14 years	
average no. of persons per household (0·8886)	pensioners (– 0·8929)
	underoccupancy (– 0·7418)
married females aged 16–29 (0·7631)	married females aged 45–59 (– 0·7529)
married females aged 30–44 (0·7077)	farmers (– 0·4567)
economically active males (0·6733)	low rateable value (– 0·4291)
postwar housing (0·5302)	
economically active females (0·4969)	
working population (0·4962)	
working wives (0·4324)	
overcrowding (0·4256)	
armed forces (0·4136)	
rented furnished accommodation (0·4034)	
Married females aged 16–29 years	
Population aged 0–14 (0·7631)	married females aged 45–59 (– 0·7752)
economically active males (0·6028)	pensioners (– 0·6893)
average no. of persons per household (0·5552)	underoccupancy (– 0·5977)
	farmers (– 0·4534)
postwar housing (0·5082)	
working population (0·4694)	
armed forces (0·4414)	
females aged 30–44 (0·4300)	
rented furnished accommodation (0·4288)	

life-cycle, although it will be seen that there are considerable problems of overlap between the stages.

(1) PROPORTION OF POPULATION AGED 0—14 YEARS AND PROPORTION OF MARRIED FEMALES AGED 16—29 YEARS

These two variables generally represent the stages of family formation but there is clearly an overlap between couples with no children and those who have already started a family. Equally there is some overlap with the next category. The correlations (greater than ± 0.4 and significant at 0.001) which link with these two variables are given in Table 3.11.

The initial point to be made about this first broad stage relates to housing tenure. Despite the fact that rented furnished accommodation is by far the least common tenure category in the countryside, there is a strong correlation with these younger, growing families. In part at least this is explained by the comparable correlation with heads of households in the armed forces. The link with other tenure groups is much less strong, though local authority renting shows a stronger correlation with children in the population (0.2518) than does owner-occupation. Overcrowding, in so far as it is a problem in the countryside, is more likely to be associated with these younger families than with other, older households.

These conditions also confirm ideas about the type of rural area where these younger families tend to be found. Essentially these are the rural growth areas where employment possibilities, probably in local towns and cities, are good both for men and women. They are seemingly less common where the agricultural economy is strongest.

(2) PROPORTION OF MARRIED FEMALES AGED 30—44 YEARS

Naturally women in this age-group will often still have children living at home and to an extent therefore there is an overlap with the previous stage. Indeed there is a high correlation with young children (Table 3.12). The significance here, though, is that this is a more established stage in the family cycle where financial circumstances may be easier and access to a preferred form of housing more possible. Dependence upon rented property is clearly much lower than at the previous stage (negative correlation with rented unfurnished accommodation of -0.4745), though the link with owner-occupation is perhaps not as high (0.2347) as might be expected. None the less the relationship with employment in the intermediate non-manual class reinforces the hypothesis of an improvement in household circumstances.

In another respect this stage has similarities with the previous stage. These families are also to be found in the accessible countryside where development since 1945 has been greatest and where the old rural economy has perhaps been overwhelmed by new employment opportunities.

Table 3.12   *Rural housing and the family life-cycle: Stage 2*

Positive correlation	Negative correlation
Married females aged 30–44 years	
population aged 0–14 (0·7077)	pensioners (− 0·8271)
average no. of persons per household	underoccupancy (− 0·6616)
(0·6875)	low rateable value (− 0·5191)
working population (0·6771)	farmers (− 0·4786)
postwar housing (0·6401)	rented unfurnished accommodation
economically active males (0·6083)	(− 0·4745)
economically active females (0·5906)	
intermediate non-manual employment	
(0·5803)	
working wives (0·5624)	
accessibility (0·4873)	
married females aged 16–29 (0·4300)	
total households (0·4184)	

(3)   PROPORTION OF MARRIED FEMALES AGED 45–59 YEARS

This group acts as a proxy for households from which children have departed and the strong negative correlation with young children supports this interpretation (Table 3.13). Household sizes are relatively small and the age structure generally high.

It is clear that rented furnished property is of little significance with these older households in contrast to Stage 1. Secondly, the relationship with low occupancy rates suggests that there may have been little movement of households since the previous stage. This leads back to a point made earlier, namely, that the inertia of older households which have put down roots and family ties in an area leads to reduced movement through the housing stock.

Table 3.13   *Rural housing and the family life-cycle: Stage 3*

Positive correlation	Negative correlation
Married females aged 45–59 years	
pensioners (0·4793)	married females aged 16–29 (− 0·7752)
underoccupancy (0·4082)	population aged 0–14 (− 0·7259)
	average no. of persons per household
	(− 0·5099)
	armed forces (− 0·4658)
	rented furnished accommodation (− 0·4485)
	economically active males (− 0·4432)
	married females aged 30–44 (− 0·3362)

(4)   PROPORTION OF POPULATION OF PENSIONABLE AGE

This represents the final stage in the cycle when children have invariably left the parental home. It naturally includes a variety of circumstances, from the elderly residual population living perhaps in straitened circumstances to the elderly, relatively wealthy immigrant to a rural area. Perhaps because of this there are no very clear links with any particular tenure group (Table 3.14). The increased positive correlation with low occupancy rates compared with the previous stage suggests that immobility *vis-à-vis* the housing stock has increased.

Table 3.14   *Rural housing and the family life-cycle: Stage 4*

Positive correlation	Negative correlation
Pensioners in private households	
underoccupancy (0·8029)	population aged 0–14 (− 0·8929)
married females aged 45–59 (0·4793)	average no. of persons per household
farmers (0·4658)	(− 0·8901)
low rateable value (0·4115)	married females aged 30–44 (− 0·8271)
	working population (− 0·8205)
	economically active males (− 0·7654)
	married females aged 16–29 (− 0·6893)
	economically active females (− 0·6720)
	working wives (− 0·5993)
	postwar housing (− 0·5729)
	intermediate non-manual employment
	(− 0·4201)

Most other factors point to the nature of the area in which pensioner households are to be found and here there is a contrast particularly with Stages 2 and 3. Pensioners were found to be linked with agricultural employment (farmers), a relationship which in part would also explain the correlation with low rateable values. In part this may also be indirectly related to poorer housing quality but there is little corroboration since correlations with housing amenity variables are much weaker.

A second way of assessing the significance of the family life-cycle upon rural housing use is by multiple regression analysis. The indicators from the correlations were adopted as the dependent variables against which the eighteen independent variables listed in Table 3.15 were regressed using a stepwise process. As in the previous section it was necessary to transform the percentile variables by an arcsine transformation to satisfy the linearity assumptions of the regression method. The equations obtained, together with their R^2 values, are given in Table 3.16.

The results confirm many of the points raised by the correlation analyses and a pattern of housing use through the cycle begins to emerge. In Stage 1 families are particularly dependent upon rented furnished accommodation,

Table 3.15   *Independent variables in family life-cycle regression equations*

Description	Code name
Percentage of households with no car	NOCAR
Percentage of owner-occupier households	OWNOCC
Percentage of households renting local authority accommodation*	LARENT
Percentage of households renting private unfurnished accommodation*	RENTUNF
Percentage of households renting private furnished accommodation*	RENTFUR
Percentage of households in non-permanent buildings	NONPERM
Percentage of households with less than 0·5 persons per room	<0·5 p.p.r.
Percentage of households lacking exclusive use of one or more basic amenities	LAKEXAMEN
Percentage of households with head in SEG 1–4	PROFEMP
Percentage of households with head in SEG 13, 14	FARMER
Percentage of households with head in SEG 5, 6	NONMAN
Percentage of households with head in SEG 8, 9, 12	SKILWORK
Percentage of households with head in SEG 7, 10, 11	MANWORK
Percentage of households with head in SEG 15	AGRICWORK
Percentage of households with head in SEG 16	FORCES
Percentage of housing stock built since 1945	NEWHSE
Percentage of rateable values > £100	HIGHRATES
Percentage of rateable values < £30	LOWRATES

Notes:

Full definitions of socio-economic groups are given in Appendix II.

Variables from the 1971 Census are marked *; all others are from the DoE Local Indicators Project.

while young married couples are also linked with postwar housing. At Stage 2 there is no clear picture of a significant tenure, but again housing (both private and public) built since 1945 comes to prominence. The new housing element is not present at Stage 3 and this again points to decreasing mobility as families age. Relatively little of the post-1945 housing would have been built by the time these Stage 3 households first formed and they have clearly not moved into it subsequently to any great extent, unlike Stage 2 and some Stage 1 families.

The differential use of the housing stock over time is also illustrated by these results. Underoccupancy is significant as a factor in all the equations, but for the first two stages, when families are growing and children are in the home, the association has a negative value implying relatively full use of the housing stock. In the final two stages this underoccupancy becomes a positive factor especially in the case of pensioner households. Again this seems to support the thesis of housing immobility in older households.

Social class, described by socio-economic group, is not particularly well represented in this analysis. It does appear, however, in the first two stages,

Table 3.16 *Rural housing and the family life-cycle: regression analysis*

Stage	Dependent variable (x)		R^2
1	population 0–14 years	$x = 0 \cdot 80 - 14 \cdot 34 < 0 \cdot 5$ p.p.r. $+ 0 \cdot 11$ RENTFUR $- 0 \cdot 14$ NOCAR $+ 0 \cdot 06$ SKILWORK $- 0 \cdot 07$ NONPERM $+ 0 \cdot 08$ MANWORK $(0 \cdot 02)\ (0 \cdot 77)\qquad\quad (0 \cdot 01)\qquad\quad (0 \cdot 02)\qquad\quad (0 \cdot 02)\qquad\quad (0 \cdot 02)\qquad\quad (0 \cdot 02)$	0·667
1	married females 16–29 years	$x = 0 \cdot 27 - 4 \cdot 93 < 0 \cdot 5$ p.p.r. $- 0 \cdot 05$ NEWHSE $- 0 \cdot 05$ HIGHRATES $+ 0 \cdot 14$ RENTFUR $+ 0 \cdot 11$ SKILWORK $- 0 \cdot 09$ NOCAR $(0 \cdot 02)\ (0 \cdot 74)\qquad\quad (0 \cdot 10)\qquad\quad (0 \cdot 01)\qquad\quad (0 \cdot 01)\qquad\quad (0 \cdot 02)\qquad\quad (0 \cdot 01)$	0·663
2	married females 30–44 years	$x = 0 \cdot 44 - 8 \cdot 07 < 0 \cdot 5$ p.p.r. $- 0 \cdot 07$ NOCAR $+ 0 \cdot 06$ PROFEMP $- 0 \cdot 05$ NONPERM $+ 0 \cdot 33$ NEWHSE $+ 0 \cdot 04$ LAKEXAMEN $(0 \cdot 01)\ (0 \cdot 46)\qquad\quad (0 \cdot 01)\qquad\quad (0 \cdot 01)\qquad\quad (0 \cdot 01)\qquad\quad (0 \cdot 06)\qquad\quad (0 \cdot 01)$	0·678
3	married females 45–59 years	$x = 0 \cdot 20 - 0 \cdot 04$ FORCES $+ 2 \cdot 19 < 0 \cdot 5$ p.p.r. $+ 0 \cdot 04$ HIGHRATES $+ 0 \cdot 03$ LOWRATES $+ 0 \cdot 03$ NOCAR $(0 \cdot 01)\ (0 \cdot 004)\qquad (0 \cdot 45)\qquad\quad (0 \cdot 01)\qquad\quad (0 \cdot 01)\qquad\quad (0 \cdot 001)$	0·423
4	pensioners in private households	$x = -0 \cdot 27 + 29 \cdot 95 < 0 \cdot 5$ p.p.r. $+ 0 \cdot 38$ NOCAR $(0 \cdot 03)\ (1 \cdot 27)\qquad\quad (0 \cdot 03)$	0·714

Notes:
Standard errors of coefficients are shown in subscripted parentheses.
All variables are significant at 0·01.

with service, semi-skilled and skilled manual workers contributing significantly to the first stage of the cycle while professional groups appear in Stage 2. The evidence is, of course, indirect but there is a suggestion of younger rural households from the lower socio-economic groups being joined at a later stage of the cycle by incoming professional groups. The implication of this interpretation is clear. Younger, newly-formed households are likely to have poorer financial resources for house purchase than the older, middle-class elements which dominate Stage 2. And if this contrast is acceptable then it could help to explain the significance of rented furnished accommodation for households with young children. A second, though related, explanation for this last point could, however, be the importance of armed forces personnel in this youngest family group, and indeed the variable relating to this category was only excluded from the regression analysis at the penultimate step.

One final characteristic of these equations should be noted. In all five equations the variable relating to car-ownership (or rather the absence of car-ownership) is significant. The interesting feature is that for the first two stages the variable has a negative coefficient, indicating that car-ownership is common in these households. On the other hand, in the last two stages the coefficient has a positive value, implying a relatively lower level of car-ownership among older households. The significance of this is not necessarily straightforward, for it could be argued that these older households live in more accessible rural areas where public transport is adequate. The balance of the argument, however, would seem to lie in the other direction. It has already been noted earlier in this chapter that it is the older households which tend to be found in the least accessible parts of the countryside and, in any case, many people would argue that private transport is essential even in the most accessible areas, particularly if older families and especially pensioners are involved.

This chapter has necessarily sketched a broad canvas, ranging from the historical development of rural housing to the use and condition of the housing stock at the present time. Although its purpose has been essentially descriptive, it has inevitably begun to suggest the outlines of a discussion on the different capabilities of groups in the countryside in relation to their different needs for housing. It is clear not only that families at different stages of development have different housing needs but also that they are able to articulate their needs in different ways. Already, for example, there is the suggestion that younger households are at a disadvantage compared with other groups and that disadvantages of a different kind emerge again at the end of the family cycle. These and other groups are all in competition for rural houses and it is the task of the next and subsequent chapters to enlarge upon this theme.

Chapter 4

Competitors for Rural Housing

This chapter discusses the various groups in the countryside which compete with each other for the stock of rural housing. It considers some of the attempts which have been made to recognise such groups and to estimate their particular circumstances and their competitive power. As such it sketches out in preliminary form many of the issues which will be considered in later chapters.

The previous chapter went some way towards recognising the important housing groups in rural areas. The pattern of tenure and the social and economic circumstances of households all help to differentiate the rural population according to their housing opportunities. It has also been seen how at the various stages of the family life-cycle different combinations of housing and housing conditions are adopted by different types of rural household. These individual factors all influence rural housing choices but previous explanations of their influence have been piecemeal and they need to be fitted together to produce a more comprehensive picture. While each household is unique, with its own combination of family structure, employment, income, aspirations, and so on, there are none the less common themes and links between them. As with any aspect of social policy, it is appropriate to base housing policy, whether public or private, on the recognition of common patterns or groups. While ultimately both the local authority housing officer and the private developer or landlord have to respond to the individual wishes and capabilities of households, they can only do so if they understand the general structure of housing in which they are operating.

This proposition can be considered in another way. The housing manager or the private landlord deals on a day-to-day basis at a clearly *tactical* level. He has to match individual households with individual houses, using a variety of criteria such as estimated need or ability to pay. To make these tactical decisions, however, he has to understand the *strategic* framework of his operations. The housing manager realises that one household's needs are relative to those of another, while the landlord or developer recognises that the level of rents or the price of houses is directly related to the rest of the market. The strategic view is thus essential to allow the tactical decisions to be made. By the same token, if the research worker is interested in the differential capabilities of households with regard to housing access, he must first outline the main groups of households which compete with each other for housing resources.

Interest in rural housing problems in recent years has tended to be focused on one or other of a number of particular groups which from time to time have been of topical interest, and little attempt has been made to put these groups into an overall framework. It is possible to recognise a largely unco-ordinated progression of concern from the early 1960s, starting with the invasion of rural areas by commuters and leading on to second homes, tied housing, mobile homes and local housing needs — each group supplanting its predecessor in media-based social concern, without any regard for these groups as part of a general structure.

URBAN HOUSING GROUPS

There has been much more progress along these lines in the study of the urban housing market and it is instructive to start there in the hope that comparisons are possible. Murie *et al.* (1976) have argued that if means of access to housing is considered important then a basic twofold distinction, between those who *can* own and those who *must* rent, provides the essential starting point. This view follows from distinctions recognised by Pahl (1975) where he listed five groupings:

1 Large property owners and capitalist speculators.
2 Smaller landlords.
3a Owners of capital sufficient to own their own houses and owning.
3b Owners of capital sufficient to own their own houses and renting.
4 Those who must rent.

This basic dichotomy between owners and tenants has already been seen to be important in Chapter 3. With the decline in the availability of privately rented housing and the expansion of the owner-occupied sector in rural areas it will be seen as a continuing theme.

Another major contribution to this line of investigation is the recognition by Rex and Moore (1967) of what they first termed 'housing classes'. Their ideas were developed not only in an urban context but more particularly in an inner city environment (Sparkbrook, Birmingham), with the additional complication of competing ethnic groups. Their work has often been substantially criticised from a variety of standpoints (for example, Haddon, 1970), notably on the grounds that a static picture based essentially on tenure status wrongly presupposes both a common access capability and also a common set of values. Moreover the concept of housing classes as applied in the urban 'zone of transition' has perhaps been weakened by the fact that Rex has variously recognised five, six or seven housing classes and confusion has naturally resulted (Saunders, 1978). The seven groups which have been recognised by Rex are:

1 The outright owners of large houses in desirable areas.
2 Mortgage payers who 'own' whole houses in desirable areas.
3 Council tenants in council built houses.
4 Council tenants in slum houses awaiting demolition.
5 Tenants of private house-owners, usually in the inner ring.
6 House-owners who must take lodgers to meet loan repayments.
7 Lodgers in rooms.

The specifically inner urban location of this hypothesised framework inevitably invalidates any attempt to transfer Rex's housing classes to rural areas in an *a priori* sense. The significance of the lodging-house and of inner area redevelopment on a major scale does not have any obvious rural counterpart, and these classes, particularly the first, are crucial to the operation of Rex's model.

SOCIAL GROUPS IN RURAL AREAS

The recognition of discrete groupings within rural areas has not been entirely neglected, although not surprisingly findings have had less impact than, say, Rex and Moore's urban housing classes. Of course, Pahl's simple classification referred to above is adaptable enough to transfer to a rural context. As in the urban situation, the evidence from rural housing studies suggests again that a main attribute of this system is the basic recognition which it gives to those who *can* own and those who *must* rent. This distinction is more than an obvious split between two well-recognised tenure types; it has significance for the actual processes of housing access – construction, municipalisation and allocation.

The substantial work carried out largely in Suffolk by Newby and his colleagues illustrates this point and further emphasises the advantages of an owner/tenant dichotomy as a useful starting point in recognising housing groups. Here it has been shown (Saunders, 1977; Newby *et al.*, 1978) how owner-occupiers who are migrants to the rural area can ally with existing owners, particularly farmers and large landowners, against tenants, especially of council houses. The alliance of these two owner groups can take several forms. Most commonly they ally to restrict further housing development by means of planning policy and to keep rates low, thus hindering investment in local authority housing. The two groups can have slightly different motives, but a common purpose. The immigrants are concerned to protect their new-found rural environment from development and also to safeguard property values, while the landowners seek to retain control over their labour through tied housing and to prevent employment competition and wage increases consequent upon population increase.

Before passing on to more detailed rural typologies it is perhaps worth noticing a second dichotomous structure which has been recognised increasingly in recent years and which has resulted in specific modifications to rural housing policy. This is the recognition of the supposed special claims to housing of local people above those of immigrants to the rural area. This topic will be discussed in greater detail later but it is worth recording here that this basic distinction has, despite the problems of definition, received considerable attention and popular support. One consequence can be seen in policy statements in many structure plans and other planning documents (for example, the Lake District draft National Park Plan), where the recognition of these two main rural housing classes has resulted in the adoption of policies of positive discrimination in favour of locals. Even before these statements, of course, this distinction was often implicitly made, in so far as a residential qualification has frequently been a necessary input to local authority housing allocation procedures in many rural areas.

There have been two main attempts to date to provide for rural areas a useful typology of social groups which might be applicable to studies of housing. These are the systems described by Pahl (1966) and, more recently, by Ambrose (1974).

Pahl's typology of social groupings is especially useful in this preliminary understanding of the structure of rural housing and it will form the basis for the review of rural housing groups which follows. Before this, however, it is instructive to consider Ambrose's system.

Ambrose recognises seven 'rough groupings of households ... based on general observation rather than empirical data'. As well as making distinctions on the basis of tenure and income capability, Ambrose stresses the significance of mobility and accessibility through the ability or inability of households to own a car in a situation of declining public transport. It might be argued that this factor rather dominates Ambrose's classification but there can be little doubt of its importance in questions of rural housing (Moseley, 1979). Ambrose's seven groups are:

1   Those who have capital, can afford a house of character and can run two cars.
2   Those who can afford a four-bedroomed house and can run a car.
3   Those who can afford a three- or two-bedroomed semi (or could until the 1972 price rises) and can run a car.
4   Those in a similar situation but who cannot run a car.
5   Those who cannot afford to purchase but whose situation enables them to gain a council house and who can run a car.

6 Those in a similar situation but who cannot run a car.
7 Those who cannot afford to purchase, cannot get a council house and who live in privately rented accommodation.

Pahl's eight main social groupings have been given wide currency, particularly as a checklist of social change in the village. It has generally been forgotten that Pahl himself suggested that his typology was of specific application to housing policy.

I very much hope that if planning consultants or local authorities are considering further research on 'villages' they will concentrate on the specific problems and housing needs of particular social groups. To consider 'the village' as a sort of average of all such groups is extremely misleading and possibly accounts for much of the confusion in rural planning. *There is no village population as such: rather there are specific populations which for various, but identifiable, reasons find themselves in a village.* (Pahl, 1966, his italics)

Accordingly it is worth examining Pahl's social groups and considering their importance for housing access, both in terms of their own housing opportunities and in terms of their power and control over other groups.

(1) LARGE PROPERTY-OWNERS

This group comprises owner-occupiers who are also property landlords. Historically it has been very important, particularly in the closed estate villages where the control of both housing and employment can be in the hands of one man. Of equal importance is its power over housing and planning policy at a wider level through formal membership and informal links with local authority committees and councils.

Until the work of Newby and colleagues (Newby, 1977; Newby *et al.*, 1978) this group had only been considered from the viewpoint of rural housing in the specific context of estate villages (for example, Havinden, 1966). It is fair to say that while such studies certainly emphasised the range of a landowner's influence they did not really provide an analysis of the pervasive nature of that influence. Indeed at times it is clear that the power and paternalism which go hand-in-hand with this situation have been uncritically accepted as a long-standing and essentially rural benevolence.

Newby *et al.* bring out the dominating influence of this group within many aspects of rural life. In particular they stress the strong position afforded to this group by virtue of its dual control over both the housing and the employment of labour. Indeed they underline the key position which farmers and landowners have in this respect, emphasising the limited opportunities for both alternative housing and alternative employment which often exist in rural areas.

The control of the large property-owners over housing and employment is extended by the political power which they exert both at a national and a local level. At a national level it is perhaps most clearly seen in the undoubted lobby strength of the National Farmers' Union and of the Country Landowners' Association. These two bodies have consistently fought against any amendment to the status of agricultural tied cottage tenants, arguing that the system was both necessary to agriculture and worked well. However, in each year prior to the Rent (Agriculture) Act 1976, there were perhaps 1,500 eviction threats, or 'cottage cases' as they have been called by the farmworkers' union, when tenants were issued with orders for eviction.

At the local level this political power is wielded through membership of district and county councils and particularly through the membership of key committees such as housing and planning. Newby found that in East Anglia as a whole in 1973 30 per cent of the membership of such committees was in the hands of farmers and others with a direct involvement in the agricultural industry (Newby *et al.*, 1978). Taking just the rural districts of the region, no less than 42 per cent of council members were members of this agricultural interest group, while the figure rose to 50 per cent when rural district councils in Norfolk alone were considered. Some years earlier, a study carried out for the Redcliffe-Maud Commission on local government reorganisation (Moss and Parker, 1967) showed that at the national level the comparable figure for this representation was 35 per cent. Changes in local government, particularly where urban areas have been joined with rural areas, may have reduced this numerical importance slightly, but there is little doubt that representation is still high and, moreover, is made more significant when it is realised how key positions such as chairmen are held by this group.

(2) SALARIED IMMIGRANTS WITH SOME CAPITAL

These are typified by Pahl as inhabiting 'period property – full of beams, latches, central heating and assorted reproduction ironmongery'. Owner-occupiers whose main influences are perhaps in the improvement and gentrification of rural housing, they subsequently ally with group (1) in preserving the countryside against development by involvement with local politics and pressure groups.

(3) 'SPIRALISTS'

Again these are owner-occupiers, though of a transient sort. The short time they are resident in a village usually precludes their conscious involvement in local government like the two above groups, but they may have an indirect influence upon housing through membership of environmental groups which seek to influence design standards in rural areas and to restrict further housing development. Having gained access to countryside amenities they, like the previous group, are reluctant to extend this access to other groups for fear of prejudicing their own enjoyment.

Pahl makes a distinction in his classification between these two groups of owner-occupiers but other than pointing out some differences of age and mobility he does not differentiate between them in terms which are significant for housing. However, it is possible to suggest certain differences. The spiralists, by virtue of their generally younger age structure and their high level of mobility, are more likely to compete at the slightly cheaper end of the owner-occupation market and particularly for newer houses. Their incomes, though high relative to local incomes, may well preclude buying expensive houses of character. Moreover the probability of moving within a few years means that they are attracted to houses which are not in need of substantial improvement or adaptation and are easily and quickly sold when necessary. The modern detached or semi-detached house on a recent development in an accessible village provides the ideal combination. Conversely, the older and more established owner-occupier may be looking for an older house, ripe for improvement with less of a premium on immediate saleability.

The impact of these groups upon the rural housing market has been studied in an area of the Peak District by Penfold (1974). Commuters working in Sheffield and seeking a pleasant rural location are able to compete very effectively for the existing housing stock. The problem is exacerbated by the development control policies employed by planners, consequent upon the designation of the area as a national park, which reduce the amount of new building that is allowed. These same pressures have been charted more recently in the Lake District by Bennett (1976) where the same combination of escalating house prices, a declining rented sector and low levels of local wages conspire to handicap local residents.

Both of these studies perhaps inevitably devote much attention to the influence of another housing group, the second home owner. Pahl does not distinguish these transient commuters in his scheme, but implicitly they might be included in one or other of these two groups of middle-class owner-occupiers. While, as both Penfold and Bennett have illustrated, the activities of the second home owner are especially noticeable in areas of high landscape value, their significance is wider than this.

There have been several studies of second homes (for example, Bielckus *et al.*, 1972; Downing and Dower, 1973; South West Economic Planning Council, 1975; Shelter, 1980) and all have stressed the influence of the development upon the local housing market. More recently criticism of the role of the second home in the rural housing market has combined with the concern for the interests of local people mentioned earlier. Thus Larkin (1978c) has been especially critical of the second home influence: 'It is immoral for people to own two homes whilst others have none, and Shelter will continue to represent the claims of those who want and need to live in the countryside, rather than those who can merely afford to do so'.

It should be noted, however, that quantitative measures of the growth of second homes upon, for example, local house prices or housing availability have generally not been possible. In practice it has been difficult to distinguish between the different pressures upon local housing markets. Thus the escalation in house prices relative to national and regional levels charted for the Peak District by Penfold can only be explained by the influence of commuters and second home owners by inference and not by direct proof.

(4) THOSE WITH LIMITED INCOME AND LITTLE CAPITAL

This group is equated by Pahl with reluctant commuters who have been forced out of the towns in the hope of finding cheaper but larger housing in rural areas in response to a growing family, as noted in the analysis of the relationships between stage in the family life-cycle and housing in Chapter 3. As a group which *can* own it has good access to housing resources, though not as wide as the wealthier groups mentioned previously.

(5) THE RETIRED

The retired population in the countryside is an important and growing element in the demographic structure, and one with some quite specific housing needs. It can be found in both the owner-occupied and tenant sectors but it is the former on which Pahl concentrates his comments. He emphasises the problems of isolation and loneliness which they may find, but of much greater significance for housing access is their purchasing power as owner-occupiers and more particularly their obvious need for and ability to gain proximity to services. Thus, as will be seen in the local studies in Part Three, this group is to be found especially in small towns and large villages where accessibility is high and service provision comparatively good.

As with the spiralist group, the retired migrant is in a good position to compete strongly for housing. Since he is looking to the small town or large village for his housing and could be expected to favour smaller, easily run houses and bungalows, the estate development of quality houses is an obvious attraction. One of the few studies of this phenomenon relates to a survey of newly built housing in what was then Ruthin Rural District in Denbighshire (Jacobs, 1974). Although land had been released for building to help a local demand for owner-occupation chiefly among young people, it was clear that it was retired in-migrants who were generally taking up the houses. No less than 64 of 152 respondents to the survey reported that they were retired, and high proportions of these new residents had moved from or were still employed outside the local area.

Although he emphasises that the retired come from 'varied financial backgrounds', the essential significance of this group for Pahl is as movers and as newcomers to rural areas. As a result the brief picture which he gives is partial in its analysis. Of equal if not greater importance, particularly in the more remote countryside, is the residual retired population, left behind by a process of selective migration and in no sense having chosen its housing environment. As such, this group has some affinities with a group which follows – the tenants of tied cottages. The local studies in Part Three will explore this relationship more directly, especially in the case of estate villages in the Cotswolds. There have been in recent years some attempts to recognise the particular problems which these long-standing retired residents have in the matter of housing. In part their needs can be met by local authority housing construction, involving sheltered accommodation as necessary. In part also a response has come from private landlords, particularly the large landowners noted earlier (for example, Shelburne, 1976 and 1978). A third approach has been through the creation of housing associations specifically dealing with the retired farmworker (Arthur Rank Centre, 1976; Buckler, 1978). All three approaches have to come to terms with the combination of old age, low income and local ties which, together with possible infirmity, make up a formidable barrier to wider access to rural housing.

(6) COUNCIL HOUSE TENANTS

This sixth group marks the definite transition to the groups which *must* rent. Pahl stresses the mismatch between council house provision and present employment structures and also the generally poorer housing quality and service provision of this group. All in all the significant feature of this group is its relative inflexibility of tenure and of location compared with the owner-occupiers.

The characteristics of council house tenants in rural areas have been neglected to date. The general circumstances of council tenants and in particular the systems and controls upon access to the local authority sector have received much attention in recent years (for a good review see Murie *et al.*, 1976) but little is known specifically about this group in rural areas. It may be argued that the urban/rural distinction is much less relevant for this group, that the basic structure is set by local authority policy on housing construction, management, allocation and the like and that such policy shows a uniformity between authorities irrespective of their location. Certainly Niner's study of Ludlow Rural District (Niner, 1975) recognised little distinction with regard to housing policy and procedures when compared with urban authorities.

None the less, there are arguments to suggest that rural council tenants may well be different from their urban counterparts. The generally smaller housing stock available for them, the poorer financial base of rural areas, the inevitably higher costs of housing construction and maintenance and the consequent concentration of the limited public housing stock in a few centres, are all factors which would suggest that, as a group, rural council tenants would have different problems which deserve individual attention.

(7)   TIED COTTAGERS AND OTHER TENANTS

Pahl makes no distinction between tied tenants and others renting from private landowners. The distinction will be seen to be important, though both subgroups have low access potential.

Tied tenants can exist in a number of employment situations, including the church, education, the catering trades, the mining industry and, as will be seen later, in the armed forces. The problems faced by these groups are very different and it is a mistake to consider them as an homogeneous group. By far the most well documented subgroup is, of course, the farmworker. The National Union of Agricultural and Allied Workers has campaigned since 1909 for the abolition of the tied cottage system in agriculture and the matter has been official Labour Party policy since the end of the Second World War. In recent years this opposition has come to a head and, although it stopped well short of outright abolition, new legislation under the Rent (Agriculture) Act 1976 has in effect given a security of tenure to the farmworker which is not dissimilar to that afforded to other private tenants (Rossi, 1977).

The number of tied agricultural cottages is only roughly known – the study by Gasson (1975) reported a figure of around 73,000 for England and Wales – but it is certain that the relative importance of the tied cottage within agriculture has increased in recent years as labour totals have decreased but low earnings and fewer opportunities for council housing in rural areas have forced more farmworkers to be dependent on the tied house. Roughly half of all farmworkers are dependent on the tied cottage for their housing, a proportion which represented some 90,000 workers and their families in Britain in 1974 (Irving and Hilgendorf, 1975).

In part at least the debate about tied agricultural cottages relates to housing conditions. In common with many private tenants, the general housing standards for the tied home dweller are significantly lower than those for council tenants or for owner-occupiers. A survey carried out in Tiverton Rural District in Devon showed that, judged both by amenity provision and by condition, agricultural tied cottages were in general in a poorer state than other rented accommodation (Fletcher, 1969), though more recent surveys suggest that agricultural tied housing may often be of a rather higher quality than other privately rented property.

The major concern expressed over the agricultural tied cottage question is, however, not one of quality but rather one of equity. Many people would argue that it is wrong to link housing with employment. Whatever attempts are made by legislation to safeguard tied tenants, there will always be a handicap resulting from such a link and the employee will always feel constrained by the system.

In terms of access to housing the farmworker is in a poor position. In the first place this relates to the low level of wages paid in agriculture despite the farming industry's high productivity record over the past thirty years and its key status, as continually stressed by the farming lobby. There is no way in which many farmworkers can aspire to owning their own home particularly in areas where house prices have been inflated by incomers from the towns. Secondly, the availability of rented accommodation is likely to be so small that a tied house provides the only chance of suitable housing. Finally, there may be an additional barrier to housing mobility as a result of local housing policy. Some local housing authorities are not prepared to view tied tenants as suitable candidates to join a waiting list. As Larkin (1978b) has stated:

> The logic is immutable: we make inadequate provision of rented accommodation; therefore people are forced into tied accommodation for want of an alternative; therefore they are adequately housed; therefore our inadequate provision was sufficient after all.

The private tenant who is not living in a tied house has, like the rural council tenant, been rather neglected. Historically, of course, this group has been far more significant than it is today: numbers have declined substantially during the present century and particularly during the last decade. Pahl equated this category (including the tied tenant) with the rural poor, linking low wages, poor housing conditions and isolation. Chapter 3 has already suggested that the second of these criteria may be true and it will be seen later how relevant the other characteristics are.

(8) LOCAL TRADESMEN AND OWNERS OF SMALL BUSINESSES

This final group is rather indeterminate in its housing characteristics and may include both owner-occupiers and tenants. From the viewpoint of housing provision some members of this group may act as landlords for rented property.

The eight social groups recognised by Pahl have provided something of a starting point in this discussion of competitors for rural housing. It remains, however, only a generalised framework and, as has been seen, some groups have been inevitably subsumed within others while other groups have been missed out altogether.

Given that second home owners, although omitted from Pahl's classification, have already been considered, there remain at least three further groups or subgroups which must be considered if a complete picture is to be given. All three tend to be tenants of some sort and all have particular problems of housing access.

In 1975 about 147,000 people lived in mobile homes located on some 9,000 sites, particularly in the south-east of England (Department of the Environment, 1977). Most of the sites were privately owned, with only 5 per cent in the hands of local authorities. Though mobile home ownership is apparently regarded by some households, for example, retired couples, as a highly suitable form of housing, the comparatively short life of the caravan is nevertheless an obvious and relatively expensive handicap. In cases where there is little capital for home-ownership or households have low eligibility for council housing, the mobile home may be regarded as a useful stopgap. Yet in general the mobile home dweller is in a disadvantageous position. His security of tenure tends to be limited, despite the Mobile Homes Act of 1975, and conditions of overcrowding and poor standards of amenity provision and necessary services are not uncommon. To complicate the picture, some local authorities seem to use mobile home sites as a convenient dumping ground for homeless or problem families (Larkin, 1978a and 1978b, and papers in Shaw, 1979 and Walker, 1978).

Larkin has argued that mobile homes represent clear evidence of the failure by local authorities to provide adequate housing. A second area where this deficiency is evident is in the provision of winter lets – that is, holiday accommodation which becomes available during the winter months and which can be used by the local authority to relieve overcrowding or homelessness, albeit only on a temporary basis. This category is in many ways, of course, generally part of the privately rented sector which was briefly considered above. It represents an element which exists uneasily between this sector and the local authority sector, neither arrangement providing the household with any real security nor opportunity to improve housing circumstances.

A final category, which has already been briefly mentioned, involves members of the armed services living in rented accommodation usually provided by the Ministry of Defence. The location of service bases in rural areas brings with it special problems, not just of housing (Miller, 1973). Service tenants share many of the disadvantages which were considered with other tied tenants. In particular, there is often a serious problem of rehousing when the employee leaves the services and since around 40,000 men leave the services every year (Shelter, 1974) this can prove a great strain upon local authority housing departments.

This review of the main competitive groups for rural housing has necessarily been built up in an incremental fashion. It has indicated the range of rural household types and suggested some of their particular strengths and weaknesses but it has only been superficial in its coverage. The remainder of this chapter will consider a more comprehensive approach to the question of classification.

A CLASSIFICATION OF RURAL HOUSEHOLDS

The previous chapter attempted to express a view of rural housing in terms of its physical nature (age, quality, and so on) and also in terms of the links between housing tenure and the social and economic characteristics of rural dwellers. Yet social variables and housing characteristics do not, of course, exist in isolation nor as simple two-way correlations. Neither can tenure, despite its central position in any consideration of housing, provide the comprehensive approach that a really useful national typology should provide. A basic starting point for this study of rural housing is the view propounded by Murie *et al.* (1976) that housing should be regarded as a system of interconnecting parts – physical, social, economic and political – and any national classification should attempt to build in as many of these factors as possible.

Comprehensiveness of content is, then, the first objective of any classification of rural housing. A second follows logically, namely, that such a classification should be national in its coverage. The characteristics of a case study may be applied on a wider scale but this is not necessarily so. Indeed some of the criticisms which have been levelled at Rex and Moore's housing classes relate to the view that conditions away from Sparkbrook are sufficiently different to make their system less useful. A scheme based on a national data set should answer this second objective.

A third objective would be for the national scheme to be applied to a more detailed examination of the nature of rural housing at the local level. Clearly the flexibility required for this transformation to be possible demands a lot from the chosen method. None the less a system which can in some degree be replicated from one area to another and yet retain common features would be extremely useful.

It can be argued that a fourth aim should be a large measure of objectivity in distinguishing between classes. This aim, perhaps, of all those considered is the one which is most prone to criticism. As will be seen, objectivity in both the choice of variables and the method of analysis is perhaps a goal which is impossible to attain. Many would argue that the application of a statistical analysis does nothing to build in supposed objectivity since the researcher has to make decisions throughout the analysis which introduce a subjective element. Others would argue that even after an attempt to keep these subjective elements to a minimum the end result is not objectivity but a crudely mechanistic system.

These criticisms are well founded but do not rule out the undoubted advantages of a rigorous statistical analysis. However, a major response to such criticisms revolves round the fact that any national analysis is bound to involve large amounts of data and if national variation is to be measured, rather than vaguely suggested, some recourse to statistical analysis is inevitable. The simple typology of rural social groups devised by Pahl, to which reference has already been made, has its uses, but only very general variations throughout the country can be suggested and then only with imprecision. A many-sided problem inevitably leads to a multivariate approach.

The multivariate approach adopted in this study is cluster analysis using as a data base the Small Area Statistics (SAS) from the 1971 Census of Population. Cluster analysis is one of a number of techniques which can be used to group together data which have a multifaceted nature and the method has the additional advantage of recognising the importance of the individual variables which lead to the differentiation of the main groupings.

Cluster analysis has been widely used by researchers in similar circumstances. In most cases the classifications have been of a broad social and economic nature, differentiating for example, between local authorities in Britain at a general level (Webber and Craig, 1976). The use of classification methods and the recognition of social indicators has naturally been particularly common for urban areas (Knox, 1978), but Webber (1977a) has produced an analysis for the rural area of Cumbria. Although, as stated earlier, most classifications have been general in their approach, they have also been designed to focus on specific social issues, such as housing (Webber, 1977b) or social deprivation (Stockford and Dorrell, 1978). The concern here is, naturally, with rural areas and, within these, specifically with housing.

The proposed cluster analysis fulfils most of the objectives which were considered earlier. Primarily because it uses the existing data base of the population census it can be relatively comprehensive in its coverage and easily accessible to any researcher or local authority. The detailed information is available for small areas (enumeration districts containing perhaps 150 households) yet the data can also be aggregated for analysis at a broader scale.

A fuller account of the cluster analysis method, interpretation and results can be found in Dunn, Rawson and Rogers (1980b). In its simplest form thirty variables relating to housing and household characteristics were aggregated from enumeration district data and analysed for the 410 rural districts of England which existed in 1971. The method successively groups the rural districts on the basis of their similarity to each other over the range of chosen variables. The numbers of clusters of districts are naturally reduced at each iteration of the process and existing clusters are linked up with those to which they have the closest affinity. Obviously the individual clusters become more heterogeneous within themselves as the clustering proceeds until finally the last two clusters fuse into one. Clearly a balance has to be struck between a manageable number of clusters on the one hand and a sufficient level of differentiation between clusters on the other.

The cluster analysis recognised a major stable solution when seven main clusters had been derived. These have been termed *rural housing profiles* and they provide the essential picture of rural housing structure at the national level which is considered here. The relative importance of the main socio-economic variables within each individual profile allows a deeper understanding of the national rural housing system than the isolated indicators of tenurial structure, social class or basic amenities. On the basis of these constituent variables, the profiles have been named as follows:

agricultural: farmworkers (42 rural districts)
agricultural: farmers (91 rural districts)
owner-occupiers: retired (42 rural districts)
transitional rural (90 rural districts)
owner-occupiers: high status (83 rural districts)
armed forces (36 rural districts)
local authority housing (26 rural districts).

The nature of these seven rural housing profiles can be seen in Table 4.1 which records the main diagnostic variables within each profile. The spatial distribution of the seven profiles is illustrated in Figure 4.1.

These seven main profiles are naturally at a generalised level and they may hide small but distinctive forms of rural housing. In part this particular problem is a function of the use of the census as a data base. Thus the scheme presented here does not recognise second home ownership, a form of rural housing which has been widely discussed in recent years, simply because this household attribute was not recorded in the 1971 Census. Similarly, households living in tied accommodation are subsumed within the privately rented category since this special tenure group has not been recognised by the census since 1961.

The second reason relates to the way in which small clusters will be subsumed within larger clusters as aggregation proceeds. For this reason it is instructive to consider the components of each individual profile and reference can be made to the dendrogram illustrated in Figure 4.2. Here the seven main profiles are seen to be made up of two, three or four constituent clusters which were recognised at a previous stable solution to the analysis. While the eighteen clusters eventually aggregate to form the seven main profiles, several of them relate to distinct subtypes of rural housing. A full tabulation of the eighteen clusters, together with brief descriptions, can be found in Dunn, Rawson and Rogers (1980a).

This dendrogram (Figure 4.2) is also useful for another reason. Because it shows the progression from eighteen clusters through to the seven named profiles, the affinities between these profiles can be grouped. It will be seen that the links between particular profiles illustrated in Figure 4.2 are directly paralleled by links in the national distribution shown in Figure 4.1.

As discussed earlier, a major distinction in English rural housing can be drawn on the basis of the four main tenure categories. This cluster analysis recognises the importance of tenure as an explanatory variable, but it also recognises what is perhaps an equally important twofold distinction between areas which have remained essentially rural in nature, and those

Table 4.1   *Rural housing profiles*

Profile 1 : Agricultural : farmworkers (42 cases)

T statistic	Variable number	Variable description	National mean	Profile mean
1·27	29	% households with head in SEG 15	6·3	12·3
0·86	17	% households lacking exclusive amenities	13·8	18·5
0·80	22	% economically active females unemployed	3·6	4·4
0·78	21	% economically active males unemployed	2·8	3·8
0·68	10	% households renting private unfurnished	20·9	26·3
0·66	6	% households with no car	32·3	37·0
−0·98	26	% households with head in SEGs 5, 6	23·5	17·9
−0·87	16	average number of rooms per dwelling	5·1	4·9
−0·76	23	% population with higher education	5·8	4·3
−0·71	24	% households with head in SEGs 1, 2, 3, 4	14·6	11·2
−0·69	8	% owner-occupier households	54·5	47·0

A high proportion of agricultural workers and low proportions of professional and non-manual workers. Above-average private rented unfurnished tenancy group and also greater than average number of households lacking exclusive use of one or more basic amenities. High unemployment rates. Low level of car-ownership.

Profile 2 : Agricultural : farmers (91 cases)

T statistic	Variable number	Variable description	National mean	Profile mean
1·10	25	% households with head in SEGs 13, 14	6·8	13·2
0·95	10	% households renting private unfurnished	20·9	28·4
0·87	15	% households with less than 0·5 persons per room	37·9	42·5
0·68	29	% households with head in SEG 15	6·3	9·6
0·63	5	% population of pensionable age	16·8	19·4
0·58	16	average number of rooms per dwelling	5·1	5·3
−0·74	26	% households with head in SEGs 5, 6	23·5	19·3
−0·68	1	total number of private households	7,799·9	4,082·6

A predominantly agricultural group with low population totals and high proportions of farmers and agricultural workers. Many households living in rented unfurnished accommodation. Low occupancy rates. Above-average proportion of pensioners.

Table 4.1 continued

Profile 3 : Owner-occupiers: retired (42 cases)

T statistic	Variable number	Variable description	National mean	Profile mean
1·72	5	% population of pensionable age	16·8	23·7
1·18	22	% economically active females unemployed	3·6	4·8
1·04	15	% households with less than 0·5 persons per room	37·9	43·3
1·02	21	% economically active males unemployed	2·8	4·1
0·76	8	% owner-occupier households	54·5	62·7
− 1·75	4	% population of working age	56·2	52·7
− 1·57	18	% males 15 + economically active	80·4	73·2
− 1·48	2	average number of persons per household	2·9	2·7
− 1·38	19	% females 15 + economically active	37·4	31·7
− 1·28	3	% population aged 0–14	24·3	21·0
− 1·16	20	% married females economically active	36·1	30·2

Large retired population. Low economic activity rates, high unemployment rates. High level of owner-occupation and underoccupancy of dwellings.

Profile 4 : Transitional rural (90 cases)

T statistic	Variable number	Variable description	National mean	Profile mean
0·94	20	% married females economically active	36·1	40·9
0·87	19	% females 15 + economically active	37·4	41·0
0·69	26	% households with head in SEGs 5, 6	23·5	27·4
0·68	4	% population of working age	56·2	57·6
0·64	3	% population aged 0–14	24·3	25·9
− 0·77	5	% population of pensionable age	16·8	13·7
− 0·74	10	% households renting privately unfurnished	20·9	15·1
− 0·73	15	% households with less than 0·5 persons per room	37·9	34·2
− 0·69	29	% households with head in SEG 15	6·3	3·1

A large profile incorporating a variety of cluster characteristics. High female economic activity rate. Above-average proportion of non-manual workers, slightly more than average percentage of children. Fewer pensioners and agricultural workers than the average for rural districts. Renting privately unfurnished is a smaller than average tenure category and there is less underoccupancy.

Table 4.1 continued

Profile 5: Owner-occupiers: high status (83 cases)

T statistic	Variable number	Variable description	National mean	Profile mean
1·12	7	% households with 2 + cars	15·8	20·7
1·11	24	% households with head in SEGs 1, 2, 3, 4	14·6	19·8
1·01	23	% population with higher education	5·8	7·9
0·86	26	% population with head in SEGs 5, 6	23·5	28·4
0·66	16	average number of rooms per dwelling	5·1	5·3
0·57	8	% owner-occupier households	54·5	60·7
− 0·74	6	% households with no car	32·3	27·0
− 0·58	14	% households with more than 1 person per room	4·4	3·7
− 0·53	22	% economically active females unemployed	3·6	3·1
− 0·52	28	% households with head in SEGs 7, 10, 11	21·6	19·6

High proportion of heads of household employed in professional and non-manual occupations and correspondingly above-average level of education. Two car ownership and owner-occupation are both above average.

Profile 6: Armed forces (36 cases)

T statistic	Variable number	Variable description	National mean	Profile mean
2·46	30	% households with head in SEG 16	2·7	16·6
2·29	11	% households renting private furnished	3·3	12·6
1·21	3	% population aged 0–14	24·3	27·4
0·87	2	average number of persons per household	2·9	3·0
0·85	18	% males 15 + economically active	80·4	84·2
0·72	14	% households with more than 1 person per room	4·4	5·3
− 0·82	15	% households with less than 0·5 persons per room	37·9	33·7
− 0·82	8	% owner-occupier households	54·5	45·6
− 0·79	5	% population of pensionable age	16·8	13·7
− 0·72	27	% households with head in SEGs 8, 9, 12	24·4	19·9

A small profile dominated by armed forces personnel and households living in rented furnished accommodation. Above-average proportion of children leading to some overcrowding. High male economic activity rate. Few pensioners.

Table 4.1 continued

Profile 7: Local authority housing (26 cases)

T statistic	Variable number	Variable description	National mean	Profile mean
2·24	6	% households with no car	32·3	48·3
2·19	27	% households with head in SEGs 8, 9, 12	24·4	38·3
1·72	14	% households with more than 1 person per room	4·4	6·6
1·57	9	% households renting from local authority	21·1	34·3
− 1·79	7	% households with 2 + cars	15·8	8·0
− 1·26	15	% households with less than 0·5 persons per room	37·9	31·4
− 1·16	2	average number of persons per household	5·1	4·9

A small group of rural districts with high proportions of households living in local authority rented accommodation. Skilled manual workers dominate the occupational structure. Relatively few households own cars. Some overcrowding of dwellings.

which have been progressively affected by urban influences.

The more truly 'rural' housing profiles may be considered first. Figure 4.2 shows three profiles (agricultural: farmworkers; agricultural: farmers; owner-occupiers: retired) as having closer links with each other than with the other four profiles. Only in the final stage of the clustering process do these three groups join up with the others. The two agricultural profiles are also seen to be closely linked with each other.

On the other hand the four remaining profiles, which as will be seen demonstrate what might be termed 'urbanising' characteristics, are more closely linked with each other than with the first three. Within these four there may be recognised two important subgroups. Local authority housing and armed forces are, not surprisingly, linked in large part because they represent concentrations of rented property whereas the owner-occupiers: high status and transitional rural profiles are joined both by virtue of a common tenure pattern and a common association of social class.

This important twofold distinction is reinforced by the national distribution of rural housing profiles (Figure 4.1). Here the agricultural and retired profiles are particularly to be found in the peripheral areas of the country – the north of England, the eastern counties, the Welsh Borderland and the South West. A line of rural districts dominated by retirement housing extends along the south coast to complete the picture. In contrast to this pattern, the profiles which emphasise owner-occupation, higher social class or government intervention in the housing market, are distributed in a central core stretching from south-east England in a broad band towards

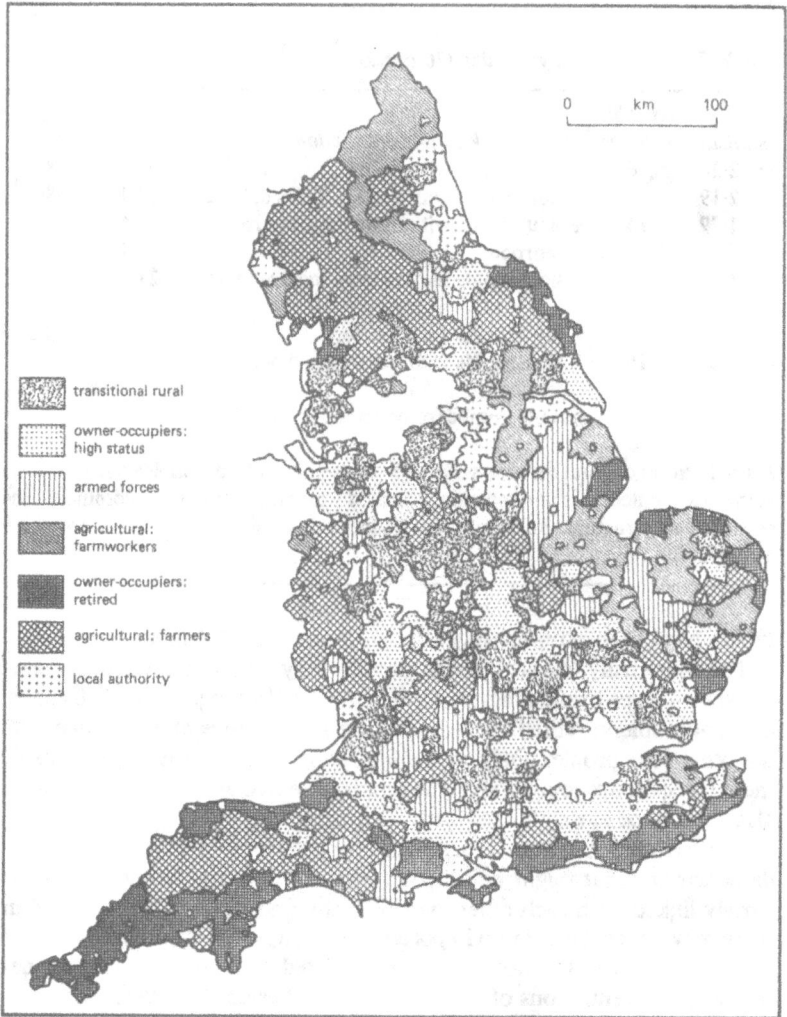

transitional rural

owner-occupiers:
high status

armed forces

agricultural:
farmworkers

owner-occupiers:
retired

agricultural: farmers

local authority

0   km   100

Figure 4.1   *Rural housing profiles, England, 1971*

the north-west. It can be argued that this represents the rural expression of
the metropolitanising zone which has been such a common theme in
postwar planning in this country (Hall *et al.*, 1973). The remainder of this
section considers in more detail the seven profiles creating this core/
periphery pattern.

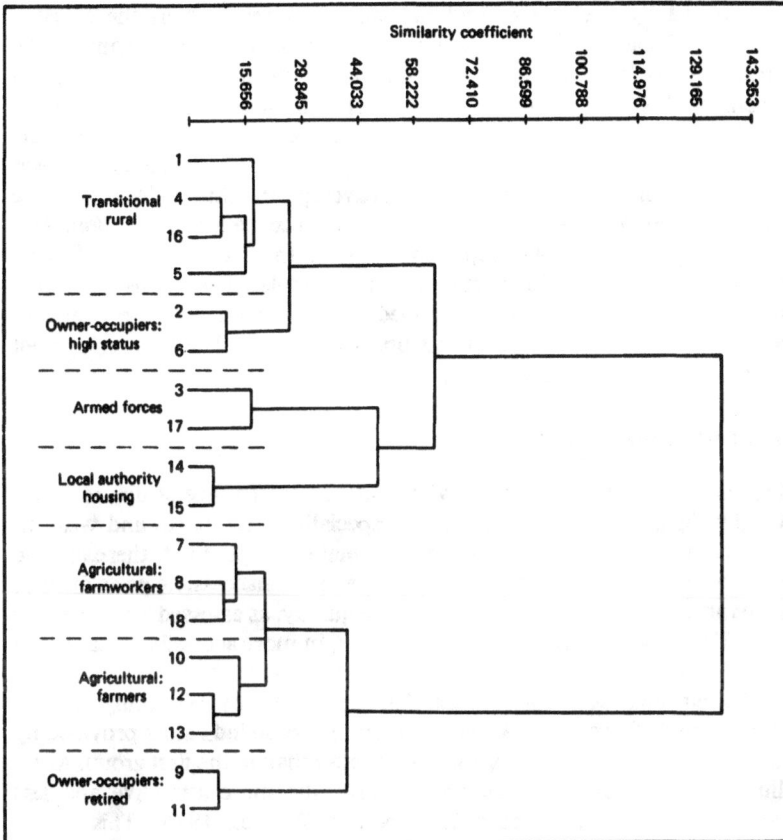

Figure 4.2 *Rural housing profiles: cluster aggregation*

AGRICULTURAL : FARMWORKERS

This profile may be regarded perhaps as the stereotype of rural housing, particularly if privately rented accommodation is tied to employment. In these areas agricultural employment is twice the national average and there are relatively fewer professional people. Housing quality, as measured by housing amenities, is significantly lower than average. Employment was above average in 1971 and car-ownership was less than the national figure. This profile is found particularly in the north of England and is also dominant in the east of England, especially East Anglia.

AGRICULTURAL : FARMERS

The rural economy of uplands of the north and west of England, where farms are smaller and where agricultural labour is more frequently represented by the farmer and his family, is reflected in the housing structure. Rented property is common and rural housing in many of the rural districts is relatively poorly equipped with the standard household amenities. There are relatively lower population totals in these more remote rural areas, and the age-structure of these areas is skewed towards the elderly, with one in five of the population being of pensionable age. Houses tend to be rather larger than the national average and this, together with the large numbers of pensioners, means that underoccupation is common. At a national level this profile represents one of the classic forms of rural housing, showing a familiar set of housing and related problems: an ageing population housed in poorly equipped housing stock with the attendant problems of poor service provision, isolation and few employment alternatives to agriculture.

OWNER-OCCUPIERS: RETIRED

This profile shares with the previous one an elderly age structure and a location in the peripheral rural areas especially of the north and west. In practice it seems to be made up of two main groups. First, there are the areas of residual population, usually in the more inaccessible parts of rural England, such as Cornwall. Here housing quality, as assessed by household amenities, is noticeably poorer than average. In more accessible areas of the countryside it is clear that the elderly age structure has been caused not just by the out-migration of a younger element but also by the in-migration of retired people from urban areas. Even by the crude indicators provided by the census, housing quality is noticeably better than in the first group. Areas illustrating this phenomenon are naturally the more attractive and less remote areas of the countryside (Law and Warnes, 1976). This profile dominates large areas of south-west England, stretches along the south coast of England and is common in coastal areas of the east coast and in Lancashire.

TRANSITIONAL RURAL

This large profile, containing nearly a quarter of all the rural districts in England, is perhaps one of the most difficult to describe. It is common in cluster analyses to find one large grouping which has greater variety in its structure than the other groups but, while this is probably the case here, this profile is important for a number of particular reasons. Both by its location within the central core of metropolitan England and by its balanced age structure and strong employment indicators, it comprises that part of the accessible countryside which has been strongly influenced by urban forces, particularly since 1945.

A further reason why this profile is important is that within its four constituent clusters (Figure 4.2) it contains some minor housing groups which are characteristic of this transition zone (see Dunn, Rawson and Rogers, 1980a). Thus, one cluster is dominated by younger married couples where both partners are working. More especially one cluster emphasises the importance in some areas of mobile homes, one of whose functions is as a transitional stage on the way to more permanent housing. The distribution of these districts – in the southern counties, especially Oxfordshire and Berkshire, but also in Lancashire – echoes the findings of the official mobile homes review (Department of the Environment, 1977).

OWNER-OCCUPIERS: HIGH STATUS

The previous profile represented a transitional stage between the rural periphery and the urbanising core of the English countryside, between the continued dominance of agricultural employment and the newer economic forces coming out of the town. Of the three remaining profiles, none is perhaps more characteristic of this urbanising trend than this owner-occupiers profile. The distinctive element is the importance of high-status households located near to the major centres of employment. A broad belt extends through the south midlands from London to Bristol and from London north-westwards through metropolitan England to Cheshire and Merseyside. The areas are generally more environmentally attractive than those found in the transitional rural profile, and they coincide frequently with green belt and similarly designated areas. The planning system is instrumental in protecting the attractiveness of rural housing in these areas by development restriction and by controlling the type of new building materials.

   Within this profile can be found a second classic rural housing formation – the 'metropolitan village' (Connell, 1974; 1978) which was particularly studied in Hertfordshire by Pahl (1965). This is the zone of the commuter and the 'new villager' (Radford, 1970) where rural housing is at its most attractive and where contrasts with the more traditional forms of rural housing are most apparent.

ARMED FORCES

This profile is perhaps the most distinctive recognised by the analysis. Though relatively small in number (thirty-six) the distribution of rural districts is widespread, stretching from Dorset and Wiltshire in the south, through Oxfordshire to East Anglia, Lincolnshire and Yorkshire, and reflecting the location of major army and air force bases.

   The dominant element here is the high proportion of heads of household employed in the armed services and the corresponding importance of privately rented furnished accommodation. Indeed in seven extreme cases within this profile (Amesbury, Andover, Barnack, Huntingdon, Oakham, Pewsey and Richmond RDs) service households make up a third of all households and privately rented furnished accommodation accounts for over a quarter of the total housing stock. A final feature which should be noted is the generally younger age structure of the population in these areas.

LOCAL AUTHORITY HOUSING

The final profile details those few rural districts where council housing had become a dominant element by 1971. In all other areas local authority involvement in housing has been far less important than in the twenty-six areas recorded here. In some twelve districts, council housing represents no less than 40 per cent of the total housing stock – twice the national average for English rural areas – and the mean figure recorded for the whole of the profile is over one-third of the housing stock.

These local authority dominated areas bring with them a distinctive socio-economic pattern of households. Nearly half the households in these rural districts have no car and overcrowding is significantly above average. The employment structure is typically based in the manual and skilled manual sectors. Spatially this profile is found particularly in the north of England, especially in fairly densely peopled urban fringe areas. These locations reflect two factors: first, the dominance of heavy industry, particularly the coalfield areas and, secondly, the role of urban overspill in the form of local authority estates on the edge of growing towns.

This chapter, and indeed the whole of Part Two, has had as its main objective a comprehensive and systematic analysis of the main features of housing structure and population movement in the English countryside. This has culminated in the recognition of the main social groups which are in competition for housing in rural areas. Part Three of this study looks in more detail at two rural areas in an attempt to elaborate on some of the general themes which have been discussed at the national level.

Part Three

Studies in Lowland England

Chapter 5

Cotswold and South Oxfordshire Districts: the Context

The synthesis of research and information on rural housing and movement through the housing stock presented in previous chapters has attempted to provide a commentary on national trends. But a detailed explanation of the processes involved requires these broad generalisations on the national situation to be tempered by the results of a closer study of particular areas where the critical elements influencing housing and household movement in the English countryside can be examined. It was the contention of Chapter 1 that, given the tendency of previous related research to concentrate upon extreme conditions such as depopulation in upland regions, attention should be focused upon lowland areas where incoming pressures resulting from urban decentralisation are significant. With this in mind, the areas chosen for comprehensive study were Cotswold and South Oxfordshire Districts.

This is not to say that the areas selected are representative of lowland problems, or that there is one set of circumstances and problems which is characteristic of lowland England. The diversity of such circumstances within an apparently homogeneous area has already been highlighted by the classification of rural districts into distinctive types, and a similar exercise undertaken at enumeration district level (reported in Chapter 6) emphasises the juxtaposition of very different rural communities in close proximity. The extent of such differentiation can be measured in a number of dimensions within the selected areas: the spectrum of population change, for example, ranges from rapid growth resulting from pressures exerted by commuters in the most accessible parts of South Oxfordshire to comparatively severe population losses in the northern and central Cotswolds. The contrasts are equally marked in terms of settlement and community, ranging from closed estate villages in the Cotswolds to 'open', formless, dormitory settlements in the Chilterns; in terms of landscape, with two designated areas of outstanding natural beauty, but also urban fringe and featureless plain; and in respect of housing patterns including concentrations of mobile homes, traditional villages, often with few concessions to modern living standards, and areas of transplanted suburbia.

The result of such diversity is a confused pattern requiring careful interpretation in order to understand the complex forces and processes associated with perhaps the most fundamental elements of settlement in rural areas: the disposition of particular households in particular houses and, equally fundamental, the chains of movement between houses which constitute the dynamics of the rural housing system. To place the detailed studies of these elements in their context, however, it is appropriate to consider briefly the main characteristics of the study areas. Parish location maps for both Cotswold and South Oxfordshire Districts are appended to this chapter (Figures 5.3 and 5.4) to aid identification of places.

The greater part of Cotswold District, an area of rolling limestone upland with a deeply indented western scarp face, is included in the Cotswold Area of Outstanding Natural Beauty. Allied to this is the intrinsic attractiveness of the built rural environment; towns such as Cirencester, Chipping Campden and Stow-on-the-Wold, whose mediaeval prosperity was founded largely on the wool trade, have more recently become important as tourist centres and as reception areas for retirement migration. The attractiveness of Cotswold villages, traditionally built of local stone, has been perpetuated by post-mediaeval isolation, which resulted in little new building in the nineteenth century and, latterly, by stringent planning conditions, including the use of traditional materials for new developments and a strong presumption against sporadic development or village expansion. Increasing pressure from commuters, second home owners and the retired on an artificially constrained housing market has, however, led to higher prices and to complaints that local housing needs are remaining unsatisfied.

The economic base of the Cotswolds is essentially agricultural, although employment in agriculture, in common with other primary industries (particularly limestone quarrying), is declining, so that the growth in tourism and the development of light industries, mainly in south Cotswold towns such as Cirencester and Tetbury, has been crucial. Where such development has not occurred, there has been a net loss of jobs; this trend has been especially marked in the former Northleach Rural District. The consequences of declining employment opportunities have included age-selective out-migration (with a corresponding increase in the proportion of the population in older age-groups, needing more, and conveniently located, services) and a contraction in the level of service provision, with community facilities, public transport services and primary education all seriously curtailed. The imbalance of need and supply in the more isolated parts of the Cotswolds perpetuates the existing problems and demands sensitive planning at the local scale if solutions are to be found.

Such problems of isolation and depopulation occur infrequently in South Oxfordshire, an amorphous district created in 1974 from parts of Berkshire and Oxfordshire. An administrative convenience rather than a cohesive region, South Oxfordshire includes part of the Chilterns and the Thames Valley, part of the comparatively unspectacular but locally important Oxford Green Belt, and, between Oxford and the foot of the Chiltern scarp, a traditional agricultural landscape which is reflected in social and economic terms in villages which, to varying degrees, retain a rural sense of purpose.

This is hardly true of the Thames Valley settlements, or of those in the Chilterns behind Reading and Henley-on-Thames. This is typical commuter country, with direct trains to London from Goring, Cholsey and other stations along the Oxford–Reading line. Between 1961 and 1971 the population of Oxfordshire (excluding the city of Oxford itself) increased by 31 per cent, and in the former Henley-on-Thames Rural District the rate of growth reached 44 per cent. This population explosion 'underlines the curious situation of Oxfordshire being officially regarded as a non-growth area ... while it ranks as one of the fastest growing counties in England' (Emery, 1974). Inevitably such a rate of population growth, resulting from the combination of metropolitan pressures and restrictive policies towards house-building adopted by some neighbouring authorities, has produced unprecedented demands for housing in the countryside, with predictable consequences for the rural environment, brilliantly portrayed in *Landscape in Distress* (Brett, 1965).

Brett's survey painted a depressing picture of twentieth-century housing in the countryside, both in the Chiltern commuter belt and in overspill country south and west of Oxford. Goring was found to be 'besieged by speculative builders on all sides', the Sonning Common mini-conurbation north of Reading 'interesting as showing twentieth-century residential development in its pure form undistorted by planning ... As country, which it claims to be on all maps, it is a write-off.' Russell's Water, near Henley, 'is now a mess of bungalows and Builder's Allsorts. Summer weekends see London cars creeping up every lane looking for a site or a cottage.' In overspill country, 'Benson appears to be a village gone mad. The few remaining cottages have been swallowed into the maw of a sprawl of speculative building', while 'the less said about Chinnor the better. It contains within or tacked on to its curious quadrilateral of roads just about all the sorts of ugly housing this country has produced since World War I.'

From these few paragraphs of highly abbreviated description it can be appreciated that within the Cotswold and South Oxfordshire Districts there is a diversity of environment, of population change and of housing which embraces the spectrum of conditions existing in rural areas in lowland England, and which, in addition to providing suitable material for the detailed survey, is also representative of major contemporary rural planning problems. These problems are summarised later in this chapter in conjunction with the response of the local planning authorities, but first they are set in the context of recent population changes in the two areas.

POPULATION STRUCTURE AND CHANGE

Total population change at rural district level between 1951 and 1971 is set out in Table 5.1. The broad trends indicated are a reversal of population decline in the Cotswolds as a whole, with a modest increase in the second decade; this compares with accelerated growth in South Oxfordshire, where relatively rapid development in the 1950s had intensified into dramatic and apparently uncontrollable growth in the second decade, despite the presence of such supposedly inflexible, rigorous controls as green belt and area of outstanding natural beauty status. The paradox of rapid growth in areas of strict control, identified in Hertfordshire by Pahl (1965), and in areas beyond the green belt, suddenly vulnerable as pressures for housing development leapfrogged the area of strictest development control (Radford, 1970) was equally apparent in South Oxfordshire.

Table 5.1   *Population change in Cotswold and South Oxfordshire Districts, 1951–71*

Rural district	Population 1951	% change 1951–61	Population 1961	% change 1961–71	Population 1971
Cirencester	15,218	− 4·7	14,507	7·6	15,605
North Cotswold	21,925	− 7·7	20,229	0·9	20,422
Northleach	8,621	− 8·8	7,870	− 9·6	7,106
Tetbury	6,625	− 1·7	6,510	2·7	6,684
COTSWOLD TOTAL	52,389	− 6·3	49,116	1·4	49,817
Bullingdon	34,890	19·8	41,803	29·8	54,240
Henley	20,009	10·3	22,067	44·1	31,803
Wallingford	15,598	22·4	19,092	25·7	24,001
SOUTH OXFORDSHIRE TOTAL	70,497	17·7	82,962	32·6	110,044

Source: Population Census, 1961, 1971.

Population growth was not universally the case even in the 1960s, however, and in Northleach Rural District the rate of population loss actually increased from 8·8 to 9·6 per cent. Table 5.2 considers further the 1961–71 figures and reveals the extent to which increases in population in Cotswold District were dependent upon the excess of births over deaths in the indigenous population. In each of the four former rural districts gains due to natural increase were reduced, if not outweighed, by a negative migration balance, suggesting that the attractiveness of the area for retirement in-migrants and commuters was a less significant influence upon population change than the factors tending to increase out-migration, such as relative isolation, and lack of local employment opportunities. In all parts of South Oxfordshire both natural increase and the migration balance were

Table 5.2   *Composition of population change in Cotswold and South Oxfordshire Districts, 1961–71*

Rural district	Population 1961	Population 1971	Total change (%)	Natural increase (%)	Balance including migration (%)
Cirencester	14,507	15,605	0·73	0·84	−0·11
North Cotswold	20,229	20,422	0·09	0·33	−0·24
Northleach	7,870	7,106	−1·02	0·24	−1·28
Tetbury	6,510	6,684	0·26	0·52	−0·27
COTSWOLD TOTAL	49,116	49,817	0·31	n.a.	n.a.
Bullingdon	41,803	54,240	2·64	1·42	1·37
Henley	22,067	31,803	3·72	0·77	3·13
Wallingford	19,092	24,001	2·31	1·42	1·01
SOUTH OXFORDSHIRE TOTAL	82,962	110,044	2·82	n.a.	n.a.

Note: All percentages relate to percentage change per annum. Total change figures are calculated on a cumulative annual basis, and are therefore not directly comparable with the decennial change figures in Table 5.1.
Source: Population Census, 1961, 1971.

positive, largely reflecting incoming pressures from nearby urban areas.

The population statistics thus far considered relate to the total population enumerated in the census and as such they include population not in private households – for example, in armed forces establishments, or in institutions such as boarding schools, hospitals and prisons. The institutional population is rarely significant at the district level (the population not in private households comprised 3·5 per cent of the total population in Cotswold District, 4·2 per cent in South Oxfordshire District), but, as Jackson (1968) has established in respect of the north Cotswolds, it can be very important indeed locally, and patterns of private migration can be seriously distorted. Figures 5.1 and 5.2, which attempt to indicate local variations in population change, therefore exclude the institutional population and present information for changes in the population in private households for Cotswold and South Oxfordshire Districts. Significant differences between 'total' and 'private' population change occurred in some twenty of the 198 parishes, and could be ascribed, for instance, to reductions in aircraft establishments (Fairford and Kempsford, Cotswold District), growth in school populations (Nuneham Courtenay, South Oxfordshire District; Rendcomb, Cotswold District), and changes in hospital residents (Checkendon, South Oxfordshire District).

Figure 5.1 illustrates a typically complex pattern of local population growth and decline, with the juxtaposition of gains and losses in adjoining parishes a common feature. Losses were, however, both commonest and

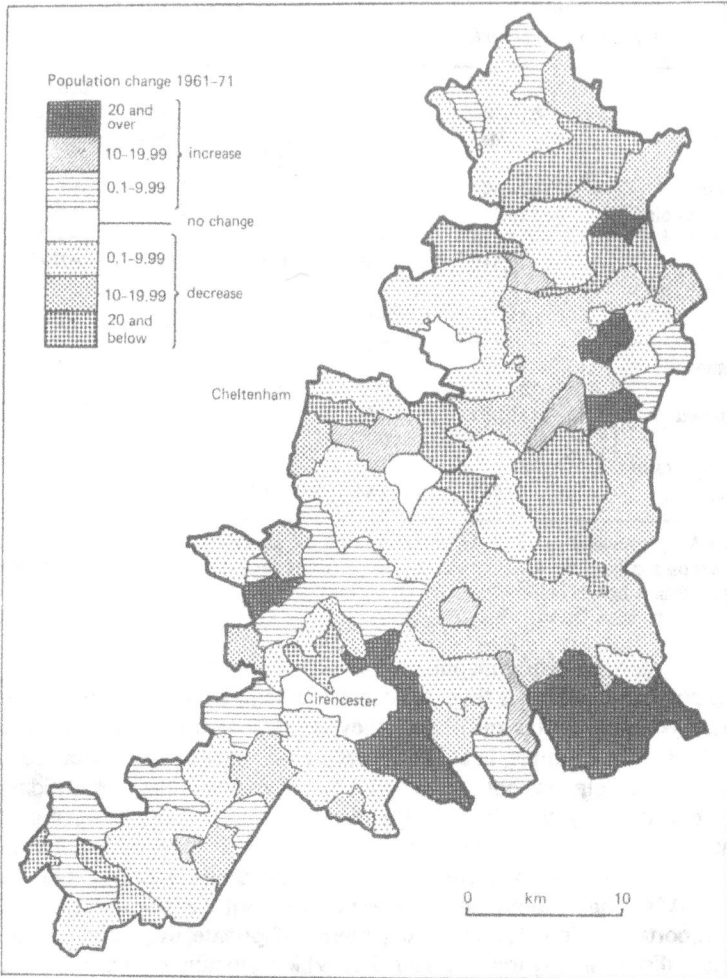

Figure 5.1   *Population change, 1961–71, Cotswold District*

most severe in the central Cotswolds, where seven parishes in the former
Northleach Rural District registered losses of 20 per cent or more between
1961 and 1971. Further north there is a contrast between isolated,
depopulating parishes such as Adlestrop and Clapton and parishes such as
Maugersbury which have seen considerable recent housing development.
In the south of Cotswold District, the provision of local authority housing
has led to concentrations of growth at Siddington and South Cerney, and
substantial growth has also taken place in villages such as Kempsford and
Preston. Even here, however, there are pockets of depopulation in remoter

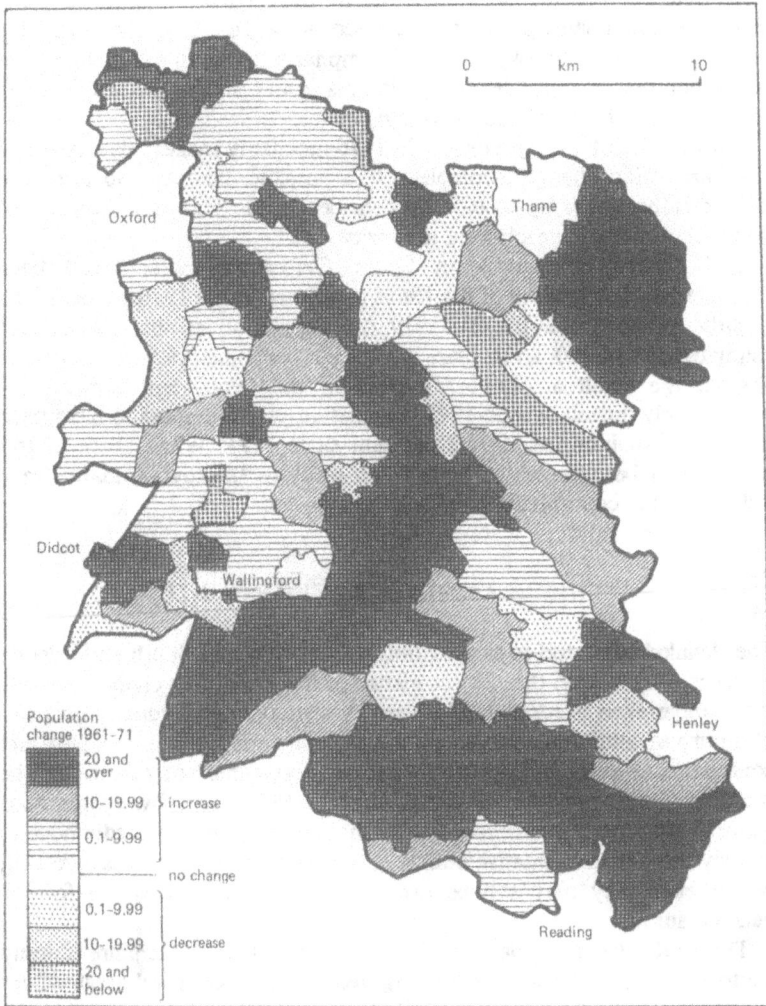

Figure 5.2 *Population change, 1961–71, South Oxfordshire District*

parishes including Ozleworth and Rodmarton. A similarly complicated picture of population change existed in South Oxfordshire (Figure 5.2): the emphasis is much more upon growth, however, and the figures for parishes in the mini-conurbation north of Reading underline the scale of growth involved: Sonning Common (+ 92 per cent, to 3,830), Eye and Dunsden (+ 154 per cent, to 4,831), Kidmore End (+ 28 per cent, to 2,085), and so on. Thames Valley settlements such as Cholsey and Goring have increased their population at a similarly dramatic rate as a consequence of in-migration by commuters. Such losses as have occurred have generally taken place in smaller settlements less accessible from motorways and the rail network, but the overwhelming emphasis in South Oxfordshire has been upon the accommodation of migrants from London, Oxford, Reading and the other towns of south-east England.

The absence of a sample census in 1976 inevitably makes this analysis of past population change incomplete. It is possible, however, to bring the picture rather more up to date by considering the mid-year estimates of population made for each local authority.

The pattern of growth in South Oxfordshire which had been characteristic particularly of the 1960s continued in the 1970s, though at a slightly reduced rate. By mid-1979 the population of this district was estimated as 134,700, an increase of 22·4 per cent since 1971. In Cotswold District the small amount of growth in the 1960s had grown very considerably indeed by mid-1979. Population was estimated to have risen to 68,400, an increase of 37·3 per cent since 1971. While much of this growth can be expected to have taken place in the towns, many small villages in the countryside must have grown too.

THE PLANNING BACKGROUND

The detailed case studies carried out in Cotswold and South Oxfordshire Districts which form the subject matter of the next three chapters clearly were undertaken in rural areas which, by virtue of extraordinary diversity of environmental and socio-economic structure mirrored in complex and contrasting patterns of population change, represented in microcosm the state of rural lowland England in the 1970s. A few paragraphs summarising the planning response to these conditions can hardly hope to convey more than a tentative outline of the problems and policies involved; nevertheless they may still be useful in providing a backcloth for the detailed surveys.

The draft structure plan for Gloucestershire (Gloucestershire County Council, 1978) recognises the varying needs of different rural areas within the county, and proposes that priority be given to the north Cotswolds and southern Forest of Dean in attracting employment, since the central aim of the strategy is 'to maintain and, where possible, improve the economic and social well-being of rural communities'. The principal housing policy states that 'a dispersal of residential development will be encouraged to main villages and their supporting settlements in areas where the possibility of rural decline is greatest, particularly in the North and South Cotswolds'. This recognition of the needs of supporting settlements in addition to main villages is translated into policy form only in the Cotswolds, rural growth in the remainder of the county being tightly restricted to main villages. Encouragement for the smaller, supporting villages was based on the recognition of the necessity for action to stabilise or increase population levels and provide local employment and housing in an attempt to retain or improve levels of rural service provision, and in particular rural transport services.

The location for the majority of development planned in the Cotswolds, however, was anticipated to be the main villages, of which thirty-three were located in the Cotswold District Council area, in addition to the towns of Bourton-on-the-Water, Chipping Campden, Moreton-in-Marsh, Northleach and Stow-on-the-Wold in the north Cotswolds and Cirencester, Fairford, Lechlade and Tetbury in the south Cotswolds. Employment would be concentrated in the towns and especially in Cirencester – a reflection of recent trends. In the north Cotswolds about half of the new housing required (1,800 houses by 1996) would be dispersed to the main and supporting villages, although priority would be given to development at Northleach in order to reverse population decline there and underpin the remaining local services in the town, which include a cottage hospital and a secondary school.

The background against which local housing and planning policies in South Oxfordshire District will be formed in the 1980s is sketched out in the *First Structure Plan for Oxfordshire* (Oxfordshire County Council, 1976), submitted in 1976 and approved by the minister in early 1979. Two alternative strategies for the county were considered, one concentrating development largely in the Oxford area and the other dispersing housing and employment to six towns (including Didcot), with strictly controlled development only around Oxford itself. It is the latter policy which is favoured in the plan.

The significance of the so-called country towns policy for the rural areas of South Oxfordshire is broadly twofold. On the one hand there is expected to be some development in Didcot – some 3,500 new jobs and 4,450 new dwellings by 1991. This concentration will account for a substantial proportion of the 7,700 new dwellings (out of a county total of 19,250) which are expected to be located in South Oxfordshire as a whole.

The remaining dwellings will be distributed among villages where there already exists a reasonable range of services and any growth in housing and employment is presumed to relate only to local needs. A key feature of the plan is the emphasis given to landscape conservation (particularly in the Chilterns Area of Outstanding Natural Beauty) and to minimising the loss of agricultural land. The strategy for most of rural South Oxfordshire is thus clear: restraint of development except to allow for limited local need and then only in the larger villages where services already exist. Elsewhere there will be no housing development and the key policies in most villages will thus relate to conservation rather than growth. The location of South Oxfordshire in so accessible a part of lowland England must, however, raise doubts about this policy of no growth. As was mentioned earlier, 'no growth' was essentially the watchword of the 1960s – and yet population growth in this district ranged from 25 to 44 per cent. A less dynamic economy and a higher relative cost of private transport might dampen the continuation of this pattern into the 1980s, but pressure upon rural housing resources from outside South Oxfordshire District seems likely to continue nevertheless.

KEY TO PARISH LOCATION MAPS

COTSWOLD DISTRICT (FIGURE 5.3)

Cirencester RD

1	Ampney Crucis	19	Kemble
2	Ampney St Mary	20	Kempsford
3	Ampney St Peter	21	Lechlade
4	Bagendon	22	Maiseyhampton
5	Barnsley	23	North Cerney
6	Baunton	24	Poole Keynes
7	Brimpsfield	25	Poulton
8	Coates	26	Preston
9	Colesbourne	27	Quenington
10	Daglingworth	28	Rendcomb
11	Down Ampney	29	Rodmarton
12	Driffield	30	Sapperton
13	Duntisbourne Abbots	31	Siddington
14	Duntisbourne Rouse	32	Somerford Keynes
15	Edgeworth	33	South Cerney
16	Elkstone	34	Syde
17	Fairford	35	Winstone
18	Hatherop		

North Cotswold RD

36	Adlestrop	55	Longborough
37	Aston Subedge	56	Lower Slaughter
38	Batsford	57	Maugersbury
39	Bledington	58	Mickleton
40	Blockley	59	Moreton-in-Marsh
41	Bourton-on-the-Hill	60	Naunton
42	Bourton-on-the-Water	61	Oddington
43	Broadwell	62	Saintbury
44	Chipping Campden	63	Sezincote
45	Clapton	64	Stow-on-the-Wold
46	Condicote	65	Swell
47	Cutsdean	66	Temple Guiting
48	Donnington	67	Todenham
49	Ebrington	68	Upper Slaughter
50	Evenlode	69	Westcote
51	Great Rissington	70	Weston Subedge
52	Guiting Power	71	Wick Rissington
53	Icomb	72	Willersey
54	Little Rissington		

Northleach RD

73	Aldsworth	86	Hazleton
74	Andoversford	87	Northleach with Eastington
75	Aston Blank	88	Notgrove
76	Barrington	89	Sevenhampton
77	Bibury	90	Sherborne
78	Chedworth	91	Shipton
79	Coln St Aldwyns	92	Southrop
80	Coln St Dennis	93	Turkdean
81	Compton Abdale	94	Whittington
82	Dowdeswell	95	Windrush
83	Eastleach	96	Winson
84	Farmington	97	Withington
85	Hampnett	98	Yanworth

Tetbury RD

99	Ashley	106	Long Newnton
100	Avening	107	Ozleworth
101	Beverstone	108	Shipton Moyne
102	Boxwell with Leighterton	109	Tetbury
103	Cherington	110	Tetbury Upton
104	Didmarton	111	Westonbirt with Lasborough
105	Kingscote		

SOUTH OXFORDSHIRE DISTRICT (FIGURE 5.4)

Bullingdon RD

1	Adwell	23	Great Milton
2	Aston Rowant	24	Holton
3	Beckley and Stowood	25	Horspath
4	Benson	26	Lewknor
5	Berinsfield	27	Little Milton
6	Berrick Salome	28	Littlemore
7	Brightwell Baldwin	29	Marsh Baldon
8	Britwell	30	Marston
9	Chalgrove	31	Newington
10	Chinnor	32	Nuneham Courtenay
11	Clifton Hampden	33	Pyrton
12	Crowell	34	Risinghurst and Sandhills
13	Cuddeston and Denton	35	Sandford-on-Thames
14	Culham	36	Shirburn
15	Cuxham with Easington	37	Stadhampton
16	Dorchester	38	Stanton St John
17	Drayton St Leonard	39	Stoke Talmage
18	Elsfield	40	Sydenham
19	Ewelme	41	Tetsworth
20	Forest Hill with Shotover	42	Thomley
21	Garsington	43	Tiddington-with-Albury
22	Great Haseley	44	Toot Baldon

45 Towersey
46 Warborough
47 Waterperry
48 Waterstock

49 Watlington
50 Wheatfield
51 Wheatley
52 Woodeaton

Henley RD

53 Bix
54 Checkendon
55 Crowmarsh
56 Eye and Dunsden
57 Goring
58 Goring Heath
59 Harpsden
60 Highmoor
61 Ipsden
62 Kidmore End
63 Mapledurham
64 Nettlebed

65 Nuffield
66 Pishill with Stonor
67 Rotherfield Greys
68 Rotherfield Peppard
69 Shiplake
70 Sonning Common
71 South Stoke
72 Stoke Row
73 Swincombe
74 Whitchurch
75 Woodcote

Wallingford RD

76 Aston Tirrold
77 Aston Upthorpe
78 Brightwell-cum-Sotwell
79 Cholsey
80 Didcot
81 East Hagbourne

82 Little Wittenham
83 Long Wittenham
84 Moulsford
85 North Moreton
86 South Moreton
87 West Hagbourne

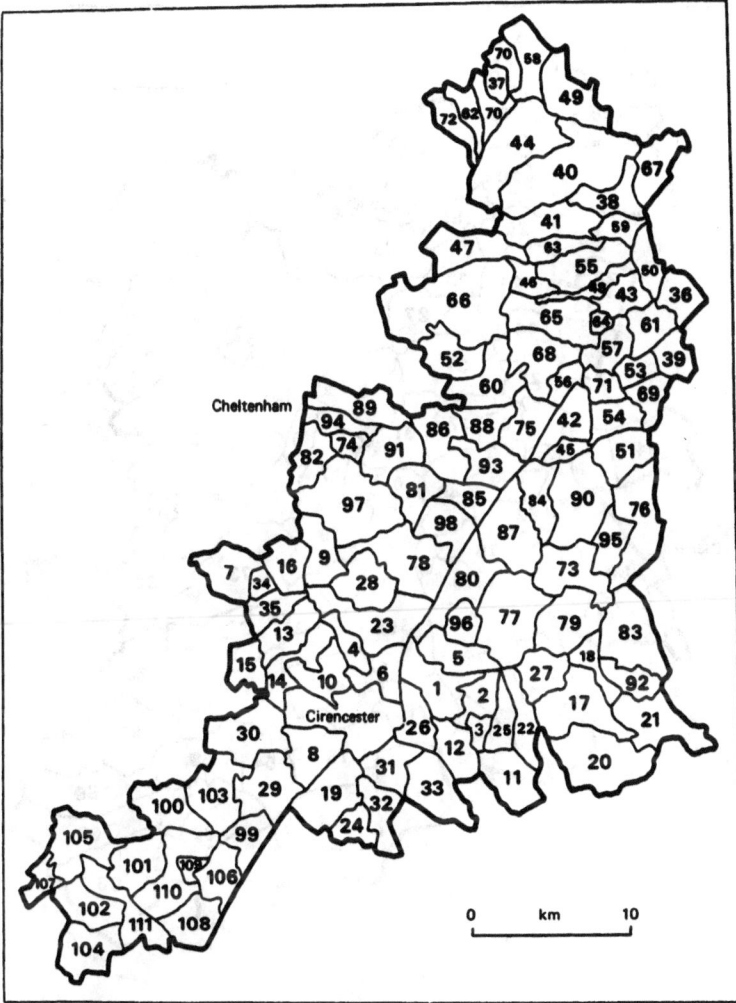

Figure 5.3 *Parish location map, Cotswold District*

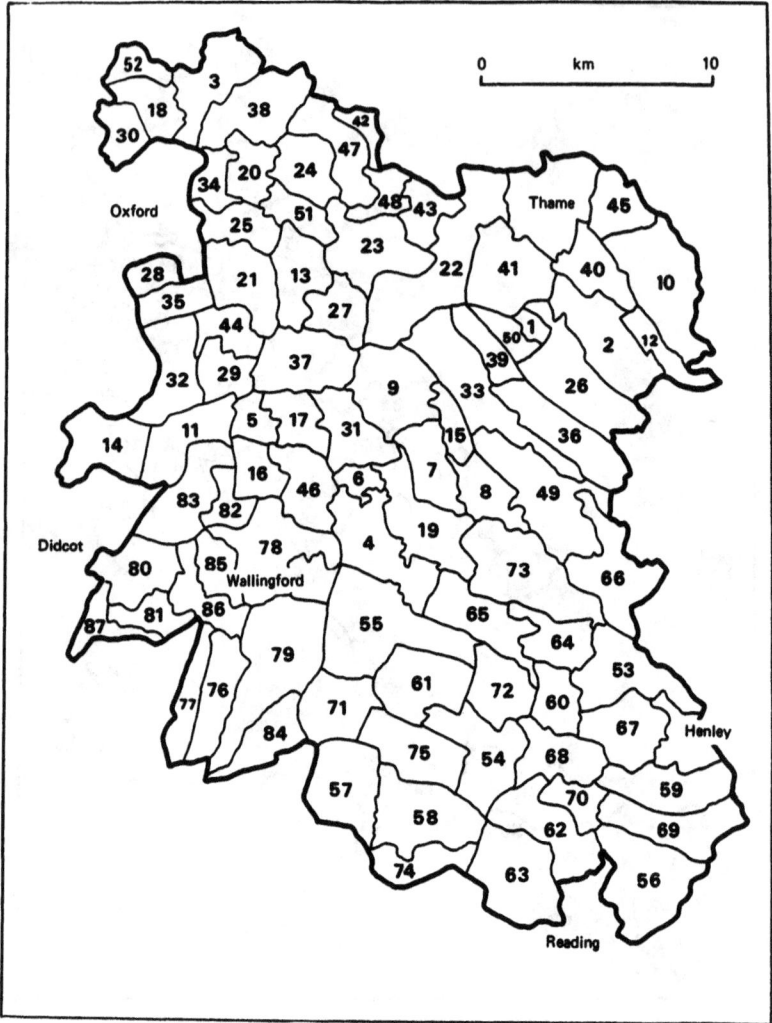

Figure 5.4   *Parish location map, South Oxfordshire District*

Chapter 6

Rural Housing at the Local Level

The aim of this chapter is to examine the nature of rural housing and rural households in the two districts chosen for case study, namely, Cotswold and South Oxfordshire. As such it develops the arguments introduced in Chapters 3 and 4 where a national review of rural housing was given, and it illustrates the variations which exist at the local level and which necessarily complicate the application of housing and related policies to individual rural areas.

After an analysis of the pattern of housing tenure and the conditions of housing in these two districts, the chapter continues with an exploration of the relationships between housing and the social and economic structure of the rural population. Finally an overall view of the structure of rural housing is attempted in the same way as the national picture was portrayed in Chapter 4. A cluster analysis technique is used to identify rural housing profiles on a more detailed scale than that employed at the national level.

The basic source of data for these analyses is the Census of Population, 1971. Although its use for housing studies is limited it remains by far the most comprehensive and accessible source of data for comparative purposes. Special surveys, such as those carried out in recent years by South Oxfordshire District Council or by central government (Department of the Environment, 1978b) may occasionally provide a valuable contribution, but comparative studies between areas are usually not possible.

The use of the population census is not without its problems and some of these have been considered in the context of rural housing studies of the two study districts (Rawson, 1978a, 1978b). In part these problems relate to slight discrepancies between the published statistics given in census volumes and the unpublished Small Area Statistics which are produced for enumeration districts. Largely because special enumeration districts, generally containing non-private households, and enumeration districts with populations of less than twenty-five persons were excluded from calculations and also because data for small enumeration districts are subject to randomisation (Office of Population Censuses and Surveys, 1973) for the sake of confidentiality, totals calculated from this source do not always coincide with those found in published census volumes. Moreover, because rural district data are rounded to the nearest five, another discrepancy between figures is introduced. In practice these discrepancies are rarely significant, but it is important to note that census data used in this chapter are invariably calculated from enumeration district data and not taken from published census volumes.

Some updating of housing data on a roughly comparable basis should be possible as a result of returns which have to be made by local authorities in connection with Housing Investment Programmes (see Chapter 11). In practice, however, definitions vary and comparisons of data are virtually impossible with the result that relatively little use can be made of this source.

HOUSING TENURE AND QUALITY IN THE COTSWOLD AND SOUTH OXFORDSHIRE DISTRICTS

From the outset, the pattern of tenure in these two districts (Table 6.1) emphasises significant differences which are essentially related to their economic structure and to the varying influence of urbanisation. In particular, the greater importance of agriculture within Cotswold District is reflected in the much higher proportion of the total housing stock in the privately rented sector, where many houses are tied cottages and tenanted farm properties. Conversely, this sector is noticeably lower in South Oxfordshire District where metropolitan influences are stronger, and owner-occupation is proportionally more important.

Table 6.1   *Housing tenure in Cotswold and South Oxfordshire Districts, 1971 (%)*

District	Owner-occupier	Local authority	Privately rented unfurnished	Privately rented furnished
Cotswold	41·0	17·7	36·3	5·0
South Oxfordshire	57·6	19·7	17·5	5·2
English rural districts	54·5	21·1	20·9	3·3

Source: Census, 1971, Small Area Statistics.

The tenancy pattern in Cotswold District in 1971 (Table 6.1; Figure 6.1) is typical of many traditional agricultural areas. There is a relatively low proportion of owner-occupiers despite retirement migrants moving into the area and buying properties. Owner-occupier households are particularly concentrated in the south-east of the Cotswold District around Cirencester,

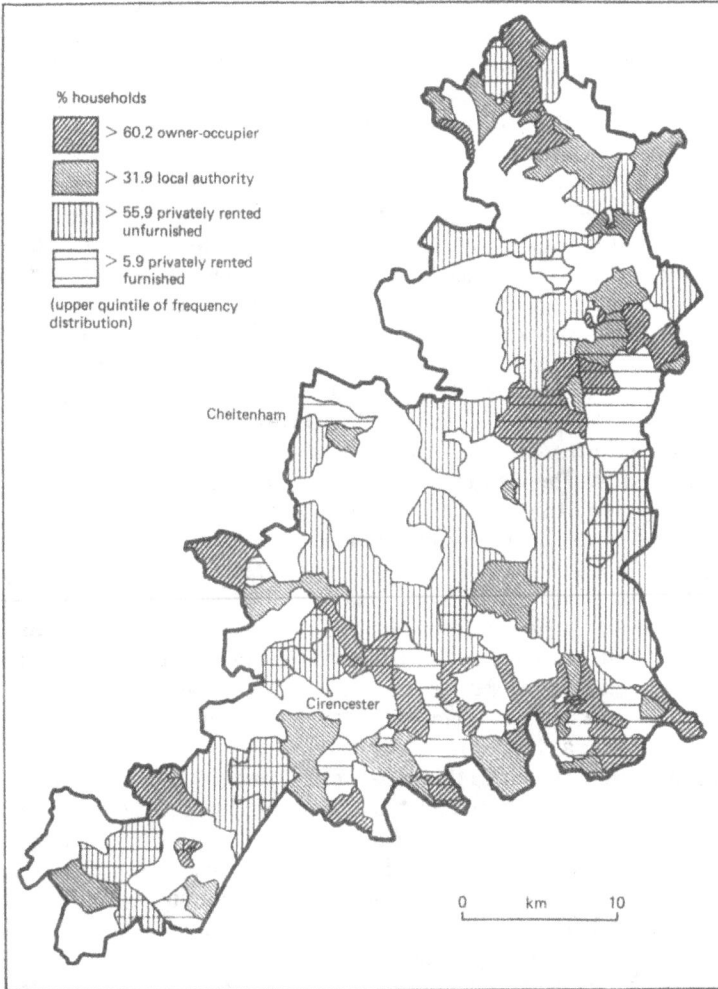

Figure 6.1 *The dominant pattern of housing tenure, Cotswold District, 1971*

and also characterise the retirement centres further north around Bourton-on-the-Water and Chipping Campden. There are relatively few owner-occupiers in the more rural areas of the eastern part of the former Northleach Rural District and to the south-west of Cirencester.

The second major tenure group in Cotswold District in 1971 relates to households renting private unfurnished accommodation. The decline in the private rented sector in Britain (from 61 per cent of total stock in 1947 to 13 per cent in 1973), especially in urban areas, has not had so great an impact in this area, where proportionately half as many households again rented private unfurnished accommodation as in English rural areas as a whole in 1971. The 36·3 per cent of households living in this sector reflect to some extent the persistence of the tied cottage and estate village elements of the agricultural scene in the Cotswolds, where 25·6 per cent of heads of households in 1971 were either farmers or farmworkers.

This tenure group is not evenly spread throughout the Cotswold District but tends to be concentrated in some of the smaller parishes and is particularly found in the east of the district in the former Northleach Rural District. In 10 per cent of the enumeration districts more than two-thirds (67·6 per cent) of all households rented private dwellings. In some villages the dominance of this tenure type is total, notably in the estate villages of the Barringtons, Aldsworth, Sherbourne and Windrush. The controversial and particular problems resulting from this total dependance upon private landlords have been especially associated with one of the villages in this area – Great Barrington (Forester, 1976; O'Donovan, 1977).

Council tenants make up a relatively small group, as they do in rural areas nationally. The distribution of council dwellings, however, is even more critical than that of privately rented accommodation. Many villages have few council houses while some centres, notably in the former Cirencester Rural District, are fairly well provided for (Figure 6.1).

Rented furnished lettings in Cotswold District (5·0 per cent of households) are rather more common than in Britain or rural areas in England. Most households are concentrated around Little Rissington, where they relate to the services component in the population, and in the Kempsford area, where they are attached to the British Aircraft Corporation base at Fairford.

Relatively little change in this broad tenure pattern seems to have taken place since 1971. Unfortunately, the Housing Investment Programme return does not allow an easy comparison. However, in 1977 24·1 per cent of households were recorded as living in public sector housing which included houses rented from the Ministry of Defence and other statutory bodies and which were considered as privately rented accommodation above. Moreover the town of Cirencester, which has a significant proportion of privately rented dwellings, is included in this 1977 total, whereas Cirencester Urban District was excluded from the census data already given.

The image of the Cotswolds as a traditional rural area may suggest that the condition of the housing stock in the more rural areas of Cotswold District would be rather poor. In fact, in this district only 11·5 per cent of households lacked exclusive use of one or more standard amenities in 1971, compared with 13·8 per cent for English rural areas. None the less, housing quality is unevenly distributed both spatially and between tenures. Table 6.2 shows how privately rented properties are in general much more likely to lack housing amenities. Moreover, in 10 per cent of the enumeration districts in Cotswold District more than 21·6 per cent of households did not

Table 6.2 Household amenities and housing density by tenure in Cotswold District and South Oxfordshire District, 1971 (%)

Tenure	Household amenities			Persons per room		
	Sharing/lacking bath	Sharing/lacking hot water	Sharing/lacking inside WC	>1·5	>1·0	<0·5
Cotswold District						
All households	7·9	6·9	9·0	0·6	4·6	42·6
Owner-occupied	6·4	5·5	6·9	0·1	1·6	53·2
Local authority rented	2·5	2·3	4·0	1·7	10·0	27·3
Privately rented unfurnished	14·5	12·9	16·7	0·5	4·5	42·1
Privately rented furnished	5·6	3·7	6·4	0·5	6·5	27·4
South Oxfordshire District						
All households	5·7	5·1	7·1	0·7	4·6	34·0
Owner-occupied	4·3	3·9	5·0	0·2	2·3	38·8
Local authority rented	2·1	1·7	5·6	1·9	10·4	20·9
Privately rented unfurnished	15·4	14·4	17·1	1·0	4·6	39·1
Privately rented furnished	10·9	9·2	11·7	1·1	6·3	24·1

Source: Census of Population, 1971, published rural district tables (not from Small Area Statistics).

have exclusive use of all basic amenities (Rawson, 1978a). These households are heavily concentrated in the estate villages in the east of the district, where the attractive façades of Cotswold stone cottages may conceal interiors with considerably less desirable conditions.

Densities of occupation in Cotswold District were low in 1971 – very few households were recorded as being in overcrowded accommodation (Table 6.2). Conversely, occupancy rates suggest that underoccupation of the housing stock may well be something of a problem, particularly for a local housing authority seeking to optimise the use of its property.

In South Oxfordshire District the most notable feature of the tenure structure is the high proportion of owner-occupiers, particularly when compared with Cotswold District (Table 6.1). On the other hand, the level of privately rented unfurnished accommodation is much lower and is, in fact, below the national rural mean also. Owner-occupiers are particularly common in the south of South Oxfordshire District, particularly the former Henley Rural District, and in 10 per cent of the enumeration districts more than 91 per cent of households were in this category. The importance of professional employment (involving 22·8 per cent of all heads of household in 1971) is an obvious linking factor here and the accessibility of the area to major employment centres like Oxford, Reading and, of course, London is a contributory influence. Away from these urban influences in the centre of South Oxfordshire District, where accessibility is less good and the economy more traditionally based in agriculture, owner-occupation levels fall.

Households renting from the local authority accounted for 19·7 per cent of all households in 1971, with the lowest levels found in the former Henley Rural District. Many council properties are found around the urban centres of Didcot, Oxford and Wallingford with some other large concentrations, notably at Berinsfield.

While the influence of urban pressures is clearly seen in the housing structure of South Oxfordshire, there are also remnants of the old rural economy which are equally reflected in the tenure pattern. In contrast to Cotswold District, the level of privately rented unfurnished accommodation is low (17·5 per cent). Nevertheless, there are areas where levels are quite high (Figure 6.2) particularly in the larger agricultural parishes. In part this relates to the question of poorer accessibility referred to above, but it may well also be related to the relics of old land-holding patterns in much the same way as the estate villages of Cotswold District reflect an older, closed economy.

This link between privately rented property and closed villages (Emery, 1974) can perhaps be most clearly seen in the case of Nuneham Courtenay which developed as part of the Harcourt Estate. Evidence provided from research at the University of Reading by Banks (1978) suggests that this explanation may also be applicable in the case of the villages of Pyrton and Shirburn which were previously part of the Macclesfield Estate and a

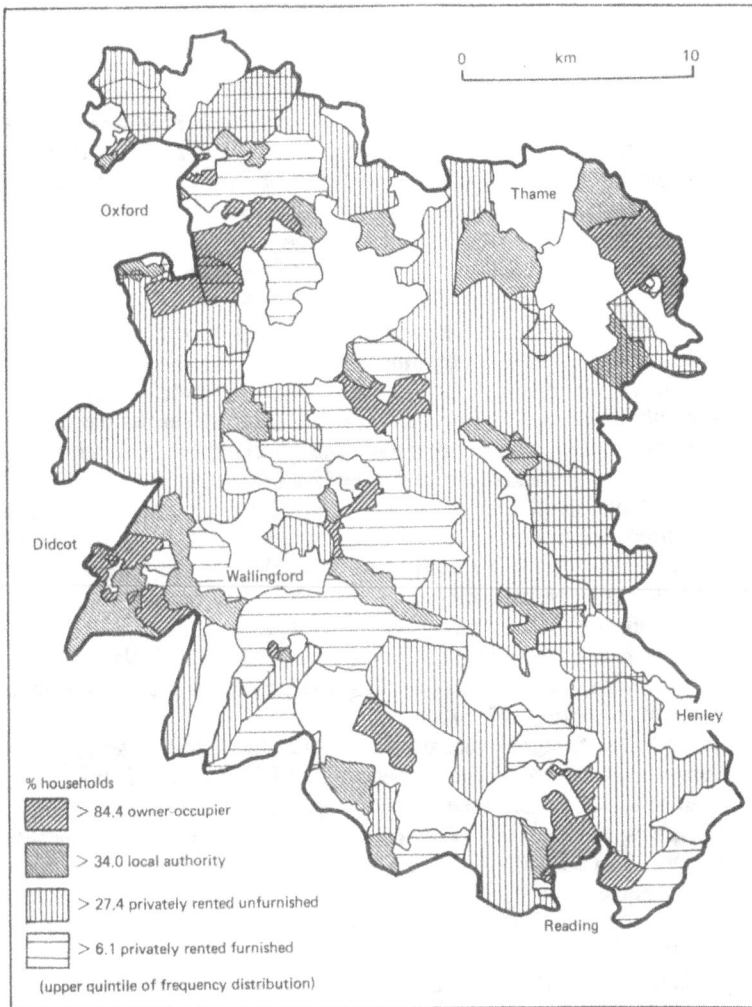

Figure 6.2
The dominant pattern of housing tenure, South Oxfordshire District, 1971

similar explanation is also possible in the case of Little Wittenham,
Moulsford and Mapledurham. In all these cases a single landlord or at most
a few large landlords were originally responsible for the growth and even
the origin of the village with the strict exclusion of development by
outsiders, and this control is evidenced today by the relatively high
proportion of private tenants and correspondingly low numbers of owner-
occupiers and council tenants.

Two further housing categories in South Oxfordshire should be noted.

Privately rented furnished property, while only making up a small (5·2 per cent) proportion of the housing stock is nevertheless important where armed service bases are found. Benson RAF base and army personnel based at Didcot (Figure 6.2) provide clear examples of this. Of equal, if not greater significance, are the concentrations of households living in non-permanent accommodation, particularly on the urban fringes of Oxford and Didcot. Some 4·4 per cent of all households in South Oxfordshire were found in these mobile homes, which were considered briefly at the national level in Chapter 3. Indeed South Oxfordshire is one of only three districts in England with more than a thousand mobile homes on private sites (Department of the Environment, 1977).

Housing quality in South Oxfordshire District is generally good. In its 1977 Housing Investment Programme (HIP) statement, the local authority recorded only 1·6 per cent of the housing stock as unfit for habitation, and that generally occurred in the privately rented sector. A similar bias is seen in the provision of household amenities (Table 6.2), where 10·7 per cent of households in 1971 lacked the exclusive use of one or more household amenities. Poor standards of amenity provision are correlated with concentrations of privately rented property within this district, particularly where estate villages are found. For example, amenity provision is noticeably lower in Nuneham Courtenay (where 25 per cent of households lacked exclusive use of basic amenities in 1971) and in Stanton St John. The latter village has in the past been largely in the hands of New College, Oxford and seems to repeat the pattern associated with closed villages noted above (see also Larkin, 1978b).

Poor facilities and some overcrowding are also found in the same areas as concentrations of mobile homes, especially the fringe areas of Oxford and Didcot, and it is likely that the two factors are related. Underoccupation is far less prevalent than in Cotswold District, probably because the age structure of the population is younger, with fewer pensioners and more children in households.

RURAL HOUSEHOLDS AND RURAL HOUSING

The structure of housing in a rural area as seen through its basic pattern of tenure is not an isolated phenomenon. Housing tenure relates essentially to the different attitudes of members of society and to the opportunities and handicaps which they face in realising their aspirations. Looking behind the simple fourfold division of tenure which was explored above, the researcher can find a common pattern of association between housing tenure and the social and economic characteristics of rural households. This was the approach adopted in Chapter 3 and it will be followed again here.

A simple correlation analysis of census variables shows this pattern of association between housing and households. Table 6.3 records for both the

Table 6.3 *The links between rural housing tenure and rural households, 1971*

Tenure	Cotswold District Positive correlation	Cotswold District Negative correlation	South Oxfordshire District Positive correlation	South Oxfordshire District Negative correlation
Owner-occupiers				large households (−0·5092) households lacking cars (−0·4621)
Local authority	skilled manual workers (0·4858) female activity rate (0·4160) households lacking cars (0·5018) overcrowding (0·4135) total households in enumeration district (0·4102)	underoccupancy (−·4466) two-car households (−0·4324)	large households (0·6203) households lacking cars (0·5980) unskilled manual workers (0·4364) household size (0·4455) overcrowding (0·4257)	underoccupancy (−0·4117)
Private tenants (unfurnished)	agricultural workers (0·4766)	total households in enumeration district (−0·5697)	agricultural workers (0·4974) farmers (0·4019) vacant houses (0·4331) two car households (0·4042) underoccupancy (0·5655)	total households in enumeration district (−0·5369)
Private tenants (furnished)	young married couples (0·4137) households with children (0·4940) armed forces employment (0·8557) number of children (0·4815)		armed forces employment (0·9106)	

Notes: All correlations are greater than ± 0·4; significant at 0·001. Tenure-based variables are omitted (see text).
Source: Analysis of Census enumeration district data, 1971. For list of variables, see Appendix III.

study areas the main correlations which were found between the four main tenure categories and other variables. It does not show reciprocal correlations between tenures such as where high levels of owner occupation (understandably) correlate with low levels of privately rented houses, nor does it record correlations below a value of ± 0·4. Immediately it is possible to expand on the simple structure of rural housing in the two study districts which has so far been presented.

Owner-occupiers, as the dominant category in both areas, are treated least satisfactorily by this analysis. Not only are they the largest group, they also come from a comparatively wide range of social and economic backgrounds. Only in South Oxfordshire are the links sufficiently strong to suggest that in this district at least owner-occupiers tend to make up smaller rather than larger households and less often households with no private transport.

Council tenants form a much clearer group in these rural areas and the clear similarity between the two areas suggests that this pattern would be repeated elsewhere. Moreover the pattern matches the national picture given in Chapter 3. Households in local authority housing tend to be larger and rather more crowded than other tenure groups. They are more likely to be without a car and, at least in Cotswold District, are likely to be found in larger, rather than smaller, settlements. Heads of households are generally to be found in skilled or unskilled manual occupations.

Private tenants, too, are clearly differentiated by this simple analysis and both tenure types link strongly with one important group in the countryside. For unfurnished property this is clearly the agricultural worker in both study districts. Moreover, in South Oxfordshire tenant farmers also come into the picture. In both cases also there is a strong negative correlation (Cotswold, − 0·57; South Oxfordshire, − 0·54) with population size, suggesting that this type of housing is more likely to be found in smaller rather than larger places with consequent problems of accessibility and service provision.

An even clearer correlation relates to the smallest of the tenure categories, tenants of furnished property. Here the link is very clearly with households where the head is employed in the armed services. The pattern of correlations in Cotswold District is more comprehensive. It stresses the importance of these houses for young households, particularly those with children. The implication is that this form of housing fulfils quite a specific role relating both to employment and to particular stages in the family cycle. This suggested role will be examined further later in this chapter.

The relationships noted above are shown in diagrammatic form in Figures 6.3 and 6.4. Here again correlations greater than ± 0·4 are shown, though here the reciprocal tenure variables have been included. Not only do these diagrams make clearer the links already discussed, but they also suggest some important points about the distribution of the main housing tenures. The strong negative correlations between council housing,

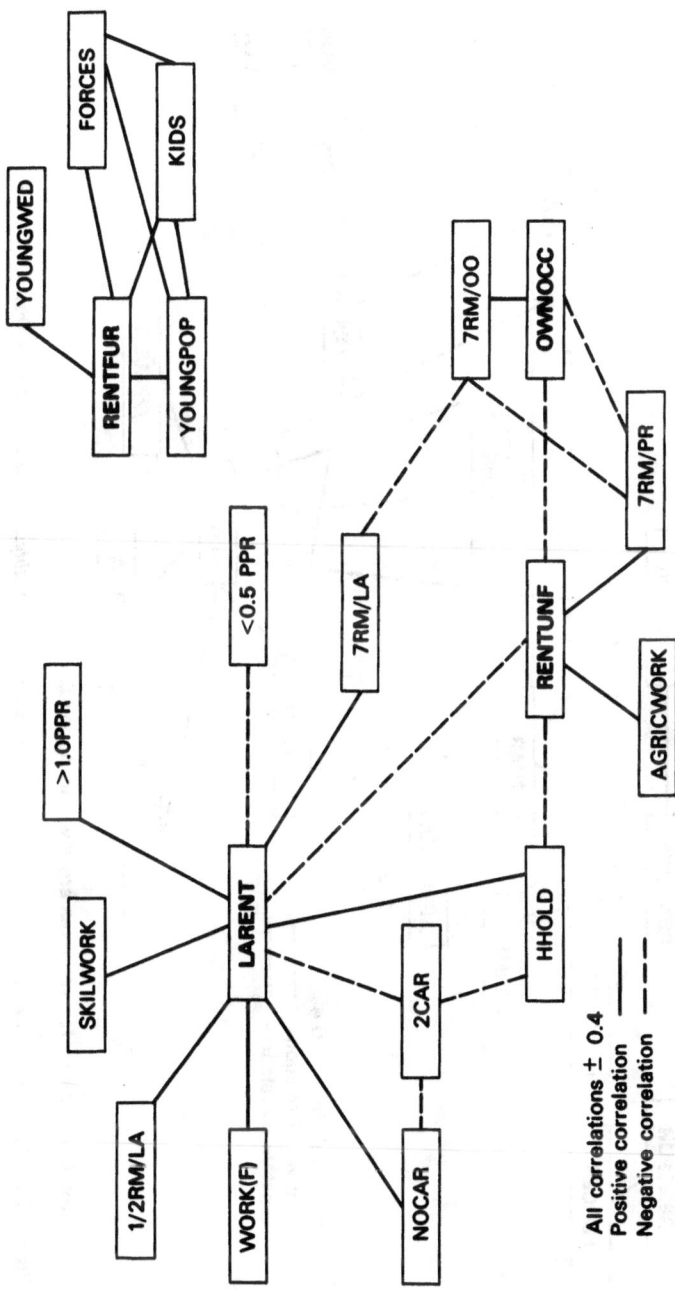

All correlations ± 0.4
Positive correlation ————
Negative correlation – – – –

Note: Code names for variables are given in Appendix III

Figure 6.3 *The links between housing tenure and socio-economic variables, Cotswold District, 1971*

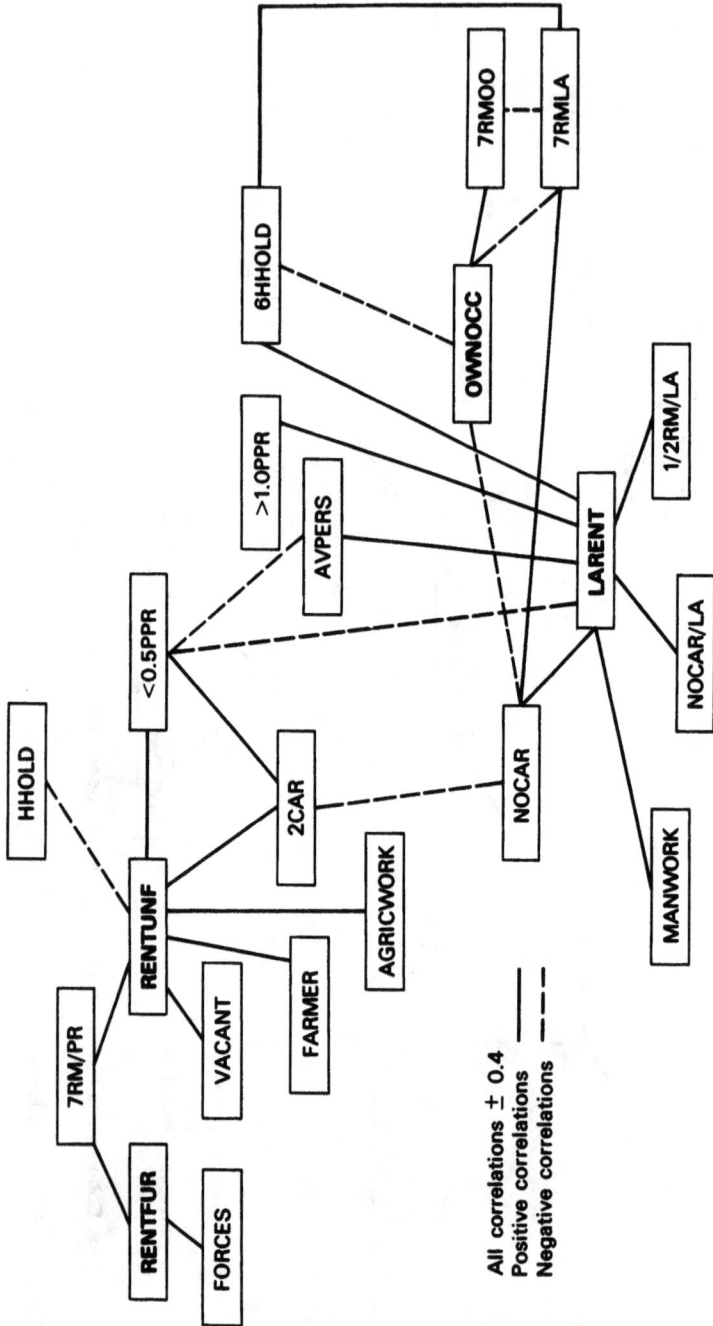

All correlations ± 0.4
Positive correlations ——————
Negative correlations ---------

Note: Code names for variables are given in Appendix III

Figure 6.4 *The links between housing tenure and socio-economic variables, South Oxfordshire District, 1971*

unfurnished rented property and areas of owner-occupation in Cotswold District suggest a polarisation of housing choice within some parts of the area. Similar links are evident in South Oxfordshire. Thus, where owner-occupation is dominant, households unable to enter this sector and dependent on local authority housing or privately rented property will invariably have to move to obtain housing.

HOUSING PROFILES AT THE LOCAL LEVEL

The national view of rural housing which was presented in Chapters 3 and 4 culminated with a classification of rural households to give seven rural housing profiles. This broad brush approach set the two study districts in their national context. Most of Cotswold District (the former North Cotswold, Northleach and Cirencester Rural Districts) fell within the profile termed 'agricultural: farmers', while the southern part of the Cotswold District (Tetbury Rural District) was classified in the 'transitional rural' category.

This largely agricultural image suggested for the Cotswold area contrasts with the profiles seen in South Oxfordshire District. Here, much of this district (Bullingdon and Wallingford Rural Districts) was grouped as 'transitional rural', while the higher status areas of the south of South Oxfordshire District (Henley Rural District) were classed as 'Owner-occupiers: high status'.

The other national classifications which have been mentioned previously, notably Webber's typologies at various scales and Cloke's indices of rurality serve to confirm this broad picture of the two study districts. South Oxfordshire was grouped by Webber and Craig (1976) as part of the 'suburban and growth areas' while Cotswold District was assigned to the 'rural and resort' family. Cloke's (1977) typology of the former rural districts also confirms this pattern, for example, stressing the less rural aspect of the area around Tetbury in the south of Cotswold District and grouping all the rural districts in South Oxfordshire as 'extreme non-rural'.

These broad national classifications are eminently suitable for the general description of the two study districts and for placing them within their national context. They are of much less use, however, as an aid to local policy. The enthusiasm for the use of social indicators and the creation of typologies has been tempered with a feeling by some authorities that these broad descriptive patterns are inappropriate for local planning. Thus, Openshaw and Cullingford (1979) have argued that, while an area-based approach to recognising rural deprivation is necessary, the broad scale of, for example, Webber's work is of little help in this respect. Moreover the fact that most of the national classifications have been limited to the census as a source of data has also been criticised. Local variations in housing and other factors can often be of such a specific and particular nature that the nationally oriented data from the census would miss the real significance of these special circumstances and local planning would therefore take little or no account of them.

These are valid criticisms which have to be answered by those who favour the use of social indicators in this respect. They are answered in part in this section where a more detailed analysis of the housing structure of the two study districts is made using cluster analysis. Though the data are taken only from the 1971 Census, they are examined in detail at the level of the enumeration district, and, as will be seen, the individual peculiarities of housing structure within each district, which were barely evident at the national level, are made clear at this scale.

The recognition of these more detailed housing profiles at the district level has therefore three objectives. First, it is considered as a natural progression from the analyses presented earlier in this chapter in the general understanding of rural housing and rural households. Secondly, it is put forward as a further example of the use of social indicators and classifications in the appreciation of local policy. Finally, it serves a distinctly practical purpose as the first step in a sampling frame for further research. The realisation that within the general mass of rural housing there existed less widespread, though not necessarily less important, types and tenures meant that these minority groups (for example, armed forces households or mobile home dwellers) had to be recognised at an early stage and sampled accordingly. By carrying out a cluster analysis it was possible to do this.

A far greater number of variables (seventy-five) was used in this analysis when compared with the national classification reported in Chapter 4. In the main this large number was justified because of the dangers of using a restricted number of variables with the small absolute numbers which are sometimes involved at the enumeration district level. If the criticism of lack of detail at the local level is to be answered, this is one way in which the method may be improved. The particular variables chosen for the analysis are given in Appendix III.

Two separate analyses were undertaken to classify the 178 enumeration districts in Cotswold District and the 233 enumeration districts in South Oxfordshire. The most stable solutions derived by cluster analysis identified five rural housing profiles in Cotswold District and six profiles in South Oxfordshire. There was little evidence of the patterns being distorted by the effects of chaining, and interpretation of the characteristics of the profiles revealed that the distinctive properties of the smaller clusters were such that intuitively one would have expected them to be very small.

The pattern of the five profiles in Cotswold District is shown in Figure 6.5, while the main characteristics of the profiles are described in Table 6.4. The predominantly agricultural character of the Cotswolds was evident in the largest group of enumeration districts, profile 1. Housing quality was relatively high, possibly relating to the generally prosperous agriculture of

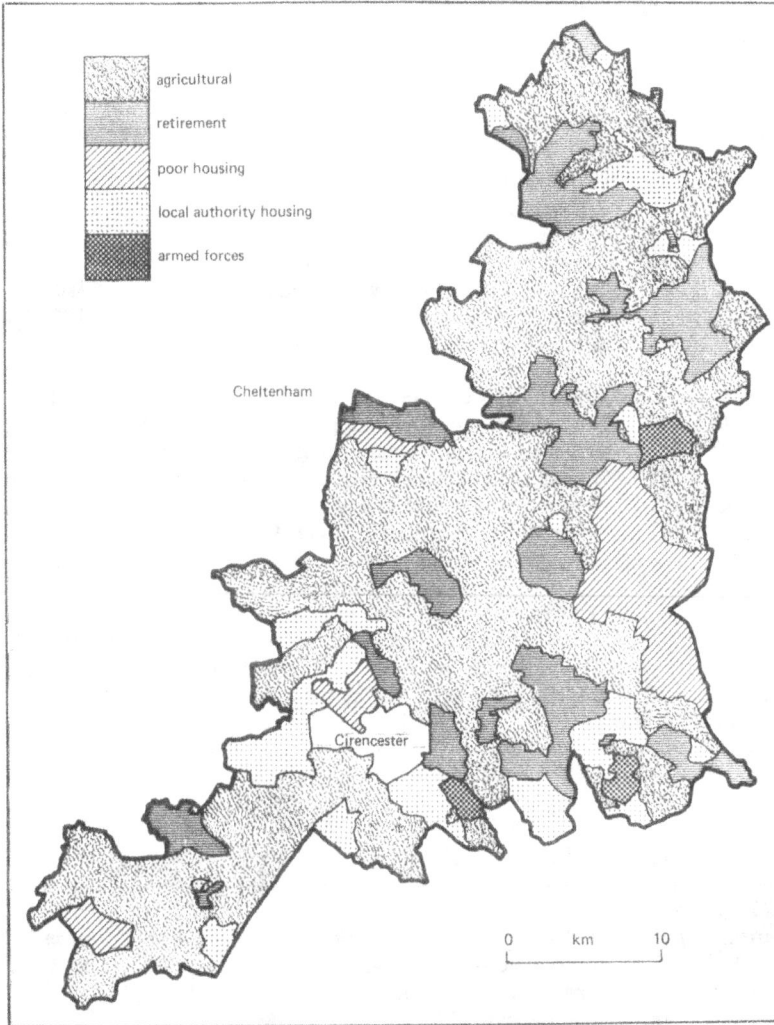

Figure 6.5 *Rural housing profiles, Cotswold District, 1971*

the area, and the profile was widely represented throughout the Cotswold District rather than concentrated in specific areas, thus reflecting the nature of this cluster as the traditional profile of the Cotswolds, one which survives everywhere except where local circumstances of landownership, planning policy or housing market forces have dictated a change in emphasis.

Profile 2 (retirement) provides some evidence of urban intrusion in the form of retirement migrants moving to areas which still retain strong rural characteristics, as noted in the national analysis in Chapter 4. The profile

Table 6.4   *Rural housing profiles in Cotswold District, 1971*

Profile 1 : Agricultural (88 cases)

T statistic	Variable number	Variable description	District mean	Profile mean
0·47	11	% households with 2 + cars	20·2	24·1
0·44	23	% households renting privately unfurnished	36·4	46·3
0·30	69	% households with head in SEG 15	14·5	20·8
0·29	35	average number rooms per dwelling	4·9	5·0
0·24	38	% 2-person households with 5 + rooms	68·3	71·6
0·22	6	% population of working age	57·8	58·9
0·22	65	% households with head in SEG 13, 14	11·1	14·7
− 0·44	10	% households with no car	29·7	25·4
− 0·41	54	% private renting share/lack hot water	11·9	7·6
− 0·40	1	total number of private households	94·0	73·4
− 0·38	22	% households renting from local authority	17·7	9·5
− 0·37	12	% owner-occupiers with no car	17·1	12·3
− 0·37	67	% households with head in SEG 8, 9, 12	20·7	14·3
− 0·36	57	% private renting share/lack inside WC	15·3	10·8

Much the largest cluster and therefore average in many respects, but predominantly agricultural in character, with high proportions of both farmers and farmworkers, many living in relatively high-standard privately rented accommodation. Higher than average level of car-ownership. Relatively small enumeration districts.

Profile 2 : Retirement (42 cases)

T statistic	Variable number	Variable description	District mean	Profile mean
1·01	7	% population of pensionable age	19·3	26·3
0·96	19	% pensioner households	29·5	39·3
0·94	18	% households with 1 pensioner living alone	11·8	17·2
0·86	15	% 1-person households	17·6	24·1
0·81	21	% owner-occupier households	41·1	57·7
− 1·03	2	average number persons per household	2·9	2·5
− 0·85	17	% households with children	33·6	24·3
− 0·81	5	% population aged 0–14	22·8	18·0
− 0·69	58	% males 15 + economically active	81·0	75·7
− 0·60	16	% households with 6 + persons	6·3	3·7

A group dominated by retired people, with greater than average numbers of small households, pensioners and owner-occupier households, but few households with children and a smaller proportion of the population economically active.

Table 6.4 continued

Profile 3: Poor housing (10 cases)

T statistic	Variable number	Variable description	District mean	Profile mean
2·91	47	% households share/lack hot water	7·4	24·9
2·82	46	% households share/lack bath	8·4	28·0
2·77	48	% households share/lack inside WC	9·5	29·5
2·30	45	% households lacking exclusive amenities	11·5	29·7
2·08	54	% private renting share/lack hot water	11·9	33·2
− 0·81	73	% population changing address in last 5 years	37·6	21·5
− 0·77	35	average number rooms per dwelling	4·9	4·6
− 0·68	5	% population aged 0–14	22·8	18·8
− 0·68	1	total number of private households	94·0	59·2
− 0·67	74	% 5-year in-migrants that are children	13·2	2·2
− 0·65	21	% owner-occupier households	41·1	27·7
− 0·64	17	% households with children	33·6	26·6

A small cluster exhibiting very poor housing conditions. Very small enumeration districts, predominantly with small houses lacking exclusive use of basic amenities, and with a very immobile population consisting largely of older households. A very high proportion of households renting privately unfurnished accommodation (36·4 per cent of the Cotswold District mean; 58·4 per cent of the profile mean).

Profile 4: Local authority housing (34 cases)

T statistic	Variable number	Variable description	District mean	Profile mean
1·56	22	% households renting from local authority	17·7	50·6
0·98	43	local authority 7 + rooms as % of all households 7 + rooms	4·1	17·3
0·92	29	% households with more than 1·0 person per room	4·5	7·8
0·85	2	average number persons per household	2·9	3·2
0·78	10	% households with no car	29·7	37·2
0·76	67	% households with head in SEG 8, 9, 12	20·7	34·0
− 0·95	30	% households with less than 0·5 persons per room	44·5	34·8
− 0·82	11	% households with 2 + cars	20·2	13·5
− 0·80	23	% households renting private unfurnished	36·4	18·4
− 0·58	7	% population of pensionable age	19·3	15·3
− 0·57	21	% owner-occupier households	41·1	29·3

A group of enumeration districts with high proportions of dwellings rented from a local authority. High average household size, with a certain degree of overcrowding; low level of car-ownership; a high proportion of heads of household are skilled manual workers.

Table 6.4 continued

Profile 5: Armed forces (4 cases)

T statistic	Variable number	Variable description	District mean	Profile mean
6·01	24	% households renting private furnished	5·0	65·8
5·70	70	% households with head in SEG 16	3·1	71·9
3·35	17	% households with children	33·6	69·9
2·94	5	% population aged 0–14	22·8	40·0
2·54	8	married persons per 1,000 aged 15–24	243·6	608·7
− 2·55	30	% households with less than 0·5 persons per room	44·5	18·3
− 2·30	19	% pensioner households	29·5	5·9
− 2·25	7	% population of pensionable age	19·3	3·9
− 1·49	18	% households with 1 pensioner living alone	11·8	3·2
− 1·49	15	% 1-person households	17·6	6·3
− 1·38	59	% females 15 + economically active	37·5	17·3

A very small group dominated by armed forces personnel living in furnished privately rented accommodation. Most households have young families, thus reducing the proportion of females able to work. Very few retired people and, conversely, a large number of children.

---

underlines a characteristic housing type found particularly in areas of attractive landscape, such as the north Cotswolds. It emphasises that this characteristic, although not overwhelmingly typical of Cotswold District to the extent that it is picked up in the national analysis (Chapter 4), is nevertheless of considerable significance in such areas. The enumeration districts making up this profile are normally located in and around the smaller towns and larger villages of the area, for example, Chipping Campden and Lower Slaughter, rather than in more isolated and open countryside, reflecting the importance to the elderly of access to services, transport and other facilities, normally available only in the larger settlements. The low rate of car-ownership of retired households was emphasised earlier in this chapter.

Some of the traditional rural characteristics of profile 1 are found in a more extreme form in profile 3. Poor housing conditions are the major characteristics here where high proportions of households shared or lacked exclusive use of one or more standard amenities. Areas with a high level of privately rented accommodation were characteristic in this profile. The profile focused particularly on the agricultural 'estate' villages, which still seem resilient to change and which are particularly found in the south-west of Cotswold District, including Great Barrington, Sherbourne, Aldsworth and other settlements in the Leach and Windrush valleys. A relatively elderly population with low levels of mobility was recognised through the housing stock, living in rented (and probably tied) accommodation. The evidence from subsequent field surveys confirmed the view that employment was (or had been) largely on the local estate.

Profile 4 (local authority housing) was particularly concentrated in the former Cirencester Rural District, where the provision of local authority housing was clearly accorded greater priority than in the other pre-1974 authorities which make up the present Cotswold District. The four enumeration districts constituting profile 5 (armed forces) were associated with housing estates for service personnel at Little Rissington and for employees of the British Aircraft Corporation at Fairford.

The six rural housing profiles recognised for South Oxfordshire are described in Table 6.5 and their distribution is mapped in Figure 6.6. Whereas in Cotswold District agricultural elements were of overriding importance, in South Oxfordshire metropolitan influences become dominant.

The largest group, profile 2 (established professional), illustrates the relatively prosperous conditions characteristic of an accessible rural area falling within the zones of influence of London, Oxford and Reading. The quality of housing exceeds the South Oxfordshire District average and it appears to be essentially the preserve of established professional groups. Profile 4 (younger owner-occupiers) resembles profile 2 in some respects but is populated by generally younger families. It is tempting to suggest that the two profiles represent part of a continuum of rural housing use with younger owner-occupiers, as they become more established, perhaps moving locally to improve their level of housing provision. If this hypothesis is valid, profile 4 could represent a zone of transition in rural areas which are subject to rapid population growth and intense metropolitan pressure, a concept resembling the theories advanced in early studies of competition for housing in urban areas (Park *et al.*, 1925). At the national scale this latter profile was seen to fit in to the broader category recognised as 'transitional rural', and it would seem probable that this is a common picture in those rural areas which have seen heavy postwar growth and the increasing influence of urban centres. The distribution especially of profile 2 underlines this argument. It is found particularly in the south of this district, near Henley and Reading, where there is good road and rail access to London. Many settlements in the Chilterns belong to this profile. Profile 4 is also found in the south of the district, but other concentrations are found to the north, around Chinnor, near the M40 motorway, and in the urban-dominated areas of Didcot and the Oxford urban fringe.

Profile 6 (poor housing) reflects a comparatively localised but significant housing problem found in South Oxfordshire but not in Cotswold District. The ten enumeration districts in this profile relate to areas of mobile homes, a phenomenon strong enough to cause both Bullingdon and Wallingford

Table 6.5 *Rural housing profiles in South Oxfordshire District, 1971*

Profile 1: Traditional rural (52 cases)

T statistic	Variable number	Variable description	District mean	Profile mean
0·97	23	% households renting private unfurnished	17·5	33·4
0·95	47	% households share/lack hot water	6·4	13·1
0·91	49	% owner-occupiers share/lack bath	3·5	8·0
0·91	52	% owner-occupiers share/lack hot water	3·3	8·1
0·90	48	% households share/lack inside WC	8·8	17·2
0·88	45	% households lacking exclusive amenities	10·7	20·1
0·83	65	% households with head in SEG 13, 14	4·8	13·6
− 0·74	1	total number of private households	147·5	96·1
− 0·54	5	% population aged 0–14	25·9	22·4
− 0·53	66	% households with head in SEG 5, 6	19·3	11·6
− 0·48	17	% households with children	41·1	35·2
− 0·45	58	% males 15 + economically active	84·4	81·4
− 0·42	2	average number persons per household	3·0	2·9
− 0·41	21	% owner-occupier households	57·5	46·7

A group of relatively small enumeration districts with a high proportion of households renting unfurnished accommodation. The standard of housing is generally much lower than average, especially where households are owner-occupiers. A higher than average proportion of farmers; average age higher than the South Oxfordshire District mean, with fewer children than average.

Profile 2: Established professional (99 cases)

T statistic	Variable number	Variable description	District mean	Profile mean
0·43	7	% population of pensionable age	13·5	16·2
0·41	19	% pensioner households	21·4	25·3
0·39	64	% households with head in SEG 1, 2, 3, 4	22·8	29·8
0·38	30	% households with less than 0·5 persons per room	35·3	39·7
0·34	35	average number rooms per dwelling	5·0	5·1
0·32	42	owner-occupiers 7 + rooms as % of all households 7 + rooms	69·1	78·5
− 0·42	8	married persons per 1,000 aged 15–24	305·9	220·0
− 0·36	17	% households with children	41·1	36·7
− 0·33	58	% males 15 + economically active	84·4	82·2
− 0·26	5	% population aged 0–14	25·9	24·2
− 0·25	57	% private renting share/lack inside WC	15·2	11·2
− 0·24	46	% households share/lack bath	7·1	5·2

Naturally, as the largest group, fairly average in many respects, but weighted towards older age-groups and higher social classes, living in slightly larger houses in good condition. Fewer households with children and fewer young married couples.

Table 6.5 continued

Profile 3 : Local authority (24 cases)

T statistic	Variable number	Variable description	District mean	Profile mean
2·23	22	% households renting from local authority	19·7	73·8
2·13	43	local authority 7 + rooms as % of all households 7 + rooms	6·2	47·5
1·56	16	% households with 6 + persons	5·9	12·1
1·38	2	average number persons per household	3·0	3·5
1·23	29	% households with more than 1 person per room	5·0	10·1
1·21	10	% households with no car	27·3	41·2
− 1·37	21	% owner-occupier households	57·5	21·3
− 1.26	30	% households with less than 0·5 persons per room	35·3	20·6
− 1·19	42	owner-occupiers 7 + rooms as % of all households 7 + rooms	69·1	34·5
− 0·95	11	% households with 2 + cars	18·4	8·9
− 0·87	25	% vacant dwellings	3·8	0·9
− 0·85	37	% 1-person households with 5 + rooms	47·2	27·1
− 0·81	63	% population with higher education	7·5	1·8
− 0·80	23	% households renting private furnished	17·5	4·3

A cluster dominated by large households in local authority accommodation, with generally low car-ownership and a relatively low terminal educational age. High level of use of the housing stock (low vacancy rate), with a moderate degree of overcrowding.

Profile 4 : Younger owner-occupiers (42 cases)

T statistic	Variable number	Variable description	District mean	Profile mean
0·94	21	% owner-occupier households	57·5	82·2
0·79	17	% households with children	41·1	50·8
0·75	58	% males 15 + economically active	84·4	89·3
0·73	8	married persons per 1,000 aged 15–24	305·9	454·6
− 0·94	19	% pensioner households	21·4	12·6
− 0·90	7	% population of pensionable age	13·5	8·1
− 0·89	15	% 1-person households	12·9	7·7
− 0·86	18	% households with 1 pensioner living alone	8·0	4·0
− 0·76	10	% households with no car	27·3	18·5

A group consisting largely of younger owner-occupiers, often with children, and with a high proportion of young married households. Conversely, few pensioners – hence a high proportion economically active – and few households without a car.

Table 6.5 continued

Profile 5: Armed forces (6 cases)

T statistic	Variable number	Variable description	District mean	Profile mean
5·64	24	% households renting private furnished	5·2	67·9
5·64	70	% households with head in SEG 16	3·6	77·3
2·23	44	private renting 7 + rooms as % of all households 7 + rooms	15·4	54·9
2·09	17	% households with children	41·1	66·7
2·02	5	% population aged 0–14	25·8	38·8
− 1·76	7	% population of pensionable age	13·5	3·0
− 1·72	19	% pensioner households	21·4	5·2
− 1·71	21	% owner-occupier households	57·5	12·4
− 1·66	60	% married females economically active	45·7	28·7
− 1·51	59	% females 15 + economically active	41·9	30·0

A small and very distinctive group of enumeration districts, dominated by armed forces personnel living in rented furnished accommodation. Many have young families, hence the reduced number of married women able to work.

Profile 6: Poor housing (10 cases)

T statistic	Variable number	Variable description	District mean	Profile mean
3·92	26	% households in non-permanent buildings	4·4	61·5
1·82	28	% households with more than 1·5 persons per room	1·1	4·4
1·80	8	married persons per 1,000 aged 15–24	305·9	670·3
1·78	48	% households share/lack inside WC	8·8	25·5
1·71	45	% households lacking exclusive amenities	10·7	28·9
− 2·50	35	average number rooms per dwelling	5·0	3·8
− 1·86	38	% 2-person households with 5 + rooms	63·5	28·2
− 1·38	37	% 1-person households with 5 + rooms	47·2	14·9
− 1·08	30	% households with less than 0·5 persons per room	35·3	22·7
− 1·02	2	average number persons per household	3·0	2·7

A small cluster dominated by poor housing conditions: a remarkable proportion of households in non-permanent dwellings, many lacking some or all basic amenities, and with a considerable degree of overcrowding. Generally small households, often consisting of young marrieds, but in very small accommodation.

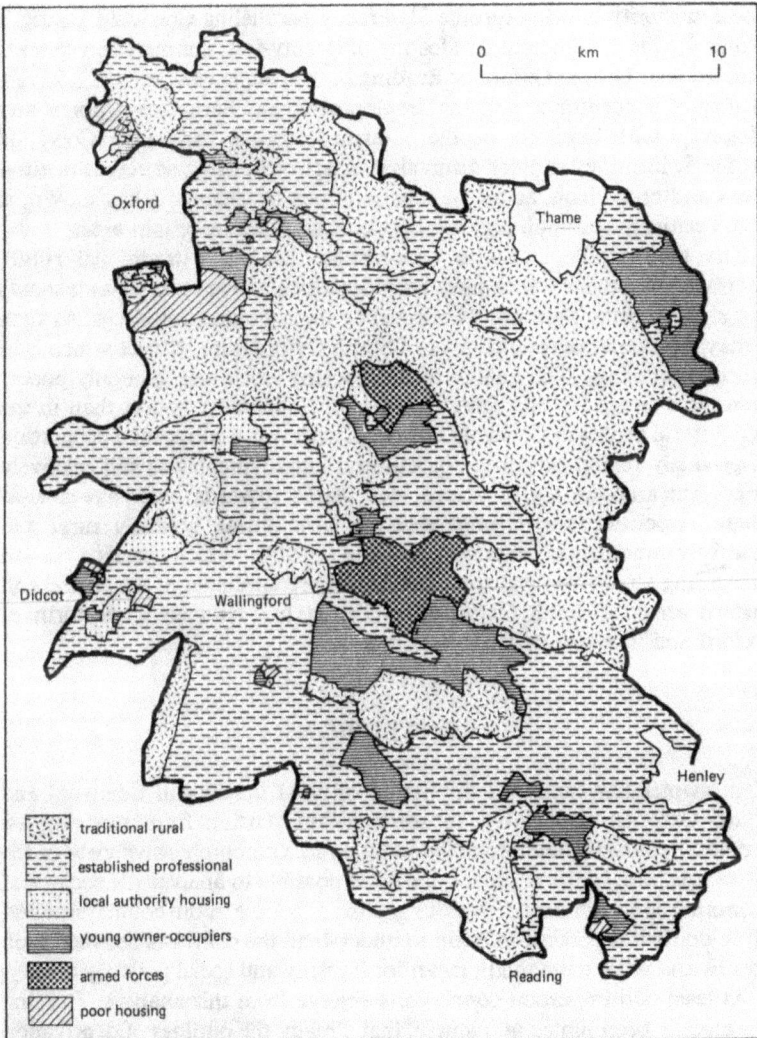

Figure 6.6 *Rural housing profiles, South Oxfordshire District, 1971*

former rural districts to be included in the mobile homes cluster of the national transitional rural profile. Mobile homes are generally located on licensed sites owned and operated by the local authority or private owners. They are commonly found in urban fringe locations and often signify urban housing problems transferred across the boundary to cheaper land.

Two other profiles reflect distinctive housing types which have limited spatial coverage and which are therefore generally too small to be recognised in South Oxfordshire at the level of a national classification. Local authority housing (profile 3), directly paralleling Cotswold District's profile 4, was the predominant feature of twenty-four enumeration districts situated near Didcot, Oxford or Reading or in specific villages which have a history of concentrated housing development, like Berinsfield (Morris and Mogey, 1965). Similarly profile 5 (armed forces), paralleling Cotswold profile 5, identifies another distinctive aspect of housing structure in rural areas and one which, as the national analysis in Chapter 3 has shown, is both relatively common and spatially concentrated in certain areas.

The final profile in South Oxfordshire, profile 1 (traditional rural), contrasts with those which have been described above in so far as it shows few signs of being significantly affected by metropolitan influences. As such it may represent the residual area of South Oxfordshire District which is in process of change. The quality of the housing stock was generally poorer than the average for this district and also, incidentally, poorer than in the agricultural profile in Cotswold District. There was a substantial proportion of privately rented property. Agricultural employment was still relatively important and the age structure was biased towards older age-groups. These associated factors emphasise the agricultural, typically rural and relatively unchanged character of this profile which persists in an urbanising accessible rural area. The profile predominates in the central and eastern areas of South Oxfordshire District but with enclaves north of Oxford and in a few parishes near Reading.

CONCLUSION

This chapter has examined the nature of rural housing in Cotswold and South Oxfordshire Districts in some detail, starting from the simplest division by housing tenure and building up to a comprehensive view of the overall picture. In the process it has been possible to analyse the social and economic circumstances of various groups of people in the countryside and by so doing it is possible to begin to understand the contrasts between such groups and what these might mean for housing and social policy generally.

At least two important conclusions emerge from this analysis. The first has already been hinted at, namely, that already the outlines of deprivation and advantage in rural housing are emerging. This theme provides the focus for the next two chapters and it will be examined in detail there.

A second conclusion is that the recognition of small but important and often socially disadvantaged groups in the countryside is only possible when local and detailed analyses are carried out. To this extent the findings of this chapter agree with those critics of national classifications who stress the importance of local problem recognition in any approach involving social indicators. An interesting corollary of this point arose when the profiles which were reviewed in the latter part of the chapter were discussed with local authority officers in the two study districts. It was very evident that the more formalised approach of the cluster analysis not only confirmed the personal experience and knowledge of individual officers but was also in sufficient detail for them to realise perhaps more clearly the significance of minority housing groups within the general structure. The experience of local officers, as will be seen in Chapter 11, is frequently a very significant and yet personal and individual element in problem recognition and policy formulation. The more formalised approach allows personal judgements to be checked against more objective indicators and also allows personal experience to be shared and put on a common footing.

A final point relates to the question of change. For reasons that have been made clear, the analyses detailed above have been based on conditions in 1971 and it is certain that changes have occurred since that time. Many of these changes will be evident in subsequent chapters (particularly Chapters 7 and 8) which rely on more recent surveys, but some indications of probable changes since 1971 should be given here.

In Cotswold District the surveys produced relatively little evidence of changes in tenure structure within the housing profiles. The only notable change seemed to have occurred in the local authority profile where the village of Kempsford, though retaining a significant proportion of council houses, had been noticeably affected by an increase in owner-occupation since 1971. The other main change was recorded within the poor housing profile covering the estate villages, where housing conditions, in terms of basic amenities, appeared to have improved considerably since 1971. In South Oxfordshire District metropolitan influences seem to have encroached into the more traditional rural areas of profile 1, where in 1971 there were only minor commuter and second-home influences; by 1977 these groups seemed to have competed successfully in the housing market and were firmly established in villages such as Marsh Baldon and Maidensgrove.

Chapter 7

Deprivation and Advantage in Rural Housing

A constant theme in this book has been the attempt to recognise different social groups in the countryside on the basis of contrasts in their material circumstances, their lifestyles and their opportunities. This chapter continues this process by examining in some detail the theme of deprivation and advantage in rural housing.

Deprivation has become an over-used word and, although the recognition of a specifically rural aspect has come much later than its urban counterpart, deprivation in the countryside has been searched for with every bit as much desperation and righteous polemic. An inevitable result has been the rejection by some authorities of the term 'deprivation' largely on the grounds that it has become vague and indeterminate. There has also been an equally inevitable reaction against the very existence of rural deprivation at any significant level, and which accordingly regards with suspicion the approach implicit in reviews such as that by Shaw (1979) and Walker (1978) and in official reports such as those produced by the Association of District Councils (1978) and the Association of County Councils (1979).

The approach adopted by the present authors steers, it is hoped, a suitable middle course. On the question of the topic of deprivation we agree wholeheartedly with the opinion voiced by Rutter and Madge (1976) that the debate about the meaning of deprivation may be too easily dismissed as 'academic disputation not worthy of further consideration were it not for the fact that behind the words lie people who continue to suffer from various forms of personal and social disadvantage. The term may generate semantic confusion but the human predicament is real enough.'

These remarks were made in a broadly urban context, but the message is no less applicable to rural areas. Those who maintain that poverty and deprivation are no longer to be found in the countryside are deluding themselves and continuing a myth of rural plenty which is belied by the facts. The claim to rural harmony and the absence of poverty in rural areas is invariably made on the basis of superficial judgements of the attractiveness of the rural landscape and on the absence of visible social unrest such as militant trade union activity, tenants' action groups and the like. The claim is equally to be seen in the context of direct and adverse comparisons with urban areas and is a reflection more of an idealised view of country living than of the real nature of some rural lifestyles. As such, the attitude may be considered as a direct continuation of the long-standing views of an harmonious countryside set against a harsh and brutal city, so ably described by Raymond Williams in his classic *The Country and the City* (1973).

Unbiased comparisons of deprivation in rural and urban areas are few and far between, but some evidence on this point can be found in the massive study of poverty in the United Kingdom carried out in the late 1960s by Peter Townsend (1979). The broad picture is one which stresses far fewer differences between urban and rural areas than the conventional wisdom supposes. On the specific question of poverty, indeed, a slightly higher percentage of the rural sample population (9 per cent compared with 8 per cent in urban areas) were found to have net disposable incomes below the state poverty level. In some other respects rural areas fared slightly better than did their urban counterparts, generally because of the advantages brought by a rural environment. Thus:

> ... markedly fewer of the population lacked gardens, and almost none complained of air pollution. Slightly fewer lacked a reasonable number of consumer durables. Roughly the same proportion as in urban Britain were socially deprived and had poor housing facilities. Fewer of those who worked indoors had bad conditions of work, but more worked outdoors, and some of them had dangerous work or very poor conditions. More owned their homes and substantially fewer had council tenancies. Perhaps surprisingly, slightly more of the adults had had more than ten years education, and about the same proportion had non-manual occupations. (Townsend, 1979, p. 549)

Deprivation, then, undoubtedly exists in rural Britain and in the main areas of incomes, social contacts and housing the levels of deprivation and poverty are as significant as they are in the towns. This chapter concentrates only upon deprivation and advantage as they can be seen to exist in rural housing. This particular theme has been considered, as has already been mentioned, in the reports by Walker and Shaw, and housing deprivation was an important element in the case for rural deprivation argued by the local authority associations. Here the concern lies entirely with the evidence for housing deprivation in the two study areas in Oxfordshire and Gloucestershire. A more detailed account of this theme, backed up by substantial statistical material, can be found in Dunn, Rawson and Rogers (1980a).

ASPECTS OF DEPRIVATION AND ADVANTAGE IN RURAL HOUSING

This account starts from the premise that there are four main aspects of housing deprivation which have to be considered – housing tenure, housing quality, housing use and the crucial aspect in rural areas of accessibility.

Each of these four aspects needs to be seen in the light of the particular circumstances of rural households. Broadly these circumstances are twofold and they lead on directly from the previous analyses in this book. First, the family life-cycle which, as was seen in Chapter 3, exerts a powerful influence upon all the four aspects of housing mentioned above. The term 'life-cycle poverty' was first used by Rowntree (1901) to describe the changes in earning power and expenditure levels which occur at different stages of an individual's life. Thus childhood, the early years of marriage and childbearing, and old age have been suggested as the three main periods of relative poverty. The cycle has been shown to be relevant to the present day in both national and urban studies (for example, Abel-Smith and Townsend, 1965; Young and Willmott, 1973), but there has been little application to rural areas.

Secondly, the social and economic status of the household is critical, acting primarily through the influence of financial resources. Household income varies over time in relation to life-cycle stages. Professional and managerial workers reach their peak earning power in middle age, but manual workers are often at their peak earning potential much earlier in life, when physical fitness and strength are assets. Agricultural workers provide an obvious example. Equally, job security, susceptibility to unemployment and the availability of pension and superannuation benefits to mitigate the financial effects of retirement are all linked to social and economic status.

Income, location, social group and household type all influence access to particular housing tenures. A clear illustration of this can be seen in building society and local authority allocation policies. Building society lending rules generally restrict mortgages to applicants with regular, stable employment, with sufficient savings to supply a deposit and with a considerable number of years of earning potential remaining. Even if a household qualifies for a mortgage by these criteria, access to owner-occupation is ultimately decided by housing availability and thus by price. The extent to which this effectively prohibits access to owner-occupation for a high proportion of rural dwellers is considered further in Chapter 11.

If income provides a central element in deciding access to owner-occupation, household circumstances are perhaps even more critical when it comes to local authority housing. Thus households with lower incomes, and particularly those with children, generally have more chance of access to council accommodation. As far as the privately rented sector is concerned, income and availability of housing probably provide the two most important factors in deciding access.

A crucial aspect of housing tenure in relation to deprivation and advantage is clearly security. Here owner-occupiers and local authority tenants are in the most advantageous position. Private tenants in rented accommodation have security under various Housing Acts and, with some provisos, that security is now extended to agricultural workers under the Rent (Agriculture) Act 1976. Farmers, however, have had tenancies which have been granted increasing security in common law since the middle of the nineteenth century. Such security was confirmed by the Agricultural Holdings Act of 1948, and in recent years it has even been extended to the successor of the tenant if the succession is within the family.

In terms of financial return there is little doubt that owner-occupation provides far and away the most advantaged position. Even with high interest rates, the fiscal advantages given to the owner-occupier make his investment a particularly attractive one. As Townsend (1979) has pointed out, mass owner-occupation is a relatively new phenomenon in Britain, but it is certain that the second half of the twentieth century has seen a great increase in the amount of inheritable wealth in the form of housing which has in general accrued to the middle classes and to their descendants. In contrast, while the evidence suggests that subsidies to keep council house rents relatively low have in recent years been given at broadly the same level as the tax advantages given to owner-occupiers, the council tenant has no commensurate benefit of wealth at the end of his tenancy since the equity still lies with the local authority. Even more disadvantaged in this respect is the private tenant who equally does not benefit from capital appreciation and who, despite attempts to control the level of rents, is often forced to pay high rates to gain access even to mediocre-quality housing.

Chapter 3 emphasised the great improvement in housing quality which has occurred since the Second World War. It also demonstrated that unfitness, as judged by the Housing Act 1957 (s. 4) and amended by the Housing Act 1969 (s. 71), is still to be found in rural, as in urban, areas and that there are still rural households which lack amenities such as hot water or inside toilet facilities. Such circumstances are, for example, to be found in those rural areas which have substantial numbers of mobile homes.

Problems of housing use, particularly involuntary sharing and overcrowding, can also still be found, although here urban areas are certainly more disadvantaged. While officially the measure of 1·5 persons per room is regarded as being satisfactory, this does not, as the Milner-Holland Report (1965) notes, meet more contemporary views of socially acceptable living standards which now favour a measure of one person per room. At the other end of the spectrum, some households own second homes or urban flats in addition to their main homes and are thus in a decidedly advantaged position.

The final aspect of accessibility is as important in deciding on the extent of disadvantage as any of the more strictly housing aspects. Studies such as that by Moseley (1979) have clearly demonstrated the deprivation suffered by households lacking private transport in the way of access to shops, social facilities and recreation. Moreover access to employment is equally important since reliance on local employment frequently implies a small range of jobs and relatively low incomes. By the same token, households with two or more forms of private transport are in a relatively advantageous position.

A MODEL OF HOUSING OPPORTUNITY

The extent to which these aspects of housing tenure, quality and use, and of accessibility are closely inter-related has already been made clear. Within the broader context of rural deprivation generally these elements of housing have been seen as an inevitable spin-off of the so-called rural deprivation cycle (Figure 7.1). In this construct, Shaw views housing largely as a consequence of the deprivation seen in income, opportunities and mobility. While this is certainly true, the model does not emphasise the fact that housing is as much a symptom of deprivation as a consequence. Housing circumstances (tenure, quality, use and location) may well be responsible, in part at least, for the handicaps which a household suffers in relation, for example, to financial resources (for instance, low capital accumulation in tenancy situations), poor employment opportunities due to location and accessibility, low levels of medical, shopping and other services due to isolation and adverse influences, for example, upon the mental and physical development of children, due particularly to poor housing conditions and crowding.

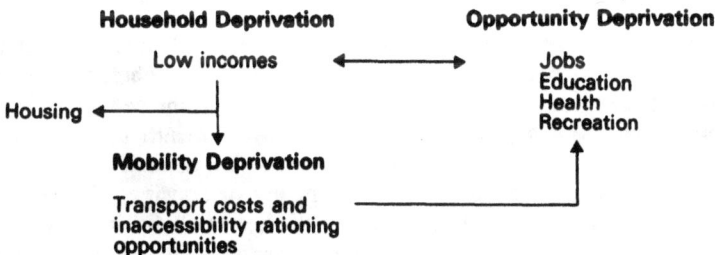

Figure 7.1   *The rural deprivation cycle*
           Source: Shaw (1979)

The cycle of rural deprivation noted above is unsuitable as a tool for a deeper understanding of housing deprivation because it does not emphasise the central importance of housing tenure in deciding relative deprivation or advantage. That central position is recognised more clearly in Figure 7.2 which attempts to pull together the various aspects of rural housing which have been considered above in relation to the main household attributes of socio-economic status and the family life-cycle. The result is a simple model not so much of housing deprivation as of housing opportunity, since it itemises the various forces which work to give both advantage and disadvantage in housing.

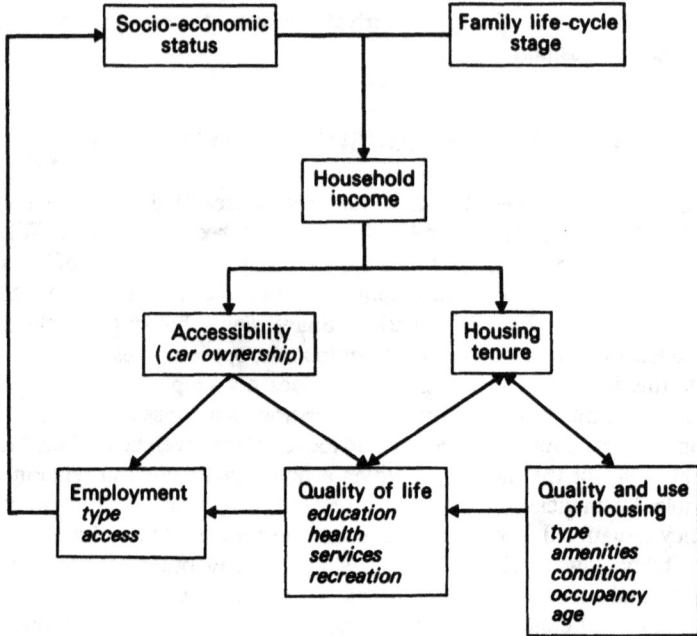

Figure 7.2   *A model of rural housing opportunity*

Stage in the family life-cycle and socio-economic status provide the essential starting points for this model. For most households these two provide the key to household income and thence to the central aspect of tenure, though for a growing minority inherited wealth in the form of property will provide an equally important starting point. The next stage, the links between housing tenure and quality of housing, lifestyles and employment have already been traced at the national level in Chapter 3.

An element of mobility between housing classes is implicit in this model and as such it is to be viewed as a model of opportunity rather than a necessary cycle of deprivation which continually re-emphasises and repeats the disadvantages of already deprived households. The path from, say, a large household through a low income to privately rented accommodation of poor quality is not necessarily a one-way route. Poor housing quality and overcrowding may, for example, result in the household moving back through the filter of tenure to improved housing conditions in the local authority sector. As a concomitant of this move it may be that aspects of the quality of life are also improved and even employment prospects are transformed.

By the same token, the model does allow for change over time, perhaps between generations. In an ideal world the route from humble origins through the rented housing sector might lead, by means of Smilesian thrift and industry, to self-improvement, wealth and owner-occupation. In another scenario the local authority sector provides the necessary impetus to improve a household's housing and life-chances and thus lead on to further gains. But for many households it must be recognised that the route is in fact a one-way path with poor housing, low access to services and employment leading to a true cycle of deprivation over time.

THE BACKGROUND TO HOUSING DEPRIVATION AND ADVANTAGE

The preceding general discussion has particularly emphasised the role of family stage, social class, income and tenure as necessary base points for an understanding of housing deprivation and advantage. This background to the two study areas is outlined in Tables 7.1–4. With regard to household type (Table 7.1), the more vibrant demographic structure of South Oxfordshire District was reflected in a higher proportion of households with children, though there were also more childless couples. In contrast, Cotswold District recorded a higher proportion of pensioner households. South Oxfordshire, as would be expected, recorded more heads of households in professional and non-manual occupations (Table 7.2), and skilled workers were also more important here than in Cotswold District. Conversely, agricultural workers and farmers were naturally more important in the latter area.

There was a very clear difference in income levels between the two areas (Table 7.3). The approximate average annual level of manual wages at the time of survey (£3,000) was taken as an arbitrary standard below which households might be financially disadvantaged, whereas twice this level was taken as representing positive advantage in income. In Cotswold District, where agricultural and unskilled workers were well represented, half of the households had low incomes while less than one in five grossed high incomes. This bias towards low incomes was far less evident in South Oxfordshire, where there was a more even spread across income groups.

Housing tenure (Table 7.4) provides the fourth base point for a consideration of housing deprivation. Owner-occupation was, as might be expected, rather more important in South Oxfordshire than in the Cotswold area, although this area was more important for those owning their houses outright. Conversely, the tied house was more important in the Cotswold area, as were other private tenancies.

These basic household characteristics do not, of course, exist

Table 7.1   *Household types in the study areas, 1977 (%)*

Household type	Cotswold District	South Oxfordshire District
Single persons	6·2	6·2
Couples without children	14·4	21·4
Couples with 1–3 children	29·8	35·8
Large families	2·8	1·7
Pensioners	16·2	10·3
Lone pensioners	8·8	8·0
Other	21·8	16·6
TOTAL	100·0	100·0
TOTAL NUMBER	500	650

Notes: Single persons and couples without children exclude those under 65 years; large families = four or more children; pensioners = two or more persons of pensionable age; other households = one-parent families and relatives/friends living together.

Table 7.2   *Socio-economic structure of the study areas, 1977 (%)*

Socio-economic group		Cotswold District	South Oxfordshire District
1–4	professional	18·6	24·5
5–6	manual	12·2	20·0
13,14	farmer	8·2	2·9
8,9,12	skilled manual	18·4	28·5
7,10,11	unskilled manual	18·0	12·2
15	agricultural worker	12·8	3·2
16	armed forces	5·2	4·5
17	indefinite	3·4	3·5
18	retired (if not coded elsewhere), students, etc.	3·2	0·7
TOTAL		100·0	100·0
TOTAL NUMBER		500	650

Table 7.3   *Income levels in the study areas, 1977 (%)*

Gross annual income	Cotswold District	South Oxfordshire District
<£3,000	50·9	31·8
£3,000–£6,000	32·6	38·2
£6,000 +	16·5	30·0
TOTAL	100·0	100·0
TOTAL NUMBER	334	474
RESPONSE RATE (%)	66·8	72·9

Table 7.4   *Tenure in the study areas, 1977 (%)*

Tenure	Cotswold District	South Oxfordshire District
Own outright	31·4	27·2
Buyer (1st time)	6·6	14·5
Buyer (not 1st time)	10·8	21·4
All owner-occupiers	48·8	63·1
Local authority	16·6	18·5
Private unfurnished	11·0	6·6
Private furnished	2·2	1·8
Tied	21·4	10·0
TOTAL	100·0	100·0
TOTAL NUMBER	500	650

independently of each other and certain important correlations should be noted. Low-income households in both areas were frequently pensioners and also single-person households, whereas the high-income households tended often to be couples without children. Households where employment was in the armed services were usually households with children, while at the time of survey these households in the Cotswold sample were also frequently characterised by being temporarily headed by mothers with the fathers away on active service in Ireland. Inevitably there was a strong correlation between socio-economic group and income. In both areas, poorer households made up at least two-thirds of each of the groups representing unskilled manual workers and farm labourers, while a similar proportion of professional workers recorded high incomes in both samples.

THE EVIDENCE FOR DEPRIVATION AND ADVANTAGE

HOUSING TENURE

Housing tenure provides the first indicator in terms of which some households hold a relatively deprived position in rural housing and some appear as privileged. On *a priori* grounds it would be expected that owner-occupiers were richer and would tend to come from higher social groups than tenants. This generalisation is found to be broadly true, as Tables 7.5–7 demonstrate, but there are notable divergences from this simple picture which should be noted.

Owner-occupiers tended to be households with children where the head of the household was in the professional or non-manual grades and was earning at least twice the average manual wage in 1977. Within this group,

Table 7.5 Household type by tenure in the study areas (% households)

Household type	Own outright	Buyer (1st time)	Buyer (not 1st time)	All owner-occupiers	Local authority	Private unfurnished	Private furnished	Tied
Cotswold District								
Single	8·9	3·0	7·4	7·8	4·8	5·5	—	4·7
No children	12·1	15·2	24·1	15·2	6·0	9·1	18·2	18·7
Children	18·5	45·5	50·0	29·1	38·6	21·8	27·3	29·0
Large family	0·6	—	5·6	1·6	4·8	5·5	—	2·8
Pensioner	30·7	—	1·8	20·1	13·3	20·0	9·1	8·4
Lone pensioner	14·6	—	—	9·4	10·8	10·9	45·4	0·9
Other	14·6	36·3	11·1	16·8	21·7	27·2	—	35·5
TOTAL	100·0	100·0	100·0	100·0	100·0	100·0	100·0	100·0
TOTAL NUMBER	157	33	54	244	83	55	11	107
South Oxfordshire District								
Single	5·1	8·5	4·3	5·6	4·2	9·3	25·0	7·7
No children	18·6	23·4	27·4	22·7	14·2	18·6	16·7	12·3
Children	13·0	48·9	53·2	34·9	30·0	20·9	41·6	61·6
Large family	1·7	1·1	1·4	1·5	2·5	4·7	—	—
Pensioners	24·9	—	2·2	11·5	8·3	20·9	—	1·5
Lone pensioner	16·4	—	—	7·1	11·7	18·6	—	1·5
Other	20·3	18·1	11·5	16·7	29·1	7·0	16·7	15·4
TOTAL	100·0	100·0	100·0	100·0	100·0	100·0	100·0	100·0
TOTAL NUMBER	177	94	139	410	120	43	12	65

Table 7.6 Socio-economic groups by tenure in the study areas (% households)

Socio-economic group		Own outright	Buyer (1st time)	Buyer (not 1st time)	All owner-occupiers	Local authority	Private unfurnished	Private furnished	Tied
Cotswold District									
1–4	professional	21·7	21·2	64·8	31·1	1·2	10·9	18·2	6·5
5–6	non-manual	15·3	15·2	16·6	15·6	13·3	12·7	9·1	3·7
13–14	farmer	12·1	9·1	1·9	9·4	—	10·9	9·1	10·3
8, 9, 12	skilled manual	22·3	36·4	9·2	21·3	26·5	12·7	36·4	6·5
7, 10, 11	unskilled manual	13·3	12·1	1·9	10·7	43·4	27·3	9·1	11·2
15	agricultural worker	3·8	—	—	2·4	9·6	14·5	—	39·3
16	armed forces	1·3	—	1·9	1·2	1·2	—	—	20·6
17	indefinite	5·1	6·0	1·9	4·6	—	5·5	9·1	1·9
18	retired, etc.	5·1	—	1·9	3·7	4·8	5·5	—	—
TOTAL		100·0	100·0	100·0	100·0	100·0	100·0	100·0	100·0
TOTAL NUMBER (500)		157	33	54	244	83	55	11	107
South Oxfordshire District									
1–4	professional	26·6	24·5	52·4	34·9	1·6	11·6	25·0	9·2
5–6	non-manual	19·2	27·6	25·9	23·4	11·6	18·6	16·7	15·4
13–14	farmer	5·7	—	—	2·4	0·8	2·3	8·3	9·2
8, 9, 12	skilled manual	27·7	39·4	14·5	25·9	45·8	39·5	33·3	4·6
7, 10, 11	unskilled manual	10·7	7·4	2·9	7·3	28·3	16·3	8·3	10·9
15	agricultural worker	1·1	1·1	—	0·7	—	9·3	8·3	13·8
16	armed forces	1·7	—	1·4	1·2	—	—	—	36·9
17	indefinite	6·2	—	2·2	3·5	6·9	2·4	—	—
18	retired, etc.	1·1	—	0·7	0·7	1·7	—	—	—
TOTAL		100·0	100·0	100·0	100·0	100·0	100·0	100·0	100·0
TOTAL NUMBER (650)		177	94	139	410	120	43	12	65

Table 7.7 Income by tenure in the study areas (% households)

Gross annual income	Own outright	Buyer (1st time)	Buyer (not 1st time)	All owner-occupiers	Local authority	Private unfurnished	Private furnished	Tied
Cotswold District								
<£3,000	46·3	41·2	8·1	35·2	63·9	59·4	63·6	60·3
£3,000–£6,000	28·1	41·2	37·8	32·4	33·3	31·3	27·3	33·7
£6,000 +	25·6	17·6	54·1	32·4	2·8	9·3	9·1	6·0
TOTAL	100·0	100·0	100·0	100·0	100·0	100·0	100·0	100·0
TOTAL NUMBER (334)	82	17	37	136	72	32	11	83
% EACH GROUP GIVING INCOME DATA	52·2	51·5	65·0	55·7	86·7	58·2	100·0	77·1
South Oxfordshire District								
<£3,000	42·9	16·2	6·3	22·6	50·0	68·6	22·0	31·5
£3,000–£6,000	30·3	55·9	33·0	37·3	39·3	22·9	55·6	48·1
£6,000 +	26·8	27·9	60·7	40·1	10·7	8·5	22·2	20·4
TOTAL	100·0	100·0	100·0	100·0	100·0	100·0	100·0	100·0
TOTAL NUMBER (474)	112	68	112	292	84	35	9	54
% EACH GROUP GIVING INCOME DATA	68·3	72·3	80·6	71·2	70·0	81·4	75·0	83·1

however, there was a very significant minority of pensioner and lone pensioner households, often owning their houses outright and recording relatively low incomes. There is clearly a category of relatively poor owner-occupiers which must be recognised and which therefore modifies the commonly held view of advantaged owner-occupiers versus deprived tenants. To some extent the skilled manual worker seemed to have entered owner-occupation, representing more than a third of first-time buyers in both areas; equally, a significant number of households with lower incomes had recently bought houses in the Cotswold area, though this was generally not the case in South Oxfordshire. With these important exceptions, however, the owner-occupier market was clearly dominated by the stereotype of the richer, non-manual household.

In the local authority sector another stereotype emerged. This sector was dominated by manual workers, skilled workers being predominant in South Oxfordshire but unskilled workers making up the majority in the Cotswold area. Though between 30 and 40 per cent of households were pensioners, the norm here was for households with children. Incomes tended to be low – two-thirds of such households in the Cotswolds and half those in South Oxfordshire earning less than £3,000 in 1977.

The privately rented sector was, as expected, more complex. In the Cotswolds tied housing was naturally dominated by farmworkers and to a lesser extent by armed service personnel. In South Oxfordshire the position was reversed, and there was in addition a significant minority of non-manual workers. This split was reflected also in the distribution of incomes which were more evenly spread in South Oxfordshire but skewed very definitely towards the lower ranges in the Cotswold sample. Furnished tenancies in the Cotswolds were characterised particularly by pensioner households with low incomes. In South Oxfordshire households with children were more common and incomes were rather higher – a reflection of the importance of mobile homes within the area.

The strongly class- and income-based picture of housing opportunity which has so far emerged inevitably raises the much-publicised issue of the gentrification of the rural housing stock. Though limited in its extent, the survey did provide some evidence about how far the professional and middle classes have encroached upon the rural housing stock.

In the Cotswold sample a quarter of the professional households were living in housing which had, within the previous five years, been occupied by manual or agricultural workers. Equally, 4·5 per cent of owner-occupiers were living in houses which had previously been privately rented and a further 3·7 per cent lived in previously tied houses. In South Oxfordshire the process seemed to have been running at a rather lower level, at least in recent years, and the corresponding figures were 3·2 per cent and 0·9 per cent. Thus, although there was some evidence in South Oxfordshire of a reverse gentrification in that some skilled manual workers had been moving into housing previously occupied by professional people, there is enough evidence over the relatively short time-period involved to confirm some of the fears for an embourgeoisement of rural housing and a concomitant decline in the amount of privately rented housing in the countryside.

HOUSING QUALITY

The quality of housing is an area where deprivation can plainly be seen, although measures of quality are invariably phrased in terms of official standards. While crowding and amenity provisions provide fairly clear-cut evidence of poor housing conditions some aspects of housing quality, for instance, house type, are far less easy to interpret. For example, while there is a rough gradation in quality from the detached house through semi-detached and terraced housing to the mobile home, the last type may well be favoured by some owner-occupiers, such as young people in the skilled manual trades who are earning relatively high incomes.

Detached houses made up about a third of the sample in both areas and, as expected, professional and non-manual employees were the dominant social group, with farmers making up an important subgroup. In South Oxfordshire in particular detached housing was essentially the preserve of the higher-income groups. The characteristic house type associated with tenants, both local authority and private, was the semi-detached house. Here the skilled manual occupations in the middle-income groups were predominant.

As far as the age of housing was concerned, owner-occupiers tended to be found in the oldest (pre-1800) properties, particularly if they were the outright owners, and in the newer postwar houses, especially if they were first-time buyers. In both areas professional households made up the main group (one-fifth in the Cotswolds; one-third in South Oxfordshire) living in pre-1800 housing. Local authority tenants were usually living in housing built in the period 1946–70, though some properties dated from the interwar years. Tied agricultural tenants lived generally in older housing – in the Cotswolds about a third of such properties pre-dated 1800 and a further third were built in the nineteenth century. Armed forces households invariably lived in postwar purpose-built housing.

While only a relatively small proportion of households in the two areas lacked the use of basic housing amenities (Cotswold: 3·8 per cent; South Oxfordshire: 6·9 per cent), these households were clearly differentiated in terms of tenure, social class and income (Table 7.8). In the Cotswolds the disadvantaged households were mainly private tenants in unfurnished property, though outright owners provided a second group, reflecting the distinction within the owner-occupier sector which has already been mentioned. These outright owners, in fact, were the most important group in the South Oxfordshire sample, though here of course the picture of disadvantage was dominated by the owners of mobile homes. In both areas

Table 7.8 *Characteristics of households lacking exclusive use of basic amenities in the study areas (% households)*

Characteristics	Cotswold District	South Oxfordshire District
Tenure		
Own outright	26·2	37·8
Buyer (1st time)	5·3	4·4
Buyer (not 1st time)	—	—
All owner-occupiers	31·5	42·2
Local authority	—	17·8
Private unfurnished	63·2	31·1
Private furnished	5·3	6·7
Tied	—	2·2
TOTAL	100·0	100·0
TOTAL NUMBER	19	45
Household type		
Single	5·3	20·0
No children	—	8·8
Children	5·3	15·6
Large family	—	—
Pensioners	42·1	17·8
Lone pensioner	10·5	26·7
Other	36·8	11·1
TOTAL	100·0	100·0
TOTAL NUMBER	19	45
Socio-economic group		
1–4 professional	5·3	—
5–6 non-manual	—	24·4
13–14 farmer	21·1	2·2
8, 9, 12 skilled manual	21·1	48·9
7, 10, 11 unskilled manual	36·6	22·2
15 agricultural worker	5·3	—
16 armed forces	—	—
17 indefinite	10·6	2·2
18 retired, etc.	—	—
TOTAL	100·0	100·0
TOTAL NUMBER	19	45
Income (per annum)		
<£3,000	76·9	68·4
£3,000–£6,000	23·1	31·6
£6,000 +	—	—
TOTAL	100·0	100·0
TOTAL NUMBER	13	38

it was pensioner households which particularly suffered from a lack of housing amenities. More than half (52·6 per cent) of such households were made up of pensioners in the Cotswold sample and the figure for South Oxfordshire was 44·5 per cent. Of all households lacking amenities in the Cotswolds, 73·7 per cent had heads of household aged 65 or more, while in South Oxfordshire the proportion was 46·7 per cent. These households tended to be long-standing rural dwellers – two-thirds of those in the Cotswolds had been resident in their home since at least 1950.

Households lacking amenities were heavily concentrated in the lower income groups (Table 7.8). In South Oxfordshire a third of these households reported incomes of less than £1,000 per year and a further 26 per cent had incomes between £1,000 and £2,000.

Relatively few houses were reported as unfit. Where they did occur there was some concentration in the tied tenure sector in the Cotswolds and particularly in the mobile homes in South Oxfordshire. In contrast, about one in five households in each area reported that their property needed some repair. The highest proportion of complaints came from the tenants of tied housing – over 20 per cent of the Cotswold tied houses reported problems, particularly damp. In both areas houses needing repairs tended more frequently to belong to households reporting low incomes, yet of the relatively few improvement grants which were reported the majority had been used by higher-income households.

HOUSING USE

By most urban, particularly inner city, standards, there was relatively little housing deprivation in the two study areas when judged by criteria of housing use. Overcrowding (that is, where densities exceeded one person per room) only affected 6·8 per cent of households in the Cotswold area and 6·5 per cent in South Oxfordshire. About half of these were in the local authority sector in both areas, while in the Cotswold sample a further quarter was found living in tied housing. Also, about half of such households in each area were earning low incomes. Shared accommodation was virtually non-existent.

In contrast, underoccupancy (with densities of under 0·5 persons per room) was recorded at a high level. Sixty-three per cent of all households in the Cotswolds and 58 per cent of households in South Oxfordshire were underoccupying property. In many cases this clearly represented a distinct measure of housing advantage, particularly since more than half of such households in the Cotswolds and more than two-thirds in South Oxfordshire were also owner-occupiers. Yet the picture is not quite as clear as these figures seem to indicate. Underoccupancy was very closely associated with small households such as those made up by childless couples, single-person and pensioner households. Moreover, almost four-fifths of all outright owners in the two areas were underoccupying properties and a high proportion of households in this category (55 per cent in the Cotswolds; 38 per cent in South Oxfordshire) reported incomes below £3,000 per year. Underoccupancy in rural areas may therefore represent some hardship, at least in financial terms and particularly for older households – another reminder of the problem of the disadvantaged outright owner of property mentioned earlier.

Probably the most extreme example of housing advantage, particularly for a rural household, is the ownership of a second home. Between 3 and 4 per cent of households in each area were in this category.

HOUSING AND ACCESSIBILITY

The final element in the simple model of housing opportunity concerns accessibility – the all-important facility which minimises the friction between house, services, employment and social life.

The obvious starting point is personal mobility as judged by access to the use of a car. Households without a car were naturally much more dependent upon public transport. Thus in South Oxfordshire over 50 per cent of households not having a car used public transport at least once or twice a week, whereas only 9 per cent of households with two cars made the same use of the public service. As Table 7.9 shows, there is a clear relationship between personal accessibility and housing tenure, household type, social type and income, though yet again it is clear that some outright owners of property are disadvantaged by having poor levels of personal mobility. Tenants, especially in the local authority sector, recorded particularly high levels of poor accessibility as judged by car-ownership, and older households were similarly disadvantaged. In contrast, the professional or non-manual household with children, owning a house (with a mortgage) and with an income in 1977 in excess of £6,000, was most likely to own two cars.

Car-ownership is, of course, only a means to accessibility. When households were questioned on their shopping habits, however, a similar pattern emerged. In both areas almost twice as many households without cars as those with cars shopped locally, that is, in the village or town where they lived or the nearest village. Those households owning two cars tended to shop further afield where presumably the range of goods was wider and prices more advantageous. When shopping patterns were disaggregated by tenure and household type there was a clear preference for outright owners and pensioners to shop locally.

A third aspect of accessibility, access to employment, completes this picture. The unequivocal conclusion from an analysis of workplace and income was that households with easy access to employment outside the two study districts were in a much more advantageous position financially than those who were employed locally. For example, commuters out of South Oxfordshire represented two-thirds of the high-income group in the

Table 7.9   *Some aspects of accessibility, housing deprivation and advantage in the study areas (%)*

Characteristics	Households without a car		Two-car households	
	Cotswold District	South Oxfordshire District	Cotswold District	South Oxfordshire District
Tenure				
Outright owners	23·1	26·9	39·7	26·7
Buyers	1·7	13·5	30·5	51·0
Local authority tenants	30·8	37·7	7·6	10·2
Private tenants	20·4	14·3	9·0	5·3
Tied tenants	24·0	7·6	13·2	6·8
Household type				
Households with				
1–3 children	9·4	16·0	41·0	42·7
Pensioners and lone				
pensioners	51·2	41·2	10·4	5·4
Socio-economic group				
Professional and non-				
manual	13·7	26·8	47·1	58·8
Unskilled manual	31·6	32·9	7·6	2·4
Agricultural workers	15·4	5·0	4·2	1·9
Income (per annum)				
Below £3,000	84·0	66·0	16·9	9·0
Above £6,000	—	3·1	49·3	50·8

Note: Figures are percentages of households in each tenure group, household type, socio-economic group and income group.

sample but only one-third of the low-income group. In both areas the majority of lower-income households worked locally – thus some 58 per cent of the Cotswold low-income sample worked within one mile of home.

CONCLUSION

This chapter has attempted a fairly detailed analysis of the extent of deprivation and advantage in rural housing as illustrated by evidence from the two study areas. The general conclusions re-emphasise many of the themes which have already been touched on in this book. Before moving on in the next chapter to a re-examination of these themes in the light of the rural housing profiles outlined earlier, it may be useful to summarise the main conclusions. In their simplest form these are: (1) the general advantage held by owners of property over both public and private tenants when judged by housing quality, use and accessibility to services. Private tenants, in particular, were seen to have a distinct disadvantage in these respects; (2) the variation which clearly exists within the owner-occupied sector, notably between the outright owner of property and the mortgagee. The former is much more likely to have a low income, to have poorer-quality housing and to have a low level of personal mobility and access to services; (3) the relatively poor situation of those groups where the occupation of the householder is centred upon agriculture and the unskilled manual trades, particularly when compared with professional and non-manual employment; (4) the often extremely disadvantaged circumstances associated with some mobile home dwellers; (5) the evidence for gentrification, particularly in the Cotswolds, and the consequential diminution in the stock of housing for rental; (6) the problems of accessibility especially associated with older households, particularly when such households live in tenanted property; (7) the problems of older households, especially lone pensioners, whose housing is frequently older, in poorer condition and with fewer amenities than that of other groups.

Chapter 8

Housing Opportunity and Rural Housing Profiles

Chapter 6 recognised eleven types of rural housing environment or rural housing profile in the study areas. In Cotswold District these profiles were labelled agricultural, retirement, poor housing, local authority housing and armed forces. Profiles paralleling the latter three groups were also recognised in South Oxfordshire together with traditional rural, established professional and younger owner-occupiers. The role of this chapter is to integrate the detailed findings given in Chapter 7 with the structure of rural housing as set out by these rural housing profiles.

HOUSING PROFILES AND THE BASIS OF HOUSING OPPORTUNITY

The first task is to examine the composite rural housing profiles in the light of the aspects of deprivation and advantage which were set out in the previous chapter. This statistical background is provided in Tables 8.1–6 and considers each profile in relation to family structure, social group, income, tenure, the use of the housing stock and car-ownership. In part, of course, this repeats analyses which were made in Chapter 6. The concern here, however, is to take the profile analyses one stage further and to provide a judgement on the nature of rural housing types on the basis of advantage, disadvantage and opportunity. Accordingly the major features of the profiles need to be reiterated in a form which emphasises the strengths and weaknesses which they contain.

Table 8.1 shows the importance, especially in South Oxfordshire, of couples without children (and who are likely to be relatively advantaged) within the established professional and younger owner-occupier profiles. Less advantaged households such as those with large families were well represented in the Cotswold local authority profile. Pensioners and single-pensioner households were naturally found in the Cotswold retirement profile and also the agricultural and poor housing profiles of that area.

Table 8.1 *Family life-cycle characteristics of rural housing profiles (% households)*

Rural housing profiles	Single persons	Families with children	Large families	Couples without children	Pensioners	Lone pensioner	Other	Total	Total no.
				By household type					
Cotswold District									
Agricultural	2·7	30·0	1·3	16·7	20·0	9·3	20·0	100·0	150
Poor housing	8·0	22·0	2·0	12·0	22·0	7·0	27·0	100·0	100
Retirement	10·0	17·0	2·0	12·0	20·0	14·0	15·0	100·0	100
Local authority housing	4·0	49·0	6·0	15·0	7·0	6·0	13·0	100·0	100
Armed forces	10·0	12·0	4·0	10·0	4·0	6·0	54·0	100·0	50
South Oxfordshire District									
Traditional rural	4·7	29·3	1·3	19·3	11·3	12·0	12·1	100·0	150
Established professional	2·0	32·7	2·7	20·7	17·3	8·7	15·9	100·0	150
Younger owner-occupier	8·0	44·0	1·0	25·0	7·0	6·9	9·0	100·0	100
Poor housing	12·0	28·0	2·0	19·0	10·0	8·0	21·0	100·0	100
Local authority housing	8·0	38·0	2·0	17·0	3·0	5·0	27·0	100·0	100
Armed forces	4·0	60·0	0·0	14·0	8·0	4·0	10·0	100·0	50

Table 8.2 Socio-economic characteristics of rural housing profiles (% households)

| Rural housing profiles | By socio-economic group | | | | | | | | | Total | Total no. |
	1–4 pro-fessional	5–6 non-manual	13–14 farmer	8, 9, 12 skilled manual	7, 10, 11 unskilled manual	15 agricul-tural	16 armed forces	17 in-definite	18 retired etc.		
Cotswold District											
Agricultural	20·7	9·3	13·3	19·3	18·6	14·7	0·0	4·1	0·0	100·0	150
Poor housing	18·0	11·0	10·0	11·0	15·0	22·0	2·0	6·0	5·0	100·0	100
Retirement	15·0	17·0	8·0	26·0	15·0	7·0	1·0	2·0	9·0	100·0	100
Local authority	25·0	16·0	2·0	17·0	28·0	8·0	1·0	1·0	2·0	100·0	100
Armed forces	8·0	6·0	2·0	18·0	8·0	10·0	44·0	4·0	0·0	100·0	50
South Oxfordshire District											
Traditional rural	25·4	14·7	5·3	0·0	10·6	8·0	0·7	3·9	0·0	100·0	150
Established professional	29·3	26·0	2·7	18·0	14·7	0·7	2·0	3·3	3·3	100·0	150
Younger owner-occupier	40·0	27·0	2·0	18·0	10·0	0·0	0·0	3·0	0·0	100·0	100
Poor housing	18·0	22·0	0·0	43·0	9·0	3·0	1·0	4·0	0·0	100·0	100
Local authority	16·0	12·0	1·0	44·0	18·0	5·0	0·0	4·0	0·0	100·0	100
Armed forces	6·0	16·0	8·0	12·0	8·0	0·0	48·0	2·0	0·0	100·0	50

Still focusing on causes of deprivation and advantage, it can be seen from Table 8.2 that advantaged professional and non-manual groups were obviously to be found in the established professional and younger owner-occupier profiles. Less advantaged groups such as agricultural workers, when judged, say, from an economic standpoint, were found in the agricultural and poor housing profiles of Cotswold District, and unskilled manual workers were well represented in the Cotswold local authority and agricultural profiles. The income statistics (Table 8.3) reinforce the pattern of advantage emerging from social characteristics: the highest proportions of high-income households were found in the established professional and younger owner-occupier profiles. The position of disadvantage of the agricultural profile is maintained when proportions of households with low incomes are assessed, but the Cotswold armed forces profile records a higher proportion of low-income households than does the Cotswold poor housing profile. The most notable feature to emerge is, perhaps, the clear distinction between the armed forces profiles in the two study areas.

The tenure pattern varies across the two areas quite considerably (Table 8.4). In Cotswold District owner-occupation varied from being the tenure of more than one-quarter of households in the estate villages of the poor housing profile to two-thirds of households in the retirement areas, but the peak of owner-occupation was achieved in the younger owner-occupier profile in South Oxfordshire. Private unfurnished tenancies were recorded at high levels in the Cotswold estate villages and in the traditional rural profile. Tied housing was of major importance both in the armed forces profiles and in the estate villages.

Table 8.3 *Income characteristics of rural housing profiles (% households)*

| | By gross annual income | | | | |
| | <£3,000 | £3,000– | | | Total |
Rural housing profiles	p.a.	£6,000	£6,000 +	Total	no.
Cotswold District					
Agricultural	65·7	23·8	10·5	100·0	76
Poor housing	56·6	17·7	15·7	100·0	76
Retirement	42·7	37·6	19·7	100·0	61
Local authority	34·4	31·6	34·0	100·0	87
Armed forces	61·8	12·3	5·9	100·0	34
South Oxfordshire District					
Traditional rural	41·3	31·6	17·1	100·0	92
Established professional	29·7	31·3	39·0	100·0	118
Younger owner-occupier	21·6	40·5	37·9	100·0	74
Poor housing	35·1	45·9	19·0	100·0	74
Local authority	32·5	43·5	24·0	100·0	71
Armed forces	28·9	44·4	26·7	100·0	45

Table 8.5 Quality and use of housing stock in rural housing profiles (% households/houses)

Rural housing profiles	By quality of housing stock				By use of housing stock	Total no. of households
	Households lacking exclusive use of basic amenities	Unfit houses	Probably unfit houses	Households living in caravans	Households with occupancy >of 1·0 p.p.r.	
Cotswold District						
Agricultural	2·7	—	0·7	—	4·0	150
Poor housing	12·0	2·0	8·0	1·0	4·0	100
Retirement	3·0	—	—	—	8·0	100
Local authority	—	2·0	—	—	13·0	100
Armed forces	—	—	1·0	2·0	6·0	50
South Oxfordshire District						
Traditional rural	10·7	5·4	4·0	1·4	4·6	150
Established professional	3·3	0·7	1·3	0·7	3·3	150
Younger owner-occupier	5·0	1·0	3·0	—	5·0	100
Poor housing	17·0	11·0	4·0	55·0	11·0	100
Local authority	1·0	—	1·0	1·0	12·0	100
Armed forces	2·0	—	2·0	2·0	4·0	50

Table 8.4 Tenure characteristics of rural housing profiles (% households)

Rural housing profiles	Own outright	Buying (1st time)	Buying (not 1st time)	By tenure All owner-occupiers	Local authority	Private un-furnished	Private furnished	Tied	Total	Total no.
Cotswold District										
Agricultural	38·0	9·3	7·3	(54·6)	5·3	12·7	4·0	23·4	100·0	150
Poor housing	21·0	1·0	3·0	(25·0)	6·0	32·0	2·0	35·0	100·0	100
Retirement	54·0	3·0	10·0	(67·0)	19·0	2·0	0·0	2·0	100·0	100
Local authority	12·0	7·0	28·0	(47·0)	37·0	1·0	2·0	13·0	100·0	100
Armed forces	26·0	16·0	4·0	(46·0)	6·0	2·0	2·0	44·0	100·0	50
South Oxfordshire District										
Traditional rural	36·6	6·0	18·7	(61·3)	14·7	12·0	2·0	10·0	100·0	150
Established professional	34·7	6·7	29·3	(70·7)	17·3	7·3	2·0	2·7	100·0	150
Younger owner-occupiers	29·0	30·0	35·0	(94·0)	1·0	3·0	0·0	2·0	100·0	100
Poor housing	29·0	23·0	14·0	(66·0)	19·0	7·0	6·0	2·0	100·0	100
Local authority	5·0	19·0	16·0	(40·0)	52·0	2·0	0·0	6·0	100·0	100
Armed forces	14·0	6·0	4·0	(24·0)	0·0	4·0	0·0	72·0	100·0	50

Table 8.6   *Car-ownership in rural housing profiles (% households)*

Rural housing profiles	By car-ownership		Total no.
	No car	*2 + cars*	*of households*
Cotswold District			
Agricultural	13·3	32·0	150
Poor housing	29·0	24·0	100
Retirement	27·0	27·0	100
Local authority	19·0	37·0	100
Armed forces	44·0	8·0	50
South Oxfordshire District			
Traditional rural	16·0	42·6	150
Established professional	14·7	38·0	150
Younger owner-occupier	12·0	34·0	100
Poor housing	32·0	19·0	100
Local authority	25·0	21·0	100
Armed forces	8·0	22·0	50

The quality of the housing stock was, of course, worst in the two poor housing areas – one typical of a relic rural situation (in Cotswold District), another of urban housing problems overspilling into rural areas (in South Oxfordshire District). Unfit houses and households lacking amenities were concentrated in the poor housing profiles, but were also well represented in the traditional rural profile in South Oxfordshire (Table 8.5). In the South Oxfordshire poor housing profile a very high proportion (55 per cent) of households lived in caravans.

The only aspect of the use of housing stock briefly mentioned here is overcrowding since underoccupancy confers neither clear advantage nor disadvantage for any household and because sharing is such a minor feature. Overcrowding was greatest in the two local authority profiles and in the South Oxfordshire poor housing profile (Table 8.5).

Finally Table 8.6 reviews car-ownership as a surrogate indicator for assessing accessibility. The Cotswold armed forces profile had a very low level of car-ownership and this contrasted in particular with the equivalent profile in South Oxfordshire. Households with two cars were found particularly in the traditional rural and established professional profiles of South Oxfordshire with a surprisingly high proportion in the Cotswold local authority profile.

THE SPECTRUM OF RURAL HOUSING OPPORTUNITY

The evidence presented in Chapter 7 and in the first part of the present chapter has set the scene for a simple ranking of the rural housing profiles. The purpose of the ranking exercise is to suggest the relative merits, as judged by various indicators of advantage and disadvantage, of the range of rural housing circumstances which have been at the core of this study.

An exercise of this type is inevitably subjective, if only in the choice of variables which are taken to indicate deprived or advantaged circumstances. It is certain that some readers would quarrel with the inclusion of particular indicators and, therefore, with the subsequent ranking. It is hoped, however, that the detailed arguments which have been rehearsed in this study provide sufficient evidence to justify the choice of indicators. On the one hand some seemingly obvious indicators have been omitted because their effect can be both advantageous and disadvantageous. Thus the life-cycle variables of large families and households with children have been seen to fall into both advantaged and disadvantaged groups and have accordingly been excluded. Many armed forces personnel appear to be relatively advantaged in South Oxfordshire, but this is not so in Cotswold District and because the same standard cannot be consistently applied across both areas membership of this socio-economic category has not been included. Also excluded for much the same reason are the outright owners of property who have been recognised to be a diverse group, traditionally considered advantaged but in fact including some of the more disadvantaged members of the community, particularly in terms of housing condition and income.

On the other hand some indicators have been included even though it is recognised that exceptions to what has been argued as a general rule may be found. It is accepted, for example, that by no means all pensioners are disadvantaged, nor are all first-time owner-occupiers necessarily advantaged. Equally, farmers and council tenants may not view their housing circumstances as being particularly advantaged, yet the analyses which have been reported elsewhere in this study have pointed out that the

Table 8.7   *Indicators of rural housing deprivation and advantage*

Indicators of deprivation	Indicators of advantage
single persons	childless couples
pensioners	professional employees
unskilled manual workers	non-manual workers
agricultural workers	farmers
low-income households (<£3,000 p.a.)	high-income households
tenants of private unfurnished accommodation	(>£6,000 p.a.)
tenants of private furnished accommodation	buyers (1st time)
tenants of tied housing	buyers (not 1st time)
households lacking basic amenities	local authority tenants
households living in unfit houses	households with 2 + cars
households living in probably unfit houses	
households living in caravans	
overcrowded households	
households lacking a car	

status of these two groups as well-protected tenants compares them favourably with many other rural dwellers.

Table 8.7 lists the indicators of housing advantage and deprivation which have been used in this analysis.

If the rural housing profiles are ranked according to these negative and positive attributes a rough scale of housing deprivation and advantage may be constructed. It would be possible to devise a fairly sophisticated ranking method, but there is little point in carrying out such analyses on relatively unsophisticated data. Accordingly the chosen method was simply to note the two profiles with the highest scores on each positive or negative indicator (Tables 8.1–6). In the event of a tie between scores (as in the case of single persons) three areas were recorded, but where there was only one very extreme score (as for mobile homes), a second score was not tabulated.

The resulting scores are recorded in Table 8.8, together with a simple totalling of the number of indicators of housing advantage (positive) and disadvantage (negative).

The final product (Figure 8.1) represents a crude ranking of the housing profiles – a spectrum of housing opportunity which tries to reflect the complex factors involved in assessing the balance of circumstances which help or hinder the rural dweller.

CONCLUSION

The prime objective of this simple analysis has been to complete the analysis of the housing profiles which have figured so prominently in this study. The intention has been to add some rough qualitative assessments to the generally quantitative view which has been presented. The picture which emerges in general confirms the previous findings of this study, and in particular emphasises the great divide in housing circumstances which exists between, on the one hand, the established and newly arrived professional groups in rural areas and, on the other, the rest of the rural population. The relatively poor position of private tenants, particularly those in tied accommodation, is also made clear. By comparison with them the circumstances of local authority tenants are noticeably more favourable. Finally it is evident on a broader scale that the more urbanised rural areas such as South Oxfordshire are at a clear overall advantage when compared with more remote countryside such as the Cotswold area.

Table 8.8 Scores of rural housing profiles on indicators of advantage and disadvantage

Rural Housing profile	Advantage indicators	Advantage score	Disadvantage indicators	Dis-advantage score	Final score
Cotswold District					
Agricultural	farmers	1	pensioners; unskilled manual workers; low incomes; agricultural workers; private unfurnished and furnished tenancies	6	−5
Poor housing	farmers	1	pensioners; agricultural workers; private unfurnished tenancies; households lacking amenities; probably unfit houses	5	−4
Retirement	—	0	single persons; pensioners; lone pensioners	3	−3
Local authority	local authority tenants	1	unskilled manual workers; overcrowding	2	−1
Armed forces	—	0	single persons; low incomes; tied housing; no car	4	−4
South Oxfordshire District					
Established professional	childless couples; professionals; non-manual workers; high incomes; two-car households; non-first-time buyers	6	—	0	+6
Younger owner-occupiers	childless couples; professionals; non-manual workers; first-time buyers; non-first-time buyers; high incomes	6	—	0	+6
Poor housing	first-time buyers	1	single persons; private furnished tenancies; households lacking amenities; unfit houses; probably unfit houses; mobile homes; no car	7	−6
Local authority	local authority tenants	1	overcrowding	1	0
Armed forces	—	0	tied housing	1	−1
Traditional rural	two-car households	1	lone pensioners; unfit houses; probably unfit houses	3	−2

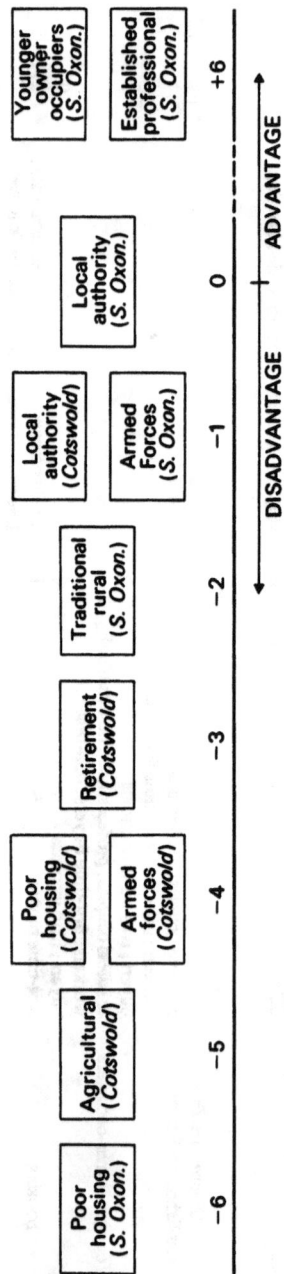

Figure 8.1 *The spectrum of rural housing advantage and disadvantage*

Chapter 9

Movement through the Housing Stock: the Dynamics of the System

The complexities of rural population movement in lowland England were described in Chapter 2; the present chapter attempts to assess the patterns of movement in the two case study areas from a number of viewpoints which are relevant to a study which is primarily concerned with the use of the rural housing stock. Attention is focused first upon the reasons for population movement and the spatial patterns of movement; succeeding sections then deal with a comparison of the characteristics of movers and stayers, and with the process of filtering through the housing stock, detailing changes in the housing circumstances of migrant households and considering the question of access to housing from the position of potential migrants – those respondents (or dependents of respondents) who would prefer to change their housing tenure, type or location. Finally, the data relating to out-migrants is examined in order to discover any differences between out-migrants and in-migrants and consequent changes in the population structure of the two study areas.

First, however, the question of the level of migration is introduced, partly to define the size of the sample involved (and to emphasise the comparatively small size of some subsamples), but also to indicate variations in levels of migration between the two study areas and between the different rural housing profiles identified in Chapter 6. The level of migration is not, of course, an unconstrained figure; the sample was stratified to comprise one-third migrants and two-thirds non-migrants, so that variations from 33 per cent result from either interviewer use of the reserve sample in different proportions or, more commonly, migration since the compilation of the electoral register issued in February 1977.

Table 9.1 summarises the situation and reveals a number of differences. A total of 446 households (38·8 per cent of the total sample of 1,150) had moved to their present address during the five and a half years preceding the survey (that is to say, they were not listed in the electoral register issued in February 1972 by virtue of their later migration). Excluding the two armed forces profiles, some 386 (36·8 per cent) of the 1,050 households

Table 9.1   *Levels of migration in Cotswold and South Oxfordshire Districts by rural housing profiles*

Rural housing profile	No. in sample	No. of migrants	Level of migration (%)
Cotswold District	500	182	36·4
Total profiles (excluding profile 5)	450	152	33·8
1 Agricultural	150	53	35·3
2 Retirement	100	27	27·0
3 Poor housing	100	30	30·0
4 Local authority housing	100	42	42·0
5 Armed forces	50	30	60·0
South Oxfordshire District	650	264	40·6
Total profiles (excluding profile 5)	600	234	39·0
1 Traditional rural	150	48	32·0
2 Established professional	150	52	34·7
3 Local authority housing	100	37	37·0
4 Younger owner-occupiers	100	46	46·0
5 Armed forces	50	30	60·0
6 Poor housing	100	51	51·0

could be defined as 'movers'. Very high levels of migration were found in the armed forces profiles; because of the involuntary nature of this movement these profiles have been excluded from the majority of the analysis, although Jackson's (1968) point about the influence of institutional populations is acknowledged. The South Oxfordshire poor housing profile also recorded a high rate of population movement, emphasising the preponderance of short-stay households in mobile homes, many seeking their first accommodation after marriage. Very low levels of migration in the Cotswold poor housing profile perhaps result from the concentration of elderly households in poor conditions but without the capital for owner-occupation or the eligibility for council housing, and hence with little alternative but to remain. Overall, the level of migration was markedly higher in South Oxfordshire.

MOTIVES FOR MOVEMENT

Recent in-migrants to the sample parishes (that is, those respondents whose move had taken place since January 1972) were asked to rank specific factors influencing their decision to move and to explain their move in their own words: responses were recorded verbatim. Tables 9.2 and 9.3 summarise the primary reasons for movement elicited in response to the second question. Although the absolute values recorded in the tables and the major obvious differences between profiles are of considerable interest,

Table 9.2 Primary reasons for in-migration in Cotswold and South Oxfordshire Districts by rural housing profiles (%)*

Reason	Cotswold District						South Oxfordshire District						
	Total profiles	1	2	3	4	5	Total profiles	1	2	3	4	5	6
Employment	40·1	44·5	18·5	30·0	35·7	73·3	33·7	25·0	38·5	21·6	37·0	86·7	11·8
Housing	30·2	27·4	40·7	30·0	42·9	10·0	35·2	41·7	30·8	54·1	32·6	6·7	39·2
Education	1·1	—	3·7	—	2·4	—	2·7	2·1	—	—	6·5	—	5·9
Marriage	6·0	5·7	3·7	10·0	4·8	6·7	13·6	6·2	12·5	13·5	13·0	3·3	29·4
Rurality	11·0	13·3	14·8	20·0	7·1	3·3	8·0	18·7	9·6	8·1	6·5	3·3	—
Friends/relatives	3·8	1·9	7·4	10·0	2·4	—	3·8	2·1	5·8	—	4·3	—	7·8
Other	7·7	7·6	11·1	—	4·8	6·7	2·7	4·2	1·9	2·7	—	—	6·0

* Figures are column percentages.

Table 9.3   *Reasons for in-migration in Cotswold and South Oxfordshire Districts (total profiles excluding armed forces profiles; %)**

| | Cotswold District | | South Oxfordshire District | |
| | Primary | Secondary | Primary | Secondary |
Reason	reason	reason†	reason	reason†
Employment	33·8	18·3	27·0	14·0
Housing	34·4	32·4	39·1	37·3
Education	1·3	2·8	3·0	6·0
Marriage	6·0	4·2	15·0	4·7
Rurality	12·6	22·5	8·6	25·3
Friends/relatives	4·6	11·3	4·3	10·7
Other	7·3	8·5	3·0	2·0

* Figures are column percentages.
† Secondary (and subsequent) reasons for movement not given by all respondents.

the bulk of this section expands the analysis by reviewing the verbatim responses of in-migrants: these are less easy to categorise but provide a more accurate reflection of the complex, involved and occasionally impulsive or irrational motives for household movement.

Tables 9.2 and 9.3 do, however, provide a convenient if oversimplified starting point. They also illustrate the atypical nature of migration behaviour in the two study areas with high levels of movement of armed forces personnel; the total sample figures in Table 9.2 are therefore discounted in favour of the statistics in Table 9.3, which exclude the two armed forces profiles. From this latter table it can be seen that housing is the reason most frequently given for movement in both Cotswold and South Oxfordshire Districts, both as a primary reason and even more pre-dominantly (as might be expected) when primary and secondary reasons for migration are combined. Employment reasons are almost as important in Cotswold District but far less so in South Oxfordshire, where movement upon marriage is a significant factor, largely but not wholly because of the nature of one of the constituent profiles in that District. Rurality is naturally more important a factor in Cotswold than in South Oxfordshire, though it formed a secondary reason for more than a quarter of migrants into South Oxfordshire, reflecting the urban origins of many of these migrants. Other reasons were of comparatively little primary significance.

But these overall impressions are of limited applicability because they do not emphasise sufficiently the complex nature of individual migration movements. The profile data in Table 9.2 read in conjunction with the reasoning of individual responses give a more profound insight into the changing character of the communities affected by highlighting the motivations, aspirations and circumstances of the households involved.

Employment reasons are particularly prominent in explaining movement into the three parishes comprising Cotswold profile 1 (agricultural), but the variety of individual motivations encompassed by this categorisation and the extent of their interplay with other motives is considerable. The high proportion of moves into tied accommodation, though primarily job-oriented, also include housing factors and other less well defined reasons: 'to a smaller shop with no employees to be managed' was the employment reason given by a village shopkeeper. Others in tied houses had found forestry or agricultural employment on completing their education, had moved to a better job, or had been made redundant and forced to find not only a new job but also a new house.

The importance of employment factors as a force precipitating movement is further emphasised by analysis of the extent to which in-migrants had changed their employment. Of the Cotswold migrants 30 per cent were now in a different job; of these a third were performing a similar task but in a different firm, nearly half were employed by a different firm but were doing a different job, and much smaller proportions were doing a different job in the same firm, had moved to retire, or had become unemployed. The same general picture was true of South Oxfordshire, though significantly more (18 per cent compared with 7 per cent) were now performing a different job in the same firm – confirming the presence of spiralists in the accessible countryside, moving upon promotion. Differentiation between profiles was generally small and usually predictable, with movement on retirement commonest in the Cotswold retirement profile and, more interestingly, in the estate villages, where movement from tied housing upon retirement was significant. Overall levels of change in employment were highest in the Cotswold traditional rural and local authority profiles, lowest in the South Oxfordshire younger owner-occupiers and poor housing profiles.

In Cotswold profile 4 (local authority housing) *housing* was the predominant factor behind in-migration, though again there were many variations upon the general theme. One household, previously sharing accommodation with parents, had secured a council house because the young couple and their two children (with another baby expected) had been living in a single room. There was a great deal of short-distance movement within a small council estate, with households seeking more (or occasionally less) room, a place for the children to play or single-storey accommodation because of disablement. One respondent said that 'the council offered this house, so we moved. First we had one room in a house on this estate, then we were put in a hotel by the council for ten weeks.' A number of cases of eviction from tied cottages occurred and the Cotswold District Council was obliged to allocate housing in these cases.

Housing reasons were also of particular significance in South Oxfordshire profile 3 (local authority housing) and profile 2 (established professional). In the former, reasons for movement were similar to those specified in the Cotswolds – the need for more room, preference for a different part of the village, the offer of council accommodation to households living with their parents or in substandard housing. In the latter, moves from nearby urban areas such as Reading and Henley for 'peace and quiet' were common, but spiralist movement to a larger house was the primary reason given by in-migrants. The particular attraction of a house in one of the more fashionable Chiltern villages inspired movement from, for example, Sonning Common, Kidmore End and other villages in the suburban sprawl north of Reading to less developed, more exclusive villages such as Rotherfield Peppard.

The attractions of a *rural environment* were, naturally enough, cited as a principal reason for movement more often by migrants to Cotswold parishes, though there was considerable variation between the housing types represented in the two study districts, with Cotswold profiles 3 (estate villages) and 2 (retirement) and South Oxfordshire profile 1 (traditional rural) pre-eminent. All of these types of environment are logical choices for households ranking rurality high in their choice of housing location, given a supply of available houses in estate villages, but the absence of the Cotswold agricultural profile, the most widespread housing profile in that district, can only be explained in terms of a shortage of available non-tied accommodation allied to restrictive planning policies in respect of new development. Clearly, rurality continues to exert a powerful influence in directing potential migrants, although there is, as the examples quoted later will show, a counter-current which contains, among others, those disenchanted with the rural way of life.

Within the estate village profile the precise motivations of in-migrants were diverse, as were their tenure characteristics: households had moved from council to rented unfurnished accommodation for 'peace and quiet', from a London flat for 'a house in the country', and for the 'freedom of country life' from Cirencester. In South Oxfordshire's traditional rural profile households had moved to the countryside from 'next to London airport' and, in a number of cases, from London because, for example, they 'wished to raise our family in a better environment': the image of the countryside is all-prevalent here, perhaps to the exclusion of the reality.

Moves into a rural environment are infrequently accomplished as a single leap of faith from conurbation to countryside, however. The process appears to be more gradual: 69 per cent of all moves into South Oxfordshire District, and 79 per cent into Cotswold District, had their origins in other rural areas or small towns. Moves direct from large towns or cities were commonest in South Oxfordshire profile 2 (established professionals: 43 per cent), profile 4 (younger owner-occupiers: 36 per cent), and profile 6 (poor housing: 43 per cent). Households in the last of these profiles were not motivated by the attractions of a rural environment, however; they can be regarded as involuntary urban overspill attracted into the mobile home sector as an apparently cheap housing option. In the case of established professionals, however, rurality was a distinct attraction for some in-migrants from smaller towns: one household moved from Wokingham to a South Oxfordshire village because 'the Wokingham area was being built up', others had moved from the suburbs of Reading to a 'better environment'. (These included, for example, residents in profile 4 villages who, as they became established, made the transition to profile 2: from Sonning Common to Rotherfield Peppard in a number of cases.)

Marriage was the primary motivating factor for 14 per cent of moves in South Oxfordshire District and 6 per cent in Cotswold District, but was particularly important in profile 6 in South Oxfordshire (poor housing: 29 per cent). In most of the cases which fell into this category in Marston, movement took place over a very short distance, from Oxford or its suburbs or from within Marston itself, and the principal attraction for the newly formed households was the availability of relatively cheap owner-occupied accommodation in a mobile home. For several households, too, this represented independence after a period of sharing with relatives. The low apparent cost was a distinct advantage for some; the extra costs consequent upon depreciation of the dwelling were either not perceived or were discounted. In other cases a mobile home was less an attraction than an inevitability: 'the only place we could find', 'the only place we could afford', or (after a divorce) 'all I could get after the house was sold'. Nevertheless, the role fulfilled by such housing in urban fringe sites should be acknowledged.

The thematic treatment of motives for migration, particular reasons in particular types of rural housing environments, in the preceding paragraphs is inevitably an over-simplification, although it has illustrated certain common motivating factors. People move to specific rural locations for a wide variety of reasons: their perceptions of the attractions of the place differ widely and may seem totally inaccurate when measured by a third party. Few moves are completely unconstrained and most are guided by a series of overlapping sets of needs and preferences. Council tenants in a Cotswold village moved because they 'wanted a bigger house with more bedrooms, and a bigger garden so that the head of the household could keep pigeons'. A widow had bought a house in the Cotswolds because 'I did not like Hove and could choose where I wanted to live in England. This area was near friends and relatives and was central for travelling around the country.' Another family had moved because they thought they would like living in a village, but were now intending to move back to a town because of the lack of shopping, social and sports facilities. On several occasions evictions from tied cottages following redundancy or a disagreement with the employers were only the immediate reasons for moves which took account of several other factors. Certainly it is true to say that for the majority of migrant households there is no single factor which is exclusively responsible for migration, except perhaps where employment acts as the trigger mechanism.

MOVERS AND STAYERS

Some further evidence relating to the determinants of migration activity can be gleaned from a comparison of the characteristics of migrants and non-migrants. The mover/stayer dichotomy, postulating significant social differences between the two groups, was first proposed by Blumen, Kogan and McCarthy (1955); empirical evidence that stayers are increasingly reluctant to become movers as their length of residence in a particular dwelling increases was adduced in a survey of Nidderdale by Johnston (1967). This question of the probability of movement, and the extent to which in-migrants to the case study areas since 1972 were more likely to move again than were stayers to make their first move (for at least five years), is returned to at the end of this section. Firstly, however, consideration is given to differences between movers and stayers, primarily in respect of key socio-economic variables.

That there were significant differences between the two groups in terms of present tenure is made amply apparent in Table 9.4. In the owner-occupied sector stayers were much more likely to own their home outright and movers to be buying their first house. This was particularly the case in South Oxfordshire, although, as the table indicates, the overall level of owner-occupation in this area was much higher than in Cotswold. Stayers were predominant in local authority housing, despite the comparatively high level of transfers reported earlier in this chapter. Cross-tabulation with other variables explains this bias towards stayers in both sectors: those owning outright were generally in older age-groups, had rather higher incomes, had more dependents and hence greater disincentives to movement, while local authority tenants, again generally in older age-groups and with a high average number of dependents, had lower incomes and therefore less ability to move even if they had the desire to do so.

Within the private rented sector, which is especially significant in Cotswold, movers accounted for the majority of households. This extremely high level of migration was greatest in tied accommodation, despite the comparatively low migration rate in the Cotswold estate village profile. Clearly the average length of residence in tied accommodation elsewhere is extremely low, partly because of the inevitable tensions between employee and employer/landlord, partly because of the desire for independence, either in owner-occupation or elsewhere in the rented sector, of a proportion of households in tied accommodation, and partly because of the generally poor condition of some tied houses, leading to a degree of rehousing in local authority accommodation.

The role played by income levels in differentiating between movers and stayers was alluded to above, and qualified support for this proposition is contained in Table 9.5. In South Oxfordshire lower incomes produce fewer movers, a clear instance of one constraint upon the housing opportunities available to low-income families. The difference is less marked with high-

Table 9.4 Present tenure of movers and stayers (%)*

Mover / Stayer	Own outright	Buying (not 1st time)	Buying (1st time)	Renting local authority	Renting private furnished	Renting private unfurnished	Renting tied
Cotswold District							
Movers	19·2	6·6	16·5	15·4	2·2	6·0	34·0
Stayers	37·9	6·9	7·6	17·4	2·2	14·2	13·9
			$X^2 = 50·77$ d.f. = 6 (significant at 0·01)				
South Oxfordshire District							
Movers	14·8	17·0	31·4	11·7	3·8	5·3	15·9
Stayers	35·0	13·7	14·2	23·1	0·5	8·0	5·4
			$X^2 = 86·23$ d.f. = 6 (significant at 0·01)				

* Figures are row percentages; chi square values, however, are calculated from absolute frequencies.

Table 9.5   *Present annual income of movers and stayers (%)**

Mover/ Stayer	Cotswold District	£3,000– £6,000	>£6,000	South Oxfordshire District	£3,000– £6,000	>£6,000
	<£3,000			<£3,000		
Movers	47·8	35·9	16·3	22·5	40·2	37·3
Stayers	53·5	31·5	15·0	38·9	36·7	24·4

$X^2 = 1·67$ $X^2 = 16·59$
d.f. = 2 (not significant at 0·05)   d.f. = 2 (significant at 0·01)

* Figures are row percentages; chi square values are calculated as for Table 9.4.

income households, since the stayers in this case include the established professional households with low levels of movement, as described earlier. The situation is less clear in Cotswold District, for a number of reasons. The overall migration rate is lower, so that any differences between movers and stayers are likely to be less marked. The pressures on the housing stock arising from migration are of a different nature and the socio-economic characteristics of the survey households are different. Most significant of all, overall income levels were markedly lower (51·5 per cent below £3,000 per annum compared with 31·8 per cent in South Oxfordshire), and hence the conventional threefold division adopted in earlier chapters and in Table 9.5 is of less relevance. If £2,000 per annum is taken as the upper limit for the first category, 22·4 per cent of Cotswold movers earned less than this figure, compared with 32 per cent of the stayers – a much more significant difference, and one which underlines the importance of income as a factor explaining levels of migration.

Mover/stayer differences described above, with the single explicable exception of income in Cotswold District, have revealed statistically significant values. The same cannot be said of differences in respect of social class (Table 9.6) although in South Oxfordshire movers include a higher proportion of social classes 1 and 2, confirming once again the continuing colonisation of parts of the area by professional groups. The statistics for car-ownership tend to support this assertion, with movers accounting for a higher proportion of two-car households and a lower proportion of households without access to a car. In both study areas households in social classes 4 and 5 were least likely to be movers, re-emphasising the constraints upon housing access for these groups of the population.

Having established the basic socio-economic differences between movers and stayers, it is now possible to consider differences in attitudes to housing, and to the wider context of the housing environment. In particular, differences in attitudes towards the type, condition and facilities of present housing, and its adequacy in fulfilling present and future housing needs, would contribute towards an explanation of the hypothesis that stayers are more likely to remain stayers than movers are to become stayers. But the

Table 9.6   *Social class of movers and stayers (%)**

Social class†	Cotswold District		South Oxfordshire District	
	Movers	Stayers	Movers	Stayers
1	27·8	26·3	29·7	25·1
2	17·2	16·6	31·3	22·6
3	23·1	15·9	12·4	16·9
4	18·9	24·7	19·7	24·0
5	9·5	12·7	6·6	10·6
6	3·6	3·9	0·4	0·8

$$X^2 = 5·74 \qquad\qquad X^2 = 12·15$$

d.f. = 5 (not significant at 0·05)   d.f. = 5 (significant at 0·05)

* Figures are column percentages; chi square values are calculated as for Table 9.4.

† Social class used rather than socio-economic group because some SEG totals are very small.

statistics in respect of type and size of house and house conditions do not suggest that stayers have to any marked degree achieved the larger and better-quality accommodation to which movers perhaps aspire. Indeed there are indications that stayers are more likely to remain stayers not because they have reached a more satisfactory housing environment, but because they have become trapped in less satisfactory ones. In South Oxfordshire a higher proportion of movers occupied detached houses (the same was true of mobile homes but there are particular reasons for this, as noted earlier), there was little variation in size of house between the two groups and only 3 per cent of houses occupied by movers were classified as unfit, compared with 8·1 per cent for stayers. There was very little difference between Cotswold movers and stayers in respect of house type or size, although once again a higher proportion of houses occupied by stayers were regarded as unfit.

The same general pattern is true of the amenities present in movers' and stayers' present houses. A higher proportion of houses occupied by stayers lacked hot water, an inside toilet, a fixed bath, connection to mains drainage, a damp course or central heating, so that the movers might be regarded as having already achieved a higher standard by their migration. But the crucial point is that a significantly greater percentage of them were still dissatisfied with the facilities offered by their present house. One indication of this greater degree of dissatisfaction is given in Table 9.7 which illustrates the fact that despite their move, movers were more likely to feel that they *still* had too few rooms, although the majority of both groups expressed the feeling that the number of rooms was adequate. The conclusion which can be drawn from this is that, despite the evidence that the standard of housing occupied by movers was of higher quality (measured in purely physical terms) than that occupied by stayers, it still does not match up to their expectations; the aspirations of the two groups

Table 9.7 *Adequacy of number of rooms in present house: opinion of movers and stayers (%)**

Movers/ Stayers	Cotswold District			South Oxfordshire District		
	Too many rooms	Right number	Too few rooms	Too many rooms	Right number	Too few rooms
Movers	4·9	75·8	19·2	6·1	64·0	29·9
Stayers	8·8	77·0	14·2	10·6	71·2	18·1

$$X^2 = 4·21$$
d.f. = 2 (not significant at 0·05)

$$X^2 = 14·42$$
d.f. = 2 (significant at 0·01)

* Figures are row percentages; chi square values are calculated as for Table 9.4.

differ more widely than their present circumstances.

This greater dissatisfaction on the part of movers was also apparent in respect of the facilities available in the immediate area. Despite the fact that movers tended to make greater use of most services and social facilities (but not of the church) they were less satisfied with the standard of provision. This was particularly the case with educational facilities and with public transport, although bus services to many of the villages studied in detail were infrequent or non-existent and the level of provision was the subject of considerable criticism from both movers and stayers. Shopping provision and welfare facilities were also criticised more widely by movers.

The inference that movers, despite their migration, were less satisfied with their quality of life is unavoidable, and it is substantiated by the statistics in Table 9.8 which illustrates the remarkable degree to which movers are more likely to move again. Given that around one-tenth of the population migrate in any period of twelve months, three-quarters of that movement in Cotswold District would derive, *ceteris paribus*, from the further migration of movers (who constituted only 36 per cent of the sample) and no less than five-sixths of South Oxfordshire movement would so derive (from 41 per cent of the sample). Inevitably such figures have to be qualified: hypothetical assessments of future behaviour are notoriously unreliable. But the differential between movers and stayers is so great that, although the exact proportions should not be taken as anything more than a general guideline, the differential itself can be accepted as further evidence of the contrasting behavioural patterns of movers and stayers.

Having already established that although the quality of the housing environment of movers is generally as good and often better than that of stayers their level of perceived satisfaction is lower, it is tempting to suggest this as the explanation for the higher propensity to migrate of movers. This is certainly a partial explanation, since high probabilities of further migration of movers are recorded for South Oxfordshire profile 4, for example (the spiralist, younger owner-occupiers: 21 per cent), but it is only

Table 9.8 Probability of household's moving within twelve months: differences between movers and stayers (%)*

Movers/ Stayers	Cotswold District					South Oxfordshire District				
	Very likely	Fairly likely	Not very likely	Very unlikely	Unknown	Very likely	Fairly likely	Not very likely	Very unlikely	Unknown
Movers	12·1	6·0	14·3	61·5	6·0	20·8	4·2	12·9	56·1	6·1
Stayers	4·1	2·5	6·6	82·3	4·4	4·9	4·2	12·7	74·0	4·2

$X^2 = 28·78$
d.f. = 4 (significant at 0·01)

$X^2 = 43·44$
d.f. = 4 (significant at 0·01)

* Figures are row percentages; chi square values are calculated as for Table 9.4.

partial. Other contributions to high probabilities of further movement result from poor housing (20 per cent in South Oxfordshire), which re-emphasises the way in which many households perceive mobile homes as a temporary solution to housing problems; from households in some traditional areas (27 per cent in South Oxfordshire), partly again through the higher proportion of older housing; and from movement of dependents within the household, especially where there was intense competition in the local housing market. There was also, perhaps surprisingly, a very high propensity to migrate from Cotswold estate villages (23 per cent). Low probabilities were found in Cotswold retirement areas (zero), the Cotswold agricultural profile (5 per cent) and the South Oxfordshire local authority and established professional profiles (both 11 per cent).

Some further light is shed on these widely varying likely rates of future movement by the verbatim responses recorded at interview, and the difficulties faced in moving again. A typical response from first-time buyers in the younger owner-occupier profile was 'to get a better house in the Sonning Common/Rotherfield Greys area'; conversely, mobile home dwellers felt that 'the caravan isn't big enough – we want a house', that the 'caravan was too small' or that their current situation offered the disadvantages of 'cramped conditions and no garden'. Households in privately rented unfurnished accommodation in South Oxfordshire wanted to move to a council house 'because of the state of their present home' or because of a closing order on the present house necessitated by persistent dampness.

Respondents, especially those wanting to change to owner-occupation, were often keenly aware of the difficulties they faced in securing new accommodation. The lack of suitable and sufficient private housing and in particular the high price of it were recurrent themes; some households had been looking for another house for a number of years. The problems were different, but no less formidable, for some potential movers within or into the local authority sector. The disadvantages for certain types of households of council points schemes for allocation were stressed by, for instance, a childless couple in a tied cottage who had been on the waiting list for eleven years; larger families whose present accommodation was too cramped – in more than one case a further child was expected, though whether this was planned to force the council's hand was left unstated; and by an older couple in tied accommodation who had been on the waiting list for a number of years, but now 'feel they will have to wait until they retire' before an offer is made. Other cases of difficulty included offspring who could not join the waiting list until they became married (but could not marry until they found accommodation) and households who claimed that 'the council aren't building the houses they promised'. Those wanting to enter the private rented sector were few in number and they recognised the problem of shortage of such accommodation.

Access to all forms of housing is constrained, therefore, by the economics of supply and demand in the case of the private sector and by the action of local authorities in defining priorities which limit the opportunities of certain types of household. Furthermore, opportunities for transfer within a particular sector are also constrained to a considerable and possibly unacceptable degree. This is a common cause for complaint amongst local authority tenants, especially where a degree of hardship is apparently incurred as a result of inflexibility in the reallocation system. For example, one couple claimed that they needed a ground floor flat because of the wife's disablement; they had been on the waiting list for a transfer for five years, despite the presence for some of that time of a doctor's certificate specifying their particular needs. Periods of up to ten years waiting for a transfer seemed to be surprisingly common and, provided that the needs of the applicant were reasonable and not too specific in terms of house type and location, could perhaps have been reduced, especially where the present house was in poor condition.

To summarise the main points considered in this section, the concept of the mover/stayer dichotomy has been substantiated by the evidence from South Oxfordshire and Cotswold Districts: major differences in the social, economic and behavioural characteristics of the two groups were discovered. Movers included higher proportions of those with higher incomes, in social classes 1 and 2 and with two or more cars, emphasising the limited housing opportunities (and hence higher proportions of stayers) of those with lower incomes. Housing provision was similar for both groups, but *attitudes* to housing varied substantially – the aspirations of movers were such that they required even better housing provision. Hence movers were more likely to move again than were stayers to move for the first time, largely motivated by their desire for better housing. The extent to which this upward filtering through the housing stock was present in their last move is the subject of inquiry of the next section.

MOVEMENT THROUGH THE HOUSING STOCK

The role of housing in motivating and directing household movement and the expectations of movers (however motivated) in respect of changes in their housing circumstances can be examined from a different perspective by analysing differences between the past and present housing of movers, particularly in terms of tenure, house type and size, facilities and house condition. The underlying premise, that movement is often used as a means of filtering upwards through the housing stock to better accommodation, is considered for the two study areas separately, and this section is concluded by a general analysis of the characteristics and effects of movement through the housing stock.

Changes in tenure consequent upon household movement are important not only in helping to identify the motivations and aspirations of migrants but also in underlining pressures upon particular sectors of the local housing market. In the Cotswolds 102 of the 167 relevant moves (61 per cent) resulted in no change of tenure (including the fifteen households who moved from the 'buying first time' to 'buying not first time' category), emphasising the financial and other constraints which, together with sheer inertia, reduce the likelihood of movement between tenures. This is particularly the case for those in tied accommodation, 76 per cent of whom remained in tied housing following their move. Households moving from tied accommodation to other tenures were predominantly housed by the local authority (and these cases, as has been shown earlier in this chapter, included movement prompted by eviction or by the imposition of a closing order on an unfit dwelling).

Despite its disadvantages, which have been rehearsed elsewhere, tied housing remains attractive in particular circumstances and this is reflected in the movement from other tenures to tied accommodation. Not all such movement, of course, is into agricultural cottages: the schoolhouse and the rectory are other examples of housing tied to specific employment. The majority of moves into tied houses in the Cotswolds, however, were into farm cottages, with instances of movement from Bristol for 'employment on a farm, and country life' and from owner-occupation upon appointment as a farm manager.

Movement into local authority housing took place exclusively from the private rented sector (discounting the one household previously in shared accommodation). The reasons for such movement from tied houses have been given above and similar reasons characterised movement from non-tied rented houses – eviction, dissatisfaction with the present house, the offer of a council property after years on the waiting list. Such movement took place, largely because of the residential criteria for eligibility for council housing, almost entirely over very short distances. In-migration by established owner-occupiers was rather different in character, with a good deal of retirement migration from London, south-east England and other towns and cities, but movement *into* the owner-occupied sector was more varied, with several cases in which the desire to own a house was the prime motivating force. In such cases movement was local, from private rented or council accommodation in nearby villages, and the perceived benefit of owner-occupation was 'a better standard of living' or 'a better house'. Longer-distance migration by new owner-occupiers was prompted by the inherent attractiveness of the area, a particularly significant factor once again for older households, and the desire to move closer to friends or relatives who were already resident in the area.

Change of tenure, therefore, was one factor in the decision to migrate of a significant proportion of Cotswold in-migrants, but other changes in the type and quality of housing also had an influence. There was some evidence of trading up in terms of house type, with two-thirds of those households previously in a flat, maisonette or bedsitter, or sharing with relatives, now aspiring to a detached or semi-detached house, and 36 per cent of those previously in a semi-detached house now living in a detached house (though 20 per cent of households formerly in a detached house had made the reverse transition). The new house was generally larger, too: three-fifths of those previously in two-bedroomed houses, and a quarter of those in three-bedroomed houses, now had more bedrooms. Furthermore, the new house was more likely to have basic facilities such as hot water, an inside toilet and a fixed bath (though these were normally available in the previous house also), and was much more likely to have central heating (68 per cent of present houses; 57 per cent of previous houses) and a damp course (78 per cent; 68 per cent), but less likely to have mains drainage available (70 per cent; 80 per cent).

The proportion of South Oxfordshire in-migrants whose tenure circumstances had remained precisely the same, together with those who had progressed from buying for the first time to buying not for the first time, was 66 per cent – higher than in the Cotswolds, perhaps because the barriers to movement between sectors, and in particular the prices of houses on the open market, were higher. Nevertheless thirty-three households (15 per cent of the migrant sample excluding those new households which had not been formed before the move) had made the transition from rented or shared accommodation into owner-occupation. One-third of these households, however, had moved into mobile homes on sites in Marston and Wheatley, at the lower end of the price range. In some cases in other profiles movement between different tenures appeared to be more or less incidental to the actual reason for migration, as with redundancy and subsequent notice to quit a tied cottage. In others renting was a short-term measure pending the completion of a new house or the appearance of a particular type of house on the market. Hence the true amount of change to owner-occupation was comparatively small; the main motivations were the high cost of rented houses in South Oxfordshire, which made owner-occupation actually less expensive in some circumstances, and the lower price of houses in the area compared with Henley-on-Thames and other towns nearer London, forcing households wanting to own their home to opt for Sonning Common, Chinnor or similar locations.

Although house prices were lower in relation to some other commuter areas they were still higher than in the Cotswolds (see Chapter 11), which may well have contributed to the high proportion of households in tied accommodation whose tenure remained the same after their movement (73 per cent). This lack of housing opportunity for the majority of households in these circumstances is reflected in the comments of those who did change tenure: in virtually all cases movement was involuntary, brought about by retirement, disability or change of employment, with the consequence that the tied house became untenable. The rest of the private rented sector saw a good deal of change, largely into owner-occupation, with a decline in the two categories (furnished and unfurnished rented) of some 60 per cent, emphasising, though from a small sample, the continuing decline in this sector and the probable eventual loss of one of the few alternatives for households with limited income and hence limited opportunities.

Movement into council housing occurred from all other tenures, although for those already in local authority accommodation before their move there was little change. New local authority tenants included one household whose private rented unfurnished accommodation had 'no [inside] toilet or bathroom and no bedroom for the children', but also former mobile home owners who were 'turned off the site' or who, for health reasons, found a mobile home inconvenient or who 'thought everyone had to move from the site because the council wanted the caravans'. Together with households evicted from tied houses, mobile home owners, who moved for the reasons outlined above or who now preferred a conventional home, accounted for the vast majority of new council tenants, although there were isolated instances of owner-occupiers moving to council houses, apparently for financial reasons.

Changes other than tenure in the housing circumstances of migrant households in the South Oxfordshire area to a large extent mirrored those of the Cotswolds, though a far lower proportion of households previously in flats, maisonettes or sharing with relatives had obtained a detached or semi-detached house. Forty-one per cent of households previously in a semi-detached house had now obtained a detached house; only 10 per cent had transferred from detached to semi-detached. Mobile homes provided the first step for 44 per cent of the newly formed households, who in turn occupied over half of the mobile homes in the sample; none of the households previously occupying a mobile home did so after their move. These various indications of the role of household movement in improving housing conditions are corroborated by the statistics on house size (households were most likely to move to a house with one extra bedroom) and amenities. As in the Cotswold area, the new house was more likely to possess the basic amenities and also would more commonly possess central heating, a damp course, a garage and a garden.

The inferences to be drawn from this section, therefore, are that some, but by no means all, households are able to treat the process of household movement as an opportunity to change tenure and improve their housing circumstances. Changes of tenure include a drift towards owner-occupation, but this is not overwhelmingly the case and the most important change, perhaps, is the movement out of the private rented sector (except for tied housing which is still very significant, especially in the Cotswolds). Changes in housing type and quality generally involve upward filtering through the stock into larger houses with better facilities, though once again there are exceptions, as with the common desire of retirement migrants for a smaller, more easily managed property. Normally, however, movement entails improvement, except where lack of power in the housing market limits the household's ability to achieve an improvement in its individual housing situation.

IN-MIGRANTS AND OUT-MIGRANTS: CHANGES IN POPULATION STRUCTURE

The fourth and final aspect of migration to be considered is a comparison between the out-migrants and the in-migrants to the same two case-study areas. An obvious difficulty arises when tackling this aspect, in that the out-migrant group is, by definition, no longer available for consultation and interview. This problem was overcome, but the data obtained were inevitably sparse and tentative. Since the out-migrants were no longer at the sample addresses, and were likely to be widely scattered, they could not be contacted directly and interviewed in depth in the same way as the in-migrants. Two sources of information remained: first, the opinions of the in-migrants in respect of the destination, motivation and other characteristics of the households they had replaced and, secondly, data from a postal survey of those out-migrants who could be traced – bearing in mind that this was a comparatively small sample, since many in-migrants were unable to recall (or would never have known) the new address of their predecessors. These two sources are considered in turn.

The quality of response to questions concerning previous occupiers was very low; this in itself necessitated the follow-up postal survey of out-migrants, but it also casts doubt upon the accuracy of the limited response which could be obtained. The results in respect of reasons for migration of previous occupiers are given in Table 9.9, from which it can be seen that the stated reasons for movement of the out-migrants closely resembled those of the in-migrants to the two study areas, with employment reasons pre-eminent in precipitating movement in the Cotswold area and housing the prime motivating force in South Oxfordshire. However, the high

Table 9.9   *Adduced reasons for migration of out-migrants (%)**

Reason	Cotswold District		South Oxfordshire District	
	(1)	*(2)†*	*(1)*	*(2)†*
Employment	21	29·2	27	34·4
Housing	16	22·2	29	38·0
Education	2	3·0	1	1·1
Marriage	4	5·1	5	6·2
To friends/relatives	4	6·1	5	6·2
Retirement	2	3·0	2	2·1
Other	22	31·2	9	12·3
Unknown	29	—	22	—

* Figures are column percentages.
† Column (2) in each case indicates adjusted percentages excluding responses of 'unknown'.

Table 9.10 *Traced destinations of out-migrants*

Rural housing profile	Total changes (1)	Changes not due to migration (2)	Total out-migrants (3)	New address traced (4)	% out-migrants traced (5)
Cotswold District					
1 Agricultural	53	13	40	3	8
2 Retirement	27	8	19	4	21
3 Poor housing	30	10	20	4	20
4 Local authority housing	42	8	34	14	41
5 Armed forces	29	3	26	0	0
TOTAL	181	42	139	25	18
South Oxfordshire District					
1 Traditional rural	48	14	34	4	12
2 Established professional	52	12	40	12	30
3 Local authority housing	37	5	32	5	16
4 Younger owner-occupiers	46	8	38	4	11
5 Armed forces	30	0	30	2	7
6 Poor housing	51	12	39	5	13
TOTAL	264	51	213	32	15
TOTAL SAMPLE	445	93	352	57	16

Notes: Figures in columns (1) to (4) are actual frequencies.
Column (1) 1976 resident different from 1971 resident.
Column (2) Previous occupier died; new house, etc.
Column (3) Column (1) minus column (2).
Column (4) Full address of previous resident available.
Column (5) Column (4) as a proportion of column (3).

percentages of unknown and (in the Cotswolds) 'other' reasons distorted the picture to some degree, as did the reliance on second-hand information, a point which is examined later. Other data supplied by the respondents in the main survey were fragmentary, although it was ascertained that out-migrants' destinations were largely rural in character (69 per cent moved to rural areas or to small country towns, only 8 per cent to major cities) and that movement generally took place over very small distances – often indeed, within the same village – in much the same way as was typical of in-migration.

To gain a greater understanding of out-migration it was necessary to conduct a follow-up postal questionnaire survey. This was carried out for all out-migrant households where new addresses could be traced, whether from information provided by respondents to the main survey or by close examination of the electoral registers. These sources were, however, able only to provide addresses for about one-sixth of the out-migrants, as is indicated in Table 9.10. Where the previous occupants had moved outside the immediate area, and the present occupant was unable or unwilling to provide a precise address, little could be done to trace the out-migrant household. Fortunately the response to the postal survey was comparatively good, completed questionnaires being returned by thirty-four out of the fifty-seven households contacted (60 per cent). The discussion which follows should naturally be regarded as merely exploratory, given that it is largely based on such a restricted sample.

To return to the question of motivation, the reasons given for out-migration (Table 9.11) are interesting in two ways: they are often very different from those characteristic of in-migrants, and they conflict with the reasons ascribed to the out-migrants by the successor households. To consider the latter question first, Table 9.12 indicates that the reasons for movement corresponded in only eighteen cases out of thirty-four, and that the successor households vastly underestimated the importance of housing factors in motivating the out-migrants.

Table 9.11 emphasises the overwhelming importance of housing reasons, compared with which employment factors are insignificant, yet in the in-migrant sample the two sets of factors were of roughly equal importance.

Table 9.11   *Out-migrants: reasons for movement*

Reason	Number	%
Employment	3	8·8
Housing	23	67·6
Education	1	2·9
Move to urban area	1	2·9
To friends/relatives	1	2·9
Retirement	1	2·9
Other	4	11·8

Table 9.12   *Comparison of adduced and true reasons for movement*

Reason given by present resident	Reason given by out-migrant			
	Employment	Housing	Retirement	Other
Employment	2	1	—	—
Housing	1	13	—	2
Retirement	—	2	1	3
Other	—	7	—	2

Note: Figures are actual frequencies.

The verbatim responses of typical out-migrants reveal a preoccupation with better or larger housing or more modern accommodation, but with some explicit references to tenure ('was living in rented accommodation and wished to have own home') and a number of more complex responses: 'family too large for house. Inconvenience due to lack of shops and distant schools. Dangerous main road nearby. Lack of sizeable garden.' Employment reasons in each case involved long-distance movement consequent upon promotion, and no other factor was the prime motivating force for more than one out-migrant household.

Changes in tenure as a result of household movement were relatively uncommon, involving seven households in all, but resulted in gains in the local authority sector and to a lesser extent in owner-occupation, and a decline of the private rented sector (Table 9.13). Movement from private rented accommodation to council housing was, predictably, related to improvement of house condition and amenities (an inside toilet or bathroom, for instance), with an appreciation of housing economics and the desire for home-ownership more prominent in the minds of those switching from renting privately to owner-occupation. Perhaps surprisingly (in terms of eligibility rather than principle) two households changed from owner-occupation to council renting; in both cases the intention was to effect an improvement in the standard of amenities available to the household.

Strictly in terms of tenure there was little evidence, from the limited sample available, of households attempting to use their movement as a

Table 9.13   *Tenure changes of out-migrants (%)**

Tenure of present occupier	New tenure of out-migrant		
	Owner-occupier	Renting local authority	Private rented
Owner-occupier	44·0†	5·9	—
Renting local authority	2·9	17·6†	—
Private rented	5·9	5·9	17·6†

* Figures are total percentages (NB $N = 34$).
† No change of tenure.

means of improving their circumstances by tending towards owner-occupation; such changes as did occur were largely explicable in terms of a combination of the condition of the present house, market forces and structural change in the mix of tenures available. More direct evidence of upward filtering is provided by changes in the type and size of house. Of those households which had moved to detached properties, four had previously occupied semi-detached houses or bungalows, two had had terraced houses and one had lived in a mobile home. Conversely, three households previously in detached or semi-detached houses now occupied one bungalow, one terraced house and one flat. Four of the households previously with one or two bedrooms now had three-bedroom properties, but for those who previously occupied larger houses there were equivalent changes towards larger and smaller house sizes.

Table 9.14   *Likelihood of further move of out-migrants within twelve months*

Likelihood	Number	%
Very likely	3	8·8
Fairly likely	—	—
Not very likely	6	17·6
Very unlikely	22	64·7
Not known	3	8·8

The out-migrant sample displayed a considerable reluctance to undertake a further move (Table 9.14), in marked contrast to the in-migrants to the Costwold area and South Oxfordshire. Only 8·8 per cent (three households) were at all likely to move again within twelve months, and these households had in two instances moved considerable distances (to Hertfordshire and to London) as a result of a change of employment. With such a small sample it is dangerous to speculate on the reasons for the existence of such a small number of potential movers, although the out-migrant sample may well have been biased towards older, established households and away from younger households and those in poor housing.

CONCLUSION

The overall impressions from this survey of migration in two areas of lowland England are of a rapid turnover of the mobile element of the population, with consequences for the household structure of the comparatively small communities involved and for the indigenous population, especially in respect of competition in the housing market. Probably the most important finding is the discovery of remarkably deep-seated differences between the perceptions of movers and stayers within rural communities in terms of attitudes to present housing and the wider aspects of life in the countryside, and of ability and willingness to move again to improve housing circumstances. Within mover groups the most important reasons for household movement were a set of factors related to housing (condition, quality, the match of house size to household size, for example) and a further batch of employment reasons; but the attractions, whether real or illusory, of the rural environment were also significant in determining the destination of migrant households. There was some evidence, too, that a proportion of migrant households geared the process of household movement towards an attempt to improve their housing circumstances. Finally, there were indications of differences in circumstances and outlook between in-migrants and the out-migrants whom they replaced, although a further, more specific survey would be necessary in order to validate this interim conclusion.

Part Four

A View of Policies

Chapter 10

Planning and Housing Policy: the National Perspective

Local housing authorities, owner-occupiers, private and public tenants – indeed all the users and suppliers of rural housing – operate within a framework of national legislation and practice. This framework provides both incentives and constraints to the working of the various markets for housing and it is important to understand this national context before assessing local policies in housing and planning policy.

This chapter reviews three main aspects of this national context. First, it considers the approach to the planning of rural settlements which has built up since the end of the Second World War, particularly the problems of providing services at an acceptable cost to village communities. The consequences for housing in rural areas are examined and then there follows a review of the way in which rural housing issues have been approached so far by structure plans. Finally there is considered the range of housing policies and practices which influence the quantity and quality of rural housing and the conditions under which such housing is occupied.

THE DEVELOPMENT OF RURAL SETTLEMENT PLANNING

Settlement policies, encouraged by the Town and Country Planning Act 1947 to concentrate upon descriptive classification and the development of hierarchies, have been slow to gain sophistication, in contrast to the advances made in urban analysis. Firmly based in development control, with concepts such as infilling within a village envelope prevalent, they have often seemed to lack the flexibility needed in dealing with a dynamic and complex situation: infilling policies, for example, are almost irrelevant to areas where the dominant pattern is one of scattered rather than nucleated settlement, yet they are still proposed for such areas.

A typical early application of standard settlement policies involved the village college concept in Cambridgeshire, which was further developed in the 1952 County Development Plan. The plan envisaged a reduction in the rate of growth of Cambridge itself, with complementary proposals for the accelerated development of a ring of key villages around the city to accommodate an extra 7,500 people, and the encouragement of growth in larger villages forming centres for a rural hinterland (Mellor, 1966). Subsequently, entirely new villages in the ring around Cambridge were proposed, and the first such settlement, Bar Hill, was initiated in 1961 and expected to house a population of around 4,000 within ten years.

The rate and direction of population change, already analysed in Chapter 2, is of course a crucial influence on the types of settlement policies which might be appropriate. Where the typical pattern is one of population growth, planning problems are often considered to be comparatively straightforward and primarily linked to decisions concerning the location and control of new development. The repercussions of population decline, on the other hand, are much more far-reaching, affecting the rural economy and the quality of social and family life through the contraction of service provision and a general decline in accessibility and opportunities.

The most significant aspect of the problem, however, is the way in which modern economic pressures, aided and abetted by the prevailing planning philosophy of centralisation (Green, 1971), have extended the area in which this contraction of economic and social provision occurs, so that the only rural areas which can expect to retain their existing services or even achieve an increase in facilities are those parts of the accessible countryside which are subject to intense growth pressures emanating from nearby towns and cities. Rural areas facing less intense pressures, even though their population is stable or gradually increasing, may find themselves served by a decreasing range and quantity of services and facilities, especially in the comparatively isolated parts of generally prosperous areas (Drudy, 1978). How development is located and services are shared out are therefore vitally important.

In population terms the emphasis of the argument has changed as rural population decline has been replaced by overall growth which conceals two important trends: continuing population losses in the less favoured parts of the countryside, and considerable changes in the composition of the rural population as a result of major differences between out-migrant and in-migrant streams. Such statistics as are available for the period after 1971 clearly indicate continuing growth in the nominally rural areas of England, but the figures are partial and incapable of useful disaggregation; if they were, it might be possible to delineate areas in which the out-migration of younger, economically active households was balanced by in-migrants consisting largely of commuters, the retired and second home owners.

This was certainly the case in Herefordshire, and the planning authority there considered the problem to be serious enough by 1969 to warrant an application to the Board of Trade for the county to be designated a development area, though the application was subsequently rejected

(Herefordshire County Council, 1969). There is little evidence to suggest that the situation has changed in succeeding years; regional policy has continued to be dominated by the needs of the West Midland conurbation, so that even the modest amount of growth proposed for Herefordshire and west Shropshire in the 1965 regional strategy (Department of Economic Affairs, 1965) had been abandoned by the time *A Developing Strategy for the West Midlands* was published (West Midland Regional Study Team, 1971).

The particular problems which call for close scrutiny in terms of the interrelationship between migration patterns and settlement planning are themselves closely interwoven, but succeeding paragraphs attempt to draw out in particular the question of social provision and the effects of the widespread endorsement of key settlement policies implying a considerable concentration of future investment. This is somewhat at the expense of direct discussion of the possibilities for employment provision, including the introduction of new small-scale rural industries and the job potential of recreation and tourism, but this issue is inevitably bound up with the question of alternative settlement strategies and therefore is not treated separately.

THE PROVISION OF SERVICES AND FACILITIES IN RURAL AREAS

The present distribution of public utilities, health and social service facilities and other vital services such as education and public transport is, in the majority of rural areas, highly concentrated in towns and a few larger villages. In the case of some facilities such as gas, this is an expression of historically stable economics of supply: it has never been feasible to supply a very dispersed population. In other cases, particularly public transport and primary education, this level of concentration is of more recent origin, reflecting greater emphasis on economic aspects (lower levels of subsidy, insistence on profit or optimal operation despite increased materials or wages costs), and by implication a lesser regard for the social consequences for the inhabitants of rural areas.

Remarkably little research has been completed on the costs and benefits of alternative levels of service provision in rural areas; least of all has there been proper consideration of social costs and benefits. Warford's study of water supply in Shropshire (Warford, 1969) is a notable exception, but even this study is not as comprehensive as might be wished. There would seem to be scope for the development of a multidimensional measure of levels of provision, preferably including some means of representing public satisfaction, since it is this perception of acceptability which influences migration decisions (Crothers, 1970; Simmie, 1972). Early, though rather inconclusive, work in this field included that of Bracey (1952) in Wiltshire and Edwards (1971) in north-east England, both of whom attempted to derive an 'index of social provision'.

Despite this paucity of conclusive evidence, however, it is widely accepted that the economic arguments in favour of increasing the degree of concentration of service provision are overwhelming (Moseley, 1971). What little evidence there is tends to support this point of view; Thorburn (1971) summarises conventional wisdom in stating that 'the larger the community the more cheaply can services such as public utilities, transport, education and retail distribution be provided'. Some attempt at quantification was made in the HM Treasury (1976) report *Rural Depopulation*, although the information used was second-hand and partly subjective; the conclusion reached was that servicing costs in rural areas were some 35 per cent higher than the national average. Confirmation of the basic trend suggested in that report, though not of the figures, was forthcoming in a case study of part of Norfolk around North Walsham. A policy of dispersed rather than concentrated development was estimated to increase costs of provision of electricity by 20 per cent, water supply by 30 per cent and telecommunications by 50 per cent. Education was estimated to cost an extra 11 to 16 per cent and the cost of school transport apparently could be up to six times greater (Norfolk County Council, 1975; Shaw, 1976 and in Moseley, 1978).

More recently, however, empirical evidence has been presented for a case study for Suffolk (Gilder, 1979) which strongly contradicts the accepted wisdom referred to above. While economies of scale were found for certain fixed services, analyses for some other services suggested that there were no such economies and, indeed, that diseconomies might set in as settlements became larger. Moreover Gilder has suggested that, in consequence, dispersed rather than concentrated growth is likely to be less costly and that the marginal costs of increasing the use of schools and other fixed assets would be less than the costs of using concentrated developments in towns and larger villages. Clearly there is a need for much more empirical work in this contentious area – indeed the Department of the Environment has already initiated a major study of this area. In the meantime there must inevitably be growing doubts about the accepted views on the economics of rural settlement strategies which, if confirmed, would in turn pose further questions about the wholesale acceptance of key settlement strategies (Cloke, 1979).

Information on the decline of public services is comparatively easy to obtain (Standing Conference of Rural Community Councils, 1978). It is much more difficult to estimate the effect of declining services on the rural population: in general terms services have been most curtailed in areas where depopulation has been greatest, but this may be an effect of out-migration (fewer services to cater for a smaller residual population) rather than a cause. The residual population is, however, likely to have a low level of car-ownership (and, since the head of a one-car household often uses the car to travel to work, an even larger proportion of the population is denied access to a car for much of the day) and is therefore dependent upon infrequent and expensive public transport services for access to work, shops and social and leisure facilities. The inadequacies of rural public transport unquestionably contribute to a potential migrant's perception of urban/ rural differentials, and hence are likely to increase out-migration in cases where accessibility is considered to be significant.

The problems encountered in providing public utilities in an area of scattered population are exemplified by those of the water supply authorities in Herefordshire. The existing pattern of supply is highly concentrated in and around Hereford and the other urban areas, with many rural areas devoid of mains water supply or mains drainage. Installation costs are highly correlated with the concentration of population, so that improvements are unlikely to be financiallly viable in an area where the population is scattered. In counties like Herefordshire mains water 'should only be provided in areas that are already [densely] populated and that have further potential for growth. This would be the most economic use of scarce resources, and over a period of time would change the present scattered settlement pattern by re-grouping the population into economically convenient settlements' (Herefordshire County Council, 1973). The implications for rural housing and employment, and hence for migration patterns, are axiomatic, since although it appears that variation in social provision is less of a primary motivating factor for migration than other factors such as jobs and housing, it may well act as a subsidiary element, guiding the final location of a household that is moving for other reasons. The ultimate effect of this imbalance in provision must surely be to guide migrants towards larger settlements with a wider range of facilities.

SETTLEMENT POLICIES: DEGREES OF CONCENTRATION

The implications of the preceding arguments in respect both of the provision of social and community facilities and the location of employment opportunities are thus uncertain. From an economic point of view a high degree of concentration of services, jobs and consequently housing is often thought necessary, while it is increasingly admitted that the social costs and benefits of such a policy are much more doubtful. Yet despite this uncertainty, the notion of employment provision only where adequate infrastructure exists, services are already provided and a sufficiently large and skilled local pool of labour is available has become a common ingredient of rural structure plan strategies; the concentration of new housing mainly in key villages is an equally standard answer in countryside planning (Darley, 1978; Cloke, 1979).

The continuing preoccupation of planners with a key settlement philosophy has been stressed by an examination of structure plans carried out for the National Council of Social Service (now the National Council for Voluntary Organisations) by Derounian (1979). While there was evidence that later structure plans took more account of problems of social deprivation in rural areas, the vast majority (eighteen of the twenty-one studied) of structure plans had opted for a key settlement strategy of some type where public services and development would be concentrated in nominated settlements. Only three plans (Cumbria, North Yorkshire and Gloucestershire) aimed to disperse development between groups of villages.

Such enthusiasm for policies of rural concentration had been fore-shadowed in a number of studies of a less obvious planning nature. For example, Newman (1964), considering the problems of part of western Ireland, argued that dispersal policies were not economically feasible and that the alternative was to provide non-agricultural employment and certain basic services in a limited number of key villages. Similarly, recognising the limited development potential of rural areas, O'Riagain (1972) stressed the need to promote industrial and other development in larger centres, but also underlined the complementary requirement that adequate provision be made for the substantial commuting element which would therefore be introduced into the non-agricultural rural population. And the inescapable corollary of such key settlement policies would seem to be the fact that smaller, non-key settlements will be subject to further contraction and selective out-migration, since 'the provision of services to the residual population becomes increasingly unsatisfactory and a further cause of rural discontent' (House and Knight, 1965).

The essence of the rural planning problem in all but the most accessible areas is therefore generally argued as the reconciliation of the social costs of continuing depopulation (or at least age- and skill-selective out-migration) in most rural settlements, represented by a diminution of the permanent community and a loss of most services, with the argument that economic progress can realistically be achieved only by concentration of development into a small number of attractive locations. The planning response, as in many other cases, has invariably been to discount the social costs, possibly because they are occasionally nebulous and often difficult to quantify precisely, and to accept uncritically the economic arguments implying a high degree of spatial concentration of resource allocations.

One example of a structure plan where the options were considered in more detail before the conventional choice was made is that of Shropshire (Shropshire County Council, 1978), where the extreme options were formalised as rigid control, with development permitted only when it could be wholly justified financially, and *laissez-faire* development taking place wherever the demand existed. Neither extreme option was considered feasible, of course, and the final choice lay between two strategies: (1) the creation of a system of main villages; (2) the creation of a system of interdependent villages, each providing some, but not all, of the services for a particular group of rural settlements. Here, then, was the opportunity for innovation and a positive approach to the planning of smaller villages and hamlets. Sadly, however, the grouped village approach was rejected because, for example, 'it would not provide a clear framework for future investment decisions', and, although the preferred approach was stated to be a compromise, most development was to be directed to main villages, with housing for local needs only in other settlements. Main villages were (inevitably) concentrated around Shrewsbury, with very few in the more isolated parts of the Welsh Borders in South Shropshire.

One factor of fundamental local importance concerning key settlement strategies is the interaction between the selected settlement and its hinterland. It can be argued that the concentration of social and economic services in the centre itself may well constitute a further major force perpetuating depopulation in the more isolated parts of its hinterland. Indeed, the growth centre concept implies just such a state of disequilibrium, since the rural hinterland, without modern facilities and functioning primarily as a labour catchment area, will be markedly less prosperous than the centre, and unless an efficient commuting network is developed, the pressures on the rural population to migrate towards the centre may be overwhelming. Hence the application of the growth centre concept, apparently acceptable in subregional terms as a method of promoting development which might not otherwise occur (as with Newtown in mid-Wales) or which might be unacceptable, in a strategy which aims to reduce the level and type of out-migration from rural areas.

The promotion of rural development was by no means the objective of the Hertfordshire structure plan, prepared for a county in which the continuation of the postwar growth spiral which had seen particularly rapid development in accessible villages was deemed to be unacceptable (Hertfordshire County Council, 1976). Nevertheless the control mechanism was still one of key villages, with development permitted only within the confines of selected villages and the greater part of the rural environment protected by one or more restrictive designations. In Nottinghamshire, too, growth in the rural areas is concentrated into a number of selected settlements in a similar way (Nottinghamshire County Council, 1978).

Recent rapid population growth in rural Cheshire, largely as a result of overspill from Manchester and Merseyside (documented in Chapter 2), has led to an equal determination in the structure plan to ensure that 'apart from a few large villages which already support a range of services, future development in villages should in general be restricted' (Cheshire County Council, 1977). The principle of discouraging village growth is intended primarily to allow the needs of local residents to be met while deflecting the much greater demand of 'people from outside' for rural housing; the mechanism by which this policy will be made effective is somewhat nebulous, however. In Suffolk, despite evidence that the existing key settlement policy was having deleterious side effects, a radical shift of policy was discounted, although some growth might be appropriate in smaller settlements, 'in some circumstances ... providing that there is no adverse impact on the environment or on highways' (Suffolk County Council, 1976). The lesson in some minds is that 'blanket negativity is the principal quality of rural planning as it emerges through structure planning' (Darley, 1978).

The application of key settlement policies probably reached its most publicised form in County Durham (Blowers, 1972), where the lowest tier of non-selected settlements was scheduled to be eradicated and the residual population resettled. This type of philosophy has, however, been more widely applied. In the West Midlands, for instance, one policy foreseen for western Shropshire and Herefordshire was the contraction of many smaller villages and hamlets to the point where they ceased to operate primarily as permanent settlements with any employment base, but were increasingly colonised by second home owners and buyers of weekend cottages (West Midland Economic Planning Council, 1970).

Employment opportunities in villages in most rural areas have never been particularly extensive or varied, and so key settlement policies which have favoured employment provision only at selected centres have probably not contributed greatly to increased concentration. Rural housing provision, however, is a much more relevant consideration: the influence of the local authority is substantially greater, partly through planning powers which make it possible for new private sector housing to be directed into specified areas, and partly through its own role as a provider of council housing. The general tendency has been for local authority housing in key villages to be built as comparatively large estates, purely in order to satisfy cost yardsticks and utilise existing facilities and infrastructure.

The overriding implication of such policies is that villages which are not selected have seen little housing development and have increasingly assumed the role of satellite settlements looking to their nearest key village for basic facilities and community services. Planning policies for such villages normally carry a presumption against any growth apart from minor infilling. What they really imply is that the rural settlement pattern is outmoded and needs to be radically altered by the demise of certain settlements, but, for political reasons, these ultimate goals are rarely acknowledged (Martin, 1976). One consequence of restrictive policies in non-key villages is to sterilise them: that is to say, to fossilise the present built form of the settlement and artificially reduce the possibility of incremental change of the type which has been present in most villages for centuries. In areas where there are strong pressures for development the effect is to increase house prices since supply is arbitrarily held back and therefore unable to meet demand, with the result that many would-be rural dwellers (some indigenous to the area in which the housing market is being distorted) are unable to find suitable accommodation in the location they have chosen. Where development pressures are less intense the effect may be to hasten the decline of smaller communities which are already disadvantaged, and thereby to perpetuate the existing imbalances in the population of such areas.

The preceding discussion has hinted at the two fundamental

disadvantages of key settlement policies: the lack of concern for the social disbenefits of such policies, and their insensitivity to the very different problems of individual communities rather than rural areas in general. The social costs of designating key villages are easily overlooked because they are less easily identified and quantified than are the economic advantages. This is largely because they are costs that fall not on the public services, which have evaded them by choosing not to offer a service to non-key settlements, but upon the remaining inhabitants of such settlements, whose time and money costs expended in obtaining services are considerably increased. Ultimately, however, the loss is more widely shared because, as is becoming recognised somewhat belatedly (Countryside Review Committee, 1977), thriving rural communities are an essential part of the countryside.

Recognition of the diversity of problems in the countryside, even where this has occurred, has not always been followed by an equivalent appreciation of the need for fundamentally different approaches to solving those problems. It can hardly be disputed that different sets of problems exist. The national housing profiles defined in Chapter 4 indicated the variety of circumstances in England, while the case studies in Part Three provided further evidence that particular problems often persist at a local scale in certain rural areas – poor housing in estate villages in the Cotswolds, or mobile home sites in the Thames Valley near Oxford and Reading, for example. These housing types, while they are spatially differentiated to some extent, are nevertheless intricately interwoven in the English countryside. But an indiscriminate application of a key settlement policy might be of little value if it failed to recognise the complex interrelationships between adjacent villages, which often do not fall into the simple pattern generated by dominant and subordinate (key and non-key) settlements.

The crucial question is this: to what extent will the policies contained in the typical structure plan dealing with rural areas help those areas which are most vulnerable either to continued depopulation and deprivation or to severe pressures for development? The answer must surely be that, because of the failure to grasp the disastrous social implications of rigidly physical and economic strategies, there will be little assistance for the remoter areas while there will be a firm emphasis on concentration of development in selected villages, often in the larger dormitory villages in the suburbanised countryside which have no need to grow further for adequate service provision. Problems of remoter communities threatened by continuing decay and insensitive rural planning will not be alleviated by policies of concentration; the end product will be a fossilised landscape populated largely by the retired, by commuters and by second home owners. Jennings' living village (Jennings, 1968) will have ceased to exist in many parts of the English countryside.

This chapter has already indicated how a grasp of the structure plan is fundamental to an understanding of the way in which authorities have approached their general rural planning problems. The second section of this chapter, therefore, attempts a more specific review of the way in which rural housing issues have been dealt with by structure plans.

STRUCTURE PLANS AND RURAL HOUSING

Under the development plan system stemming from the report of the Planning Advisory Group (1965) and the 1968 and 1971 Town and Country Planning Acts, the prime responsibility for housing policy is vested in district councils, which, as local housing authorities, provide public housing and control the scale and location of private residential development through local plans and development control. County councils are expected to establish within structure plans an overall framework to guide district council actions (Circular 4/79, s.2.1c); these plans provide, therefore, a basic statement at a subregional level of the strategy for rural areas which has been formulated by county authorities. At the scale of the district authority, local plans on the one hand and Housing Investment Programmes and associated policies on the other provide the two strands which determine local rural housing policy. These two elements of local policy provide important issues for the next chapter, while in this section the wider scale provided by the structure plan is considered.

The content of thirty structure plans submitted for English rural areas prior to December 1978 is examined here. A more detailed study of ten of these plans is contained in Rawson and Rogers (1976). Nineteen of the plans had been approved, with modifications, by the Secretary of State for the Environment at the time of writing. Such approval implies DoE acceptance of the written statement policies on rural housing. (See Appendix IV for structure plans consulted.)

Since Circular 98/74, housing has been regarded as a key issue in most structure plans and detailed housing issues are also sometimes identified. It is possible to recognise five major objectives common to the policies of most authorities:

(1)   improving the adequacy of housing in terms of structural condition and amenities;

(2)   providing sufficient land for dwellings to meet forecast housing needs and the maximum amount of choice, particularly of house type and location, commensurate with economic provision of roads and services;

(3)   satisfying a variety of planning objectives, mainly revolving around controlling the number of isolated dwellings in the countryside, avoidance of good agricultural land and fitting housing policy into key settlement strategies (as discussed in the previous section);

(4) recognising the special housing needs of some groups, particularly young couples, especially where such groups can be defined as constituting local need;

(5) encouraging a generally high level of housing design, particularly in areas of high landscape value.

A sixth objective provides a caveat to these goals, namely, an awareness of increasing costs. Improvements in services and widening the choice of housing in rural areas are mentioned in some plans as only being possible with a realistic understanding of the available financial resources.

HOUSING SUPPLY, DEMAND AND NEED

Information on the stock of rural housing presented in reports of survey is inevitably based upon published data rather than special surveys, although these have been undertaken by some planning authorities. The population census naturally provides the major data source and has generally been supplemented by construction and demolition returns, planning permissions and other accessible information.

Future housing supply is generally indicated in terms of existing housing commitments and land availability, although it is recognised, particularly by Herefordshire, that the relationship between planning permissions and the actual construction of dwellings is not very direct (see also Jacobs, 1974).

Most authorities accept the distinction between housing demand and need. The plan for East Sussex, for example, makes the distinction particularly clear (paras 4.27, 4.28). Despite the recognition of this distinction, and even accepting the point made by Crofton and Webster (1974) that structure plan authorities have tended to see calculations of housing need as essential components of their plans, the discussion of both housing demand and housing need in rural areas is generally rudimentary and largely based on future estimates of population.

Policies on future housing supply inevitably revolve around land availability in rural areas and the recognition of future levels of housing demand and need. Housing densities, dwelling types and prices and phasing elements of land allocation strategies are frequently mentioned. Future housing supply is tied closely to other policies. Thus in Oxfordshire most new housing development will be steered into or around eight towns to ensure conservation of agricultural land and open landscapes, economy in provision of services and convenient, short-distance travel from housing to employment and urban facilities (Oxfordshire H2).* Applications for fresh planning permission where an existing one has expired or is about to expire would normally be refused in the Isle of Wight unless in accordance with

*References are given for policies in written statements.

overall settlement, conservation and additional land-use policies and not causing problems with the provision of infrastructure, particularly in rural areas (5.1.2). Local authorities' intentions to ensure adequate provision of future rural housing must, therefore, be seen in the context of these other policies and, as such, they frequently appear simply as rather vague statements of good intention.

QUALITY OF HOUSING STOCK

Although the population census provides the main statistical source for reports of survey, some authorities, for example Warwickshire, Staffordshire, and Derbyshire, have undertaken special surveys of their rural housing stock to assess its physical state and provide a data base for decisions on rehabilitation or clearance programmes. Indicators of housing quality used by many structure plan authorities include provision of household amenities, age of housing, dwelling size, shared dwellings, overcrowding and underoccupancy. Rateable values, repair costs and uptake of improvement grants are sometimes also considered.

Policies relating to the stock of rural housing are in general vague and ill defined and tend to be phrased like objectives. In many cases reference is made to the relevant Housing Acts and the responsibility of the district councils to improve housing where it falls below accepted standards of structural condition and amenity provision (for example, Bedfordshire, policy 4). Where necessary, substandard housing will be demolished (Warwickshire, 4.4.9) but it is more often argued that the need for additional housing, and thus land development and resources, will be minimised and existing residential environments conserved and improved by encouraging the most effective use of existing housing stock through improvement and rehabilitation (South Hampshire, 13.2; Leicestershire, 7.16). The Department of the Environment's approach to house condition is illustrated by the East Cleveland plan where in the notice of approval a policy stating an intention to clear all unfit housing as soon as possible was deleted (E/A 10), but a policy encouraging the improvement of older housing was retained (E/A 11).

CONSTRAINTS ON RESIDENTIAL DEVELOPMENT

Many structure plans recognise constraints on future housing development in rural areas. These constraints include such items as landscape factors, pollution, community facilities, access to jobs and transport, public utilities, good farmland, historic areas, government land, green belts, and areas of conservation. From most structure plans six major constraints on development emerge:

(a) *Agricultural land.* Most plans aim to safeguard agricultural land or avoid land of high agricultural value. A few plans state that when land is released for development the location and boundaries must minimise severance and disruption of viable farm units and potential vandalism and trespass to adjoining farmland (for example, Oxfordshire, C3; Suffolk).

(b) *Green belts.* There is a general presumption against development in all those plans involving areas of statutory green belt except where such development is essential for agriculture or forestry; in these areas it should take the form of infill developments appropriate to the scale and character of the settlement (for example, Cheshire, 13.40). Several plans pledge not only to maintain the green belt but also to extend it (for example, West Sussex, B5; Central Berkshire, EN6).

(c) *Public utilities.* About half of the structure plans assessed had policies to ensure that the use of land for residential purposes reflected the ability of the necessary public services to support development (for example, Derbyshire, 4.101, 9.17; Northamptonshire, P6.3). A few plans state quite categorically that additional development will not be allowed in villages and hamlets where the necessary services and facilities do not exist and cannot be readily and economically provided (for example, Worcestershire, 4.3.1; Leicestershire, 7.9). The provision of utilities clearly remains an important argument against isolated houses (for example, Warwickshire, 4.4.1), but recent national decisions on the rating costs of cesspools may weaken the accepted policies on isolated dwellings (the *Guardian*, 1976).

(d) *Key settlements.* All local planning authorities must evolve a strategy for locating development. Some authorities intend to direct the majority of housing development to urban areas (for example, Buckinghamshire, policy 237, 238; East Berkshire, H2), considering housing for local need only in the form of residential infill in villages. About two-thirds of the authorities have clear key village policies (see Derounian, 1979). Shropshire, as was seen earlier in this chapter, undertook a detailed study of its rural settlements (Shropshire County Council, 1978) and established two categories for development purposes. In main villages housing estates would be considered, while in other rural settlements only infill development to meet local housing need would be permitted (policies 13, 14). Other structure plans have more complex categories, for example, settlements suitable for moderate expansion, limited-growth villages and remaining villages where development will be discouraged (Warwickshire, 4.3.1; Northamptonshire, P6.1, P6.2, P6.3). Generally, the only exceptions to these policies would be cases where local need can be proved, particularly if that need is related to agriculture.

(e) *Isolated dwellings.* The corollary of key settlement policies are policies restricting development of isolated dwellings in the countryside. Almost all structure plans contain a clear presumption against residential development in the open countryside, following past planning practice (Ministry of Housing and Local Government, 1969). The only exceptions are cases where residential conversions of buildings would conserve a structure of architectural or historic merit (for example, Kent, B9; Norfolk, 3.4.20).

(f) *Conservation and design.* Most plans recognise the importance of conservation and design factors in rural housing policy. Often a general intention to conserve the appearance of settlements is backed up by a policy stating that new development should have form, scale, colour, materials and location sympathetic with the character of existing settlements (for example, Peak District, 10.20, 10.59; North East Hampshire, E1, E2).

Many structure plans also refer to area-specific policies. Some authorities aim to protect and enhance the character of designated village conservation areas (for example Worcestershire, 4.9.4), while others will designate further conservation areas (for example, East Berkshire, EN13). In Areas of Outstanding Natural Beauty and areas of special landscape quality design and conservation policies will be particularly stringently applied (for example, Buckinghamshire 289; Surrey, policy 72).

Several plans mention provision of advice on building styles and scale of development (for example, Staffordshire, appendices 8 and 10). The production by councils of design guides for rural areas, as in Essex, Kent and Cheshire, will presumably aid this process.

TENURE GROUPS AND SPECIAL HOUSING CATEGORIES

Surprisingly few plans make a point of commenting on the mix of tenures within their housing stock beyond a purely descriptive level. Moreover in the few plans which do consider this aspect the statement only reflects a comment on the requirement for a range of tenure types, both private and public, to cater for the needs of different social and economic groups (for example, Oxfordshire, H6; Suffolk, 5.6.4). A few plans (for example, Leicestershire, 7.12 and East Cleveland, E/A8) single out housing associations as deserving encouragement, though they are not specific as to the particular role which associations might take in rural areas other than as some sort of replacement for the dwindling pool of privately rented accommodation. Both authorities suggest an increase in local authority rented accommodation to compensate for this shortage.

While structure plans generally have little to say on the general tenure mix of housing stock most of them explicitly recognise certain special housing categories which deserve attention. These special categories include second homes, retirement homes, agricultural dwellings, housing to meet local needs, residential caravans and temporary accommodation. It might be argued that by considering these special categories structure plan authorities are in effect recognising housing problem areas.

Second homes and retirement homes
Second homes and retirement homes are often grouped together and are considered in the reports of survey of eight plans. Some second homes may become retirement homes but to a large extent they generate different problems.

It is clear that most authorities are simply uncertain how to regard either of these developments. On the one hand, there is still a feeling in some areas that an unfavourable consequence of both developments is competition between local people and migrants. Herefordshire provides a case where this argument is keenly felt. On the other hand, many authorities recognise advantages. The increase in rates and local retail revenue coupled with the improvement of rural property seem to be more positively argued than, say, ten years ago. Thus in remoter areas of Suffolk second homes are seen as offering a new role for declining village communities, while in the Peak District second home owners are assumed to prefer remote dilapidated buildings in depopulating areas and to this extent are felt not to be in competition with local people.

Some authorities, for example, Herefordshire and Leicestershire (Rutland), are quite realistic about their lack of powers to control many of these developments, even if control were thought desirable, and very few plans have a stated policy on second homes. As regards second homes and holiday homes available for occupation all the year round, the Isle of Wight Council will wish to be satisfied that the development is appropriate for the site and location, that services and social and community facilities are available and normally that the development should be related to the existing settlement (5.1.16). Norfolk intends that no land allocations will be made where they would be likely to lead to a high level of retirement migration or second home ownership (3.4.14). On the related problems of holiday chalets, Worcestershire intends that the development of new holiday chalets will be discouraged (4.11.2), but in Shropshire they should normally conform to the siting and location requirements of caravan sites (policy 116).

Agricultural dwellings

The majority of structure plans have specific policies for agricultural dwellings. All policies share a common theme – the recognition of the special needs of agriculture in the countryside such that exceptions to the normal process of development control may be made where agricultural arguments are strong. The standard policy is that new dwellings will only be permitted in the open countryside if required to provide accommodation essential for workers engaged in agriculture, forestry or horticulture and if appropriate accommodation cannot be located within or adjoining a nearby town or village (for example, North East Hampshire, H3, H3.1; Norfolk, 3.4.20). In Worcestershire the normally restrictive policy regarding the green belt may be waived in the case of some agricultural housing (4.3.11) but in most structure plans such housing would have to be located in a village in the green belt.

The Leicestershire plan provides a more detailed illustration of the policy towards agricultural dwellings. In general agricultural housing needs will be met in existing settlements through the normal rural settlement policy

204 *Rural Housing: Competition and Choice*

(19.2). Isolated dwellings will be permitted in rural areas only where such dwellings fulfil the requirements set out in Circular 24/73 *Development for Agricultural Purposes* (18.7, 19.3). They should be sited wherever possible in existing villages or associated with existing buildings (18.7). Where a new additional dwelling of this kind is not regarded as appropriate, permission may be granted for the replacement of an existing dwelling to maintain the stock of dwellings for agricultural needs. Finally, each proposal will be decided in the light of individual circumstances (19.3).

In this way agricultural dwellings receive preferential treatment within the planning system. A major problem faced by authorities, however, is how to restrict their use to an agricultural or forestry worker. Bedfordshire (policy 9), and Surrey (policy 3) both propose the imposition of conditions on planning permission to achieve this end and such a condition was inserted in the Norfolk plan through modifications by DoE (3.4.20). The Peak District also considers tying the occupation of a rural dwelling to a particular type of occupant by legal agreements under section 52 of the Town and Country Planning Act 1971.

Housing to meet local needs

Housing problems of local people, however defined, are an increasingly common theme in structure plans. It is significant, however, that data on this topic is very limited. Only a few counties refer to specific problems (for example, Mid Hampshire, 1978) yet paradoxically most plans put forward policies. The issues of local need are emotive and popular at the present time, yet there is no consistent definition. Definitions include households resulting from natural increase in the existing population, plus the relief of homelessness, reduction of overcrowding and the replacement of substandard housing, agricultural and key sector workers, people living or employed in the area for three or more years, and people with strong ties, particularly of kinship, in the area. Several authorities follow the Isle of Wight in equating evidence of local need with the housing waiting lists, despite the acknowledged drawbacks of this approach.

Policies relating to local need tend to be vague and rather bland in their approach, strong on statements of general intent but weak on mechanism. For example, Herefordshire wants to ensure that residential development will meet the needs of all elements of the population in terms of economic resources, household composition and age; specifically it aims to persuade housing authorities and private developers to investigate ways of assisting young people and key workers who have financial problems in obtaining housing within the county (4.3). Many plans state that land and existing permissions will be allocated to meet local needs (for example, Kent, HEC1, HEC3). That such local need policies do not necessarily have official approval is, however, indicated by the deletion of such a provision in modifications made to a key settlement policy in Norfolk (4.5.37).

The plan for Worcestershire comments that it is important that people brought up in a village and wanting to continue to live there, or people who find employment in a village and want to live nearby, should be able to do so. New housing, it is argued, is often too expensive for young, local families and the authority believes that it can assist in regulating this situation by requiring that builders construct a range of dwelling types and by controlling the rate of release of planning permissions to a rate broadly equivalent to the rate of natural increase. District councils, it is felt, can help to meet local demands through their own housing programmes and by making building plots available to local families (3.40).

A rather different view is taken by East Sussex, where the plan argues that it is impractical to allocate land specifically to meet the needs and aspirations of local people who work in the immediate area, who wish to live locally upon getting married, or who wish to move to another home in the same community. The authority considers that the structure plan policies will allow a limited amount of development in certain villages and there will thus be an opportunity for local people to acquire new property. Similarly, in the plan for West Sussex it is argued that any policy concerned to meet local housing need must work through positive measures to widen opportunities for those groups for whom they might otherwise be deficient rather than through negative measures designed to keep out other people because they do not conform to some definition of 'local'. A strong line is taken in the plan for Surrey where it is argued that, since it is not possible for planning policies to determine who occupies houses once they are built, it is not practical to meet local need. Again, Surrey's solution is to improve housing opportunities generally. In contrast to several others, the East Sussex plan considers that many local people will find existing property available (9.21), though later comments acknowledge that local people are often priced out of the market (9.22). This point leads to something of an about-turn on earlier statements, for the plan proposes a policy for the possible provision of a small number of council houses to meet local need in ninety-six listed villages by agreement between the East Sussex County Council and the District Councils. In the plan for Surrey there is a similar reversal of intent when it is stated that development in settlements in the green belt will only be permitted to meet the proven needs of the locality.

Residential caravans and temporary accommodation

Staffordshire comments that it should be a basic aim of any housing programme to provide permanent housing accommodation for all those who require it. However, it may not be possible or desirable to provide permanent housing in every case because there are small groups of people who for some reason may need, or prefer, caravan or temporary accommodation. Hertfordshire assumes that the majority of people living in caravans would prefer to live in houses and many are, in fact, on local authority housing waiting lists; to this extent the authority interprets caravan sites as a perpetual source of need for permanent accommodation.

In policy terms mobile homes, including residential caravans, are generally viewed as permanent housing and subject to the same policies (for example, Bedfordshire, policy 10). A frequent caveat to this policy is that it should not be taken to imply that planning permission will be given for mobile homes on land allocated for residential development. In West Sussex a condition of the policy is that new residential caravan sites will not be permitted unless they are to be developed and operated by the West Sussex District Council as the local housing authority or the developer enters an agreement with the district council to limit the occupation of an agreed proportion of caravans to local people nominated by the council. In some areas, such as the Peak District, there is a presumption against the use of caravans as permanent homes (9.35).

STRUCTURE PLANS AND RURAL HOUSING — SOME CONCLUSIONS

This survey of structure plans emphasises above all the very general nature of these strategic documents. When viewed comparatively in the context of one major topic, housing in rural areas, some common themes emerge, but the overall impression is one of imprecision and uncertainty. Rarely can it be said that a structure plan provides a broad and definite framework in which rural housing policy can be set, and a district housing and planning authority would gain little guidance for its detailed policies from a consideration of the county structure plan.

Leading on from this imprecision, it is clear that evidence in the report of survey and policies in the written statement do not always link up. Some policy statements are apparently made in an information vacuum while in other plans survey evidence of problem areas is not followed up by policy statements. Policies, when they are stated, are often vague and uncertain.

This last point naturally reflects the limitations of the structure plan as a document primarily concerned with physical planning and not with social policy issues such as housing. Planners are on more certain ground when they are viewing rural housing in the context of settlement policies and development control. Thus these sections of plans, as the review above has shown, are more definite in their statement. But when issues of tenure choice, or of identifying households as 'locals' or 'second home-owners', are involved, the planner has moved away from his area of experience and, more particularly, from the area where he has powers to control. The effectiveness of planning permissions linked to occupancy conditions should perhaps not be dismissed as a tool for social policy in rural areas, but their usefulness seems to be limited.

ASPECTS OF NATIONAL HOUSING POLICY

This final section considers some aspects of national housing policy which particularly affect rural areas. It follows on logically from the previous accounts of the national planning system, and together they provide the background against which the local response to rural housing issues, reviewed in the next chapter, can be judged. After a broad overview of the allocation of national resources to rural housing, the chapter concludes with a discussion of a number of specifically rural issues which are important at a national level.

HOUSING EXPENDITURE

Many key issues which affect rural communities revolve around the level of public expenditure which they require, both for physical infrastructure and for services. An initial approach to the consideration of the influence of national policy on rural areas is through a review of the variations which exist in the amount of public resources spent on housing. The picture that emerges from this investigation reflects several of the conclusions already drawn in this book. Despite poor-quality housing in some rural areas, particularly in the past, and an evident need for local authority housing investment, the rate of housing expenditure by rural authorities has consistently been well below that for urban areas.

A direct comparison of capital expenditure on housing by different types of local authority was made for the period 1962–8 by Nicholson *et al.* (1975). Whereas, for example, the pre-1974 county boroughs spent on average over this period some £8,340 per thousand population, rural districts only averaged £5,120 per thousand population, and the more agricultural rural districts only spent £4,310 per thousand population each year. Moreover in terms of additions to local authority housing stock in the period 1958–61, which was taken as an indication of the impetus of a house-building programme, rural districts were found to be operating at only some two-thirds of the rate of county boroughs and this fell to under half with the more agricultural rural districts. Their conclusion was clear – 'the more agricultural the Rural District the less likely is the local authority to undertake housing' (Nicholson *et al.*, 1975, p. 82).

An examination of more recent public expenditure statistics makes a similar point in so far as the more rural regions such as the South West and East Anglia have a much lower level of housing investment than more urban regions and particularly Scotland, where public housing investment is especially heavy (Table 10.1). Compared with other fields of public expenditure, housing was ranked fourth in the South East of England and Scotland from 1969/70 to 1973/4, but eighth in the South West, and expenditure was almost twice as much per head in the South East and three times as much in Scotland as the South West. However, there has been a

Table 10.1   *Regional distribution of public expenditure on housing,*
1969/70–1973/4

Region	Average expenditure per head (£)	Index GB = 100
North	46·3	111·3
Yorks and Humberside	28·6	68·8
East Midlands	27·8	66·8
East Anglia	32·4	77·9
South East	52·4	126·0
South West	23·3	56·0
West Midlands	30·9	74·3
North West	36·5	87·7
Wales	33·0	79·3
Scotland	61·2	149·3
Great Britain	41·6	100·0

Source: Short (1978).

narrowing of the differential in housing expenditure between the above-average and below-average regions. From 1969/70 to 1973/4 Scotland suffered a 9·1 per cent decrease in the housing programme, while the South-East increased its per capita spending by 34·2 per cent and in East Anglia the increase was 55·8 per cent (calculated from Short, 1978). Yet despite the reduction in the high level of expenditure on public sector housing in Scotland and the higher costs of housing in the South East, rural regions still seem to be faring badly in bids for housing finance.

This conclusion is reinforced when housing expenditure is analysed in more detail. In the period 1969–74 overall housing expenditure was 34 per cent less per head in rural England than nationally (Table 10.2).

The level of subsidy for council house rents in rural England was less than half the national average during this period, partly because, as Chapter

Table 10.2   *Housing expenditure in rural England, 1969–74*

Classes of housing expenditure	Rural areas expressed as ratio of national average (100)
Investment in new council housing, repairs and modernisation	67
Subsidies from government and councils for rents	47
Council loans to private owners for house purchase and to housing associations	73
Renovation grants for private owners	84
Option mortgage scheme	130
TOTAL	66

Source: Internal paper, Rural Department, National Council for Voluntary Organisations; calculated by DoE from public expenditure data.

3 indicated, there are relatively fewer local authority houses in rural areas to require subsidies. Also, since a high proportion of rural local authority housing was built in the interwar and immediate postwar years, when both building costs and interest rates were low, there is a correspondingly lower level of demand for government subsidies. Thus the size and age of the rural public sector housing stock, combined with the lower level of new house starts by rural authorities leads inevitably to a 33 per cent lower capital expenditure on new building, repairs and modernisation in rural areas.

The traditional reluctance of many rural housing authorities to subsidise council rents is matched by their reluctance to provide mortgage funds, assist housing associations and allocate improvement grants. Only the option mortgage scheme claimed an above-average level of public expenditure to assist lower-income households in the competitive rural housing market. This higher figure can be explained partly by reference to the relatively high level of owner-occupation in rural areas but also because owner-occupation is often more in line with the political philosophy of local rural councils than is expenditure on public housing. Whatever the explanation, it remains a fact that, of all the tenure groups in rural areas, it is only the owner-occupiers (albeit probably the poorer ones) who have benefited at a substantially greater rate than the national average.

This record over many years of lower investment in the housing of rural areas may be completed by reference to the new system of housing finance which came with the introduction of Housing Investment Programmes (HIPs) in 1977. While other characteristics of HIPs will be considered below, it is apposite to review the evidence on financial allocations here. A study in 1979 by the Rural Department of the National Council of Social Service (now the National Council for Voluntary Organisations) showed clearly that rural housing authorities still receive substantially less housing finance than the average English local authority. Allocations made for HIPs for the year 1979/80 for all English authorities averaged £61·7 per resident. In contrast the average allocation for the sixty-three most rural authorities (defined by OPCS as those where the majority of the population was in parishes of fewer than 5,000 people, where no town had more than 25,000 people in 1971 and where population density was less than two persons per hectare) amounted to only £32·9 per resident.

In concluding this section on housing expenditure it is important to comment briefly on the sources of funds. In terms of capital expenditure, particularly of course the construction of new dwellings, local authorities generally have recourse to borrowed money for which they must obtain loan sanction from the government. Revenue expenditure by the local authority, for example, to improve the quality of housing stock, to pay the wages of local authority staff and to pay debt charges on capital borrowing is financed generally from three main sources – rates, charges for services and, by far the greatest proportion, directly from the government as the Rate Support Grant.

Although, therefore, the greater part of housing expenditure by local authorities relates to capital costs, it is necessary to note the significant changes which have occurred in the distribution of the Rate Support Grant between the cities and the shire counties because this directly affects the activities of the local housing authority. From the mid-1970s the government tended to shift grant aid from rural areas towards London and the metropolitan counties, particularly with regard to the needs element in the grant. This shift can be illustrated by examining the share of both the needs and resources elements of the Rate Support Grant between the three main types of local authority over the period 1974/5 to 1978/9 (Table 10.3).

Table 10.3   *Rate support grant: distribution between authority types*

Type of authority	Share of population 1977	Share of needs and resources elements of RSG			
		Share (%)	£ per head	Share (%)	£ per head
		1974–5		1978–9	
Non-metropolitan counties	62·4	60·0	77·88	51·1	117·27
Metropolitan districts	23·4	26·8	90·08	27·4	149·85
London boroughs	14·2	13·2	72·66	21·5	139·84
England and Wales	100·0	100·0	80·2	100·0	128·10

Source: Binder (1978).

The fairness or otherwise of this shift in the distribution of the Rate Support Grant, which is partly related to a change in the method for calculating the grant and partly related to a conscious policy to favour declining inner city areas, has been much debated. The shire counties have understandably argued that the shift has gone too far (Binder, 1978), while others have argued that it has not gone far enough (Simpson, 1977). The shift has in fact gone counter to the changes in the distribution of population. The growth of suburban and rural populations which has been mentioned several times in this study is reflected in the growth of the share of population in the non-metropolitan authorities from 61·3 per cent in 1973 to 62·4 per cent in 1977, and the trend is continuing.

The changing proportions of the Rate Support Grant and the method for deciding allocations are of concern here for two main reasons. First, although it does not relate directly to capital expenditure on housing, the evidence of lower levels of grant per head of population complement the picture which has already emerged of lower levels of spending and financial allocation in rural areas. Rural authorities spend less on housing and other services and they receive less money, both from their own rates and from the government.

The second point is very much related and concerns the method by which allocations are made. From 1974–5 the allocations were decided largely on the basis of a regression analysis of previous spending levels. The method related levels of spending in the past to spending need, and the logic, as Binder (1978) has agreed, was circuitous. The reluctance or inability of local authorities in rural areas to spend money on public services therefore led inevitably to their receiving less government finance. Though there was recognition of the disadvantages of sparsely populated areas, the system certainly failed to recognise in any real form the inevitable diseconomies of service provision in rural areas, even where, as in much of lowland England, rural populations have grown in recent years. It should be noted that, at the time of writing, there are proposals to replace the old system of local authority finance by a block grant system.

The rough justice meted out by the Rate Support Grant system may indeed not have been as unfair to rural areas in the end as some people have argued. Some counties which have well-recognised rural problems, such as Cumbria and Northumberland, fared quite well from the allocation, and allocations towards the end of the 1970s moved slightly towards favouring the non-metropolitan authorities. The point of contention lies, however, less with the relative merits of inner city areas versus the countryside than with the failure of the system of allocation to recognise specifically rural problems and with the encouragement given to some authorities to spend even less on their rural areas in the face of lower grants from government. Urban needs reflected in the grant were not necessarily the same as rural needs, and a system which equates them must inevitably be crude and contentious.

HOUSING INVESTMENT PROGRAMMES

As mentioned above, in bidding for resources for housing from central government, local authorities have operated since July 1977 within a system of Housing Investment Programmes (Circulars 18/77, 63/77, 38/78). The prodecure aims to initiate a strategic approach to housing provision so that resources can be allocated by central government according to local needs and circumstances. Much greater demands are now made upon local authorities, and many rural housing authorities, which previously relied simply upon the housing waiting list or local knowledge for the evaluation of housing needs, have had to widen their horizons by considering new topics and new approaches towards assessing needs and catering for the HIP procedure. The reluctance or inability of some of these authorities to broaden their view in this way is already clear from HIP submissions, particularly, for example, in the often very cursory treatment given to the private housing sector. More comprehensive analyses of their current position regarding housing provision should encourage more coherent planning by local housing authorities, but the system has operated for too short a time for there to be many signs that this longer-term view has been adopted.

Inevitably, perhaps, the first years of the operation of the HIP system have been confused and uncertain. None the less there must be a suspicion that some rural housing authorities have found the new system particularly irksome. The importance, especially in the smaller districts, of informal, personal approaches to housing policy at the local level will be stressed in the next chapter. In the present context it is evident that these smaller, not necessarily less able, authorities react unhappily to the formality of form-filling, hurried deadlines and complex calculations and estimates which have become part of the HIP system. While some housing authorites have clearly used the HIP statement as an important policy document, the contents of which have been debated by council members and which has obviously fulfilled that central role in local housing policy which its creators intended, other authorities have given relatively little time to the HIP statement. Some rural authorities have been content with the briefest of statements backing up their financial bid and there are suspicions that some housing departments have simply considered the HIP statement as 'just another statistical return'. Moreover, it should be remembered that a significant number of rural authorities do not even have a separate housing department. In these cases, where housing matters are subsumed perhaps with planning or environmental health, it is scarcely surprising that the HIP system has sometimes been treated with less professionalism than in the larger authorities.

Indeed even larger urban authorities have clearly had problems in this regard. In his study of the city of Oxford during the first year or so of the HIP system, Paris (1979) has shown that uncertainties about where responsibilities lay for co-ordinating the HIP submission to DoE and the existing commitments on staff made the operation of the programme very difficult. Oxford was perhaps in a fortunate position in so far as it already had available a mass of statistical data from surveys and from the structure plan submission. How much more difficult, therefore, must be the position of smaller rural authorities which have none of these advantages.

Some indication of the difficulties for rural housing authorities can be gauged from the report *Rural Recovery: Strategy for Survival*, published in 1978 by the Association of District Councils. The Association felt that the allocations which had been made so far were frequently inadequate for some rural authorities, particularly those where substantial council improvement schemes were under way. The feeling was that the high cost of building in rural areas was not sufficiently appreciated by the Department of the Environment, and the Association reported that 'many authorities complain bitterly about the sheer impracticability of planning and implementing schemes on the present one year basis, and urge the case for greater flexibility between expenditure blocks and a three or four year rolling programme' (para. 3.4). The increased demands upon local authorities consequent upon the passing of the Housing (Homeless Persons) Act 1977 and the Rent (Agriculture) Act 1976 were particularly mentioned as additional strains upon some rural housing authorities.

These dissatisfactions with the new system give some cause for concern for rural housing, since it may be that bids from some rural authorities will compare badly with their urban counterparts if they are judged as excessive or if they are less impressively put together. This contention must however remain a tentative and untested hypothesis until more research is carried out and the system settles down. What is more certain is that in the short time that the system has been in operation, and despite the contention made above that financial allocations were inadequate, a major problem has arisen of underspending on housing (Leather, 1979). One cause of this underspending has probably been an over-optimism by authorities regarding the speed of implementation of housing projects, but it has also been suggested that Conservative councils have been cutting back spending on new council houses. The influence of local political control and philosophy upon housing policy is unlikely to be lessened by the introduction of a new planning system such as the HIP. It is a point made by Paris (1979) in his study of the operation of the HIP system in Oxford, and its relevance is equally important for rural housing authorities. Indeed, bearing in mind the general political bias in rural local councils towards the Conservative Party, this argument has a particular relevance for rural areas.

NATIONAL POLICIES AND TRENDS

Housing Investment Programmes were introduced, in part at least, as an attempt to simplify and co-ordinate the task of financing and planning investment in housing. In the long term it is hoped that the HIP system will help to do away with the variety of controls and requirements made upon local housing authorities by central government. However, it is clear that progress in this direction has been slow and most of the controls, for example, over finance, building costs and housing standards, remain.

These controls and checks stem, of course, from the role given by government to local authorities (district councils since 1974) to act as housing authorities, with all the attendant responsibilities and powers. Although subsequent legislation has extended and in some cases modified these powers, they are essentially based on what has become known as the 'principal act' – the Housing Act 1957. Thus rural local authorities have responsibilities, for example, to check on and maintain housing standards within their area, to construct, maintain and manage public housing and to provide accommodation for those who are declared homeless, and they are able to call on government resources to help them in their work.

The significant point for rural housing authorities is that much housing policy has been phrased in terms which implicitly seem to favour urban areas and which, in turn, are difficult if not impossible to employ satisfactorily in the countryside. It might be argued that this bias is understandable and consequent upon the high proportion of the population living in urban areas and upon the very serious problems of urban housing, but such an argument is of little comfort to rural authorities which have to operate within this framework. Some examples will make this point clear.

The White Paper, *Widening the Choice: The Next Steps in Housing* (Cmnd 5280), published in 1973, proposed new initiatives to deal with stress areas where housing conditions and the social environment were found to be poor. Consequent upon the Housing Act 1974 which followed the White Paper, housing action areas (HAAs) were to be declared by housing authorities where both physical and social conditions were bad. The area to be designated is delimited on a map and, if the HAA is declared, the local authority is granted special powers, for example, for land acquisition, compulsory improvement and for special financial grants. The 1974 Act also made some alterations in the designation of general improvement areas (GIAs), which had originally been introduced in the Housing Act 1969. Here again the local authority has special powers regarding compulsory acquisition, levels of grant aid, and so on.

The key point about these devices to improve housing quality is that they are essentially area-based. Their designation depends upon the recognition by the local authority of a specific and clearly demarcated area where conditions are poor. This approach may be well suited to urban areas where concentrations of bad housing exist, but in rural areas poor housing, while it undoubtedly exists, is rarely found in such a concentrated and definable form. Substandard housing and the poor social conditions which frequently accompany it tend to be scattered and disparate and are not adequately covered by the provisions of this area-based policy. Accordingly it is hardly surprising that virtually no HAAs and GIAs have been declared in rural areas in the years since these designations have been in force.

A second example will illustrate the way in which national housing policy has often been unsatisfactory for dealing with rural problems. The cost yardstick set the maximum cost for new construction for which central government would provide housing subsidies. It was introduced in April 1967 and effectively limited the monies available to local authorities for house building. House construction costs in rural areas are in general significantly higher than in urban areas, where economies of scale are often possible consequent upon large development sites operated by national building firms. In rural areas construction is rarely on this scale (except perhaps in some small towns) and the prevalence of small firms and the higher cost of raw materials and transport serves to bid up the cost of building. In the remote countryside, of course, these problems are even worse (Highlands and Islands Development Board, 1974).

Early in 1980 the government announced its intention to do away with the cost yardstick, though informed opinion considered it highly likely that such abolition would have relatively little real effect. Even if the old cost yardstick were not replaced by a very similar form of financial constraint, the increasingly strict limits put upon local authority expenditure during the 1970s and early 1980s would, it was felt, have essentially the same effect.

Whether by cost yardstick limits as in the 1970s, or by the control of public expenditure generally, rural housing authorities are caught between higher costs on the one hand and restrictions on spending on the other. Moreover throughout the 1970s it was necessary for all new public housing to be built to Parker-Morris standards (Circular 36/37) and these high standards also acted as a pressure upon the financial limits imposed by the cost yardstick. Though Parker-Morris standards were abolished by the Conservative Government in 1980, the removal of this extra burden has been of relatively little comfort to housing authorities. A more critical factor in encouraging higher public building costs in rural areas remains, in so far as in national parks and designated areas of outstanding natural beauty, and also in some declared conservation areas, local planning ordinances require the use of indigenous building materials. These requirements may well add substantially to the cost of construction which must be borne by public and private builders alike.

Thus attempts at a national level to set high standards and to put increasing controls upon local authority spending have in practice served to control the amount of construction itself. Local authorities in rural areas, as is argued elsewhere in this study, have often tended for various reasons to be reluctant investors in public housing and these restrictions and limitations which flow from the blanket imposition of national policy serve to discourage them further.

A further example of the problems of applying national policies to rural areas without recognising particular rural problems concerns the sale of council houses by local authorities. Prior to 1980 a number of local housing authorities (including South Oxfordshire District Council) were prepared to sell council houses to sitting tenants, often at substantial discounts. Sales in rural areas were, however, relatively few, were generally carefully controlled and tended to be in towns rather than small villages where council house numbers were small. Equally, many local authorities, even though they were Tory-controlled and thus might be expected to favour an extension of owner-occupation, resisted pressures to sell what, with the continuing demise of the privately rented sector, was fast becoming the only source of rented property in the countryside.

The proposals by the Conservative Government which came to power in 1979 that all tenants should be given the right to buy their house, irrespective of the wishes of the local authority, was viewed with dismay by many rural housing authorities. The original safeguards for rural areas which had been promised in the Conservative manifesto were virtually useless and would have opened up sales of council houses to large numbers of people who had no claim to local need. The lower proportions of council houses in rural areas, the decline of the privately rented sector, the lower incomes of rural workers and the mounting concern for local need created a powerful lobby, involving in particular the National Farmers' Union, Shelter, the National Council for Voluntary Organisations and the county-based Rural Community Councils, which was able to realise significant amendments in the committee stage of the Housing Act 1980. Under this legislation, while council house sales are still encouraged, there are rural safeguards which restrict sales in national parks, Areas of Outstanding Natural Beauty and designated 'rural areas' where the Secretary of State for the Environment has been persuaded that pressures upon the housing stock justify the retention of a public housing sector. Sales would be restricted to local people or a ten-year pre-emption by the local authority on resale would be allowed.

The likely influence of the Housing Act 1980 upon the decline of the rural council house and the effectiveness of the rural safeguards mentioned above cannot, of course, be judged until several years have passed. There must, however, remain very grave doubts as to the effect of this legislation upon the already limited housing options available to the poorer rural dweller. At the very least it provides a clear instance of the dangers of the unthinking application of a national policy to rural areas without a true appreciation of the probable consequences.

Apart from national housing policies, rural areas are also affected by national trends in housing. A pertinent example is the decline in the private rented sector, particularly but not exclusively following the Rent Act 1974, which has inevitably affected rural areas, especially where this sector was previously dominant (Figure 3.1). Frequently the sale of former rented housing stock has allowed commuters, retirement migrants and second home purchasers to gain access to rural housing, so reducing the level of access achieved by local households.

The organisation of housing associations, stimulated by the establishment of the Housing Corporation under the Housing Act 1964, is another national trend which could be more significant for rural areas than it is at present. Housing associations, funded by the Housing Corporation, were envisaged as the 'third arm' of the housing market, providing an alternative to the declining privately rented sector. The Housing Corporation has, however, tended to give priority to urban-based associations. As an illustration of this tendency, it can be noted that the Corporation, in co-operation with the Development Commission and its programme of advance factories, allocated only 200 units of housing per year to rural housing associations in recent years.

Severe problems of realising financially viable, small-scale housing projects to meet housing needs in rural areas have to be faced by rural housing associations if they are to play an important role in rural areas. The costs of rural building mentioned previously, the shortage of building sites, the restrictions placed upon development and densities by planning authorities all conspire to constrain the progress of rural housing associations. In an informal survey of sixty-two housing association proposals within the south-east region of the Housing Corporation (Duerdoth, 1980), it was found that only four schemes had materialised. The others had failed for a variety of reasons including green belt controls, local objections, problems of access and services and legal problems. A second indication of some of these problems can be seen in the fact that only fifty housing units per year of the 200 allocated in conjunction with the Development Commission and mentioned above have in fact been allocated.

Thus, while there have been some general purpose housing associations in rural areas, most of the rural developments in this sector operate in a local area or have been created for special purposes. A notable example of such a special purpose is the development since 1976 of the National Agricultural Centre Housing Association, based at the National Agricultural Centre at Stoneleigh in Warwickshire (Buckler, 1978). The association has as its main objective 'to provide houses in villages for those living in rural areas and retiring from work in agriculture and other occupations'. It operates, together with the National Agricultural Centre Rural Trust, in the construction of small groups of houses within villages and is a direct attempt to recognise not just the declining pool of privately rented housing, but also the high proportion of agricultural workers living in tied housing and at or near retirement age.

Housing associations may well prove in the future to be a useful tool for rural housing policy, particularly when they are related to specific problems such as those of the retired rural worker. It should be re-emphasised, however, that the problems of land acquisition and construction cost which are met with by local authorities and by private developers still provide a very strict limitation to housing associations. Indeed land availability and the necessarily small scale of housing developments in villages are together probably the biggest handicap to future development. Moreover the problems faced by local authorities on their own account make it likely that they will be less than enthusiastic in helping housing associations in their area. Their attitude, particularly in times of financial stress, is likely to be that precious resources should first be used by the authority itself rather than passed on to a secondary organisation to do an essentially similar job.

Although the majority of policies and trends in housing are national and hence inevitably urban-oriented, a few policies do apply specifically to rural housing. The special arrangements regarding sales of rural council houses mentioned earlier are an example of this and a more long-standing example is legislation which relates to agricultural tied housing.

While a few agricultural workers were protected under the provisions of the Rent Act 1968 if they had a true tenancy rather than a licence, the Rent (Agriculture) Act 1976 extended security to all workers in agriculture and forestry who could qualify as protected occupiers. The details of qualification and other provisions of the Act can be found in several references (for example, Rossi, 1977) but briefly, on ceasing work for the owner of the tied cottage, the worker becomes a statutory tenant under the terms of tenancy in the Act. Provisions cover certain dependents of agricultural and forestry workers but, of course, armed forces personnel, caretakers and others with tied tenancies are not covered by the Act. Under the Rent (Agriculture) Act, apart from repossession of the dwelling under the Rent Acts, the owner can request the local authority to rehouse the tenant if the dwelling is required, in the interest of agriculture, for another employee.

The machinery for deciding on the validity of this claim for possession revolves around the operation of Agricultural Dwelling-House Advisory Committees (ADHACs), set up by local agricultural wages committees to advise local authorities on agricultural need and the degree of urgency for the farmer requiring the dwelling. If agricultural need for the dwelling is proven the local authority must use its 'best endeavours' to rehouse the current occupants. Although this obviously falls short of a mandatory requirement to rehouse, it does represent the highest level of obligation which central government can impose upon a local authority within its own jurisdiction.

As with Housing Investment Programmes, the new system for deciding tied housing issues has not been in operation long enough to assess its real effect. During 1977, 704 cases were considered by ADHACs and agricultural need was proved in 92 per cent of cases. By virtue of their endeavours, local authorities during the first half of that year rehoused 45 per cent of cottage occupants within one month of the ADHAC decision and 70 per cent within two months (Harvey, 1978). This record is regarded as a satisfactory one, at least by the farming community, and the fears which were expressed by the agricultural lobby prior to legislation seem to have been largely groundless.

Not surprisingly the National Farmers' Union and the Country Landowners' Association were adamantly opposed to any suggestion of legislation (National Farmers' Union, 1975; Country Landowners' Association, 1976). It was argued that the position of farmers seeking new employees would be made impossible by any increase in tenant security and, moreover, that the increased pressure upon rural housing authorities to rehouse workers would put an unacceptable strain on their already stretched resources. In fact no real evidence has been produced which suggests that either problem has been significant. Indeed a cynic might even suggest that the Act has worked in favour of farmers rather than against their interests. The high proportion of cases mentioned above which were proved to reflect genuine agricultural need might be taken to reflect the control which farmers and their representatives have within the ADHAC system. The argument put forward by Harvey (1978) that the system works well because it is informal and operated in a gentlemanly way may be true, but it should be remembered that this view was published in the *Farmers' Weekly*, a journal which is likely to view the farmers' position with some favour. Interestingly the other concern which farmers expressed prior to legislation – that recent entrants to farmworking would abuse the system simply to bypass the local authority waiting list – has proved unfounded.

CONCLUSION

This chapter has attempted an assessment of the national context in which both the private and the public markets in rural housing have to operate. The pressures come from two main sources, housing and planning, and it is fair to argue that in both cases these pressures result in restriction and control rather than encouragement and incentive. Whether through development control policies, financial limits or a generally low level of public expenditure, the result is to restrict the availability of housing in English rural areas. And yet, as Chapter 2 indicated, these same areas have seen a massive increase in population growth during the last thirty years which has inevitably been reflected in housing demand. It is in this context of housing pressure that local housing authorities must operate and the next chapter considers their response to this situation.

Chapter 11

Housing and Planning Policy at the Local Level

The previous chapter viewed the national context in which issues in rural housing and settlements have to be considered. This chapter moves down the scale to the local level and assesses these issues as they appear both to the suppliers (whether public or private) and the consumers of rural housing. The starting point is the strategic view of housing and planning advanced in the strategy statement produced each year by the local housing authority as part of its Housing Investment Programme (HIP) submission. This document is valuable in so far as it recognises particular problems which concern individual rural areas and suggests strategies to deal with these problems. The chapter continues with a discussion of the questions raised by the proposed strategies.

There follows a review of the vexed question of housing access – this time from the viewpoint of the system which operates to facilitate or to obstruct access to particular types of housing. As such this section is intended to complement previous chapters (particularly Chapters 7 and 8) which recognised the characteristics of the groups which have to operate within this system. As regards the public sector, the important topics covered are the system of housing allocation and management operated by the local housing authority and related issues on council building and the sale of council houses. For the private sector the key issues are rural house prices and their relation to rural wages, but the role of building societies is also briefly considered. The final part of the chapter considers the local influence of planning policies upon the location, availability and price of rural housing.

Since the focus for this chapter is local it is inevitable that the examples quoted are frequently based on experience in the two districts investigated in Part Three, namely, Cotswold and South Oxfordshire Districts. While these case studies may be illustrative, they are not necessarily typical and so some references are made to other rural areas where appropriate. It should be stressed that this review is not comprehensive, but it provides a selective assessment of the main issues which affect the operation of local rural housing systems.

HOUSING PROBLEMS: THE LOCAL AUTHORITIES' VIEW

Local housing authorities have, at least in theory, a very wide brief which makes them responsible not just for the management of their own housing stock but also for the maintenance of standards in the private sector and thus indirectly for the housing of all the population within the district. Their involvement with the private sector is necessarily partial, of course, but it is none the less pervasive. The local housing authority, for example, makes decisions on the location of new development and maintaining building standards, and if it has the resources it may provide grants for improvement and loans for house purchase.

With this overall responsibility in mind it is pertinent to start with the local authority and to see how it assesses the state of housing in its rural areas. This approach may be matched by looking at the actual record of local authority action in the recent past to see, in part at least, how local housing authorities have succeeded in solving some of their problems.

The problems of rural housing as perceived by Cotswold District Council may perhaps be taken as typical of those rural areas of England where metropolitan influences are less well developed. Based on the Housing Strategy Statement appended to the 1978/9 Housing Investment Programme submission, the problems can be listed thus:

(a) a general reduction in the quality of village life due, in many cases, to a lack of job opportunity coupled with a real difficulty for local people in obtaining housing at a reasonable cost;

(b) an increasingly elderly rural population and the resulting need for smaller houses;

(c) housing needs in respect of homeless persons and also those consequent upon the responsibility to rehouse people formerly in tied housing;

(d) the increasing selectivity of potential council tenants regarding the standard of accommodation offered;

(e) the major constraint of the lack of rural sewerage schemes in some parts of the district;

(f) a continuing concern for the poor quality of some council housing stock.

Virtually all these issues have been recognised earlier in this study. Some are the statutory obligations which local authorities have, for example under the Housing (Homeless Persons) Act 1977; others are those which seem endemic in the less accessible rural areas of lowland England, notably the ageing of the population and the problem of rural services. Item (f) in fact relates to the age of some council housing in rural areas and the need to bring it up to more modern standards.

This last point links in with item (d) – the increasing selectivity of potential local authority tenants. According to the housing manager in Cotswold District the rate of refusal on offered properties remained at about one in five until the mid-1970s. Since then this rate has doubled and it would seem that tenants are more discriminating in their choice of properties. Conclusions on this recent trend can only be tentative but there would seem to be two factors at work. First, rising aspirations in society have meant that older local authority housing is increasingly regarded as old-fashioned and poorly appointed, particularly in contrast to newer public and private housing. Secondly, it might be that real housing need has decreased and that a greater proportion of waiting list applicants are in fact able to make a choice because their present circumstances are at least basically satisfactory. The flaw in this argument is, of course, that even to be offered a property by the local authority the household must have been considered to be in need according to the specific criteria operated by the council (discussed later in this section), such as overcrowding or substandard housing. A possible explanation relates to the location of the housing rather than its quality. Households mindful of the disadvantages of isolation or location away from established family links may be prepared to move only to certain villages or towns and may thus refuse other offers.

The rural housing problems recognised by South Oxfordshire housing authority in its Housing Strategy Statement contrast with those noted above and provide a good example of a rural area where population pressure has been extreme over a longer period. Again it is possible to itemise the local authority's own assessment of the main problem areas:

(a)   Housing needs are in general the product of population growth and the rate of household formation.

(b)   Though building rates have been high, they have not met the needs generated by (a); house prices have risen and 'in turn this has meant that local families either from the second generation that followed the immediate postwar population growth or from a more deeply rooted background, have been unable to compete effectively in the private house market'.

(c)   Many families unable to find accommodation have been forced to find temporary housing in caravans, in high rent property and in shared and overcrowded housing.

(d)   The increase in small, elderly households causes special problems, particularly of underoccupation of the existing housing stock.

(e)   Two major sources of housing need arise from the high number of tied tenancies in agriculture and in the service bases in South Oxfordshire District.

(f) A proportion of the public housing stock is considered substandard, particularly that dating from the prewar period.

Some of these problems, those relating to local need, agricultural tenancies, the elderly and housing quality, are shared in common with Cotswold District. They may perhaps be taken as four key issues which are generally recognised as constituting rural housing problems today. As such they have been common threads in the previous chapters of this study; their repetition here simply confirms their importance in the eyes of local housing authorities.

Other problems are rather different, though they may have similar consequences. In particular South Oxfordshire District has two sets of housing problems which, while they are found elsewhere in rural areas, are less common. The presence of large service bases in this district frequently results in housing need to which the local authority must respond when people leaving the services, sometimes but not always with local ties, request housing in the area. Secondly, the growth in the number of caravans, particularly in the 1950s and 1960s, has meant that more than 10 per cent of permanent dwellings in the district are mobile homes. Since this form of accommodation often has a life of only about twenty years, much of the stock is either substandard now or will become so in the near future.

HOUSING STRATEGIES

The problems which are recognised by local authorities should be matched by their housing policies. These policies have now, under the HIP system, to be stated explicitly on an annual basis as a set of policy alternatives and a preferred strategy. It is appropriate, therefore, to follow this review of problems perceived by local authorities with an assessment of policies and performance developed as a response.

The problems of need associated with tied housing and with an ageing population recognised in Cotswold District could be met with a continuation of the past construction programme. In the four years 1974–7 the local authority built 500 houses and these, together with 155 from other public sources and 1,302 from the private sector, added 1,957 houses to the total stock.

The preferred strategy is, in fact, not a continued programme of construction, except where particular local difficulties exist in the market towns of Moreton-in-Marsh, Northleach and Tetbury, or where local needs and community life need strengthening. The improvement of the existing stock, together with limited purchases and improvement of unfit property and some housing association activity, is seen as sufficient to meet future needs and provide a choice of tenures. The strategy is thus a modest one; the local housing authority feels that its existing stock of housing (which represents a quarter of the total housing stock) is sufficient to cope with future demands.

The prospect in the pressure area of South Oxfordshire District is very different. Here policies have to cope with a continued shortfall in housing compared with the number of households in this district in contrast to the situation in Cotswold District. A fairly high level of new construction (300–350 units per year for five years) is one possibility, but the demands upon land availability, capital and staff resources would be high. Alternatively a lower level of new construction and joint development schemes with private developers and housing associations would probably be sufficient to meet the greatest areas of need but would not meet the housing deficit in the short term. A programme of municipalisation and improvement of existing properties provides a third component in any potential strategy.

The concern with providing housing for younger couples, particularly those with local connections, has resulted in the preferred strategy concentrating essentially upon new construction, especially of low-cost housing, given sufficient resources. Moreover the strategy envisages most of this development taking place in urban and suburban areas rather than in the villages. To quote from the HIP statement:

> It is becoming increasingly evident that future housing provision will become more localised with future developments needing to be concentrated in larger towns and urban fringes whilst developments in smaller country towns and villages will be needed mainly for local elderly or young families.

> (South Oxfordshire District Housing Strategy
> Statement, 1978, para. 1.32)

These proposals are, of course, generally in line with the broad strategy proposed by the structure plan (see Chapter 5) which envisaged growth in Didcot and general restriction in other areas.

STRATEGIES AND PERFORMANCE: SOME IMPORTANT QUESTIONS

These two strategies for two very different rural areas raise a number of major questions which are basic to a discussion of future rural housing policy. In broad terms three main issues follow from the juxtaposition of the problems and the strategies mentioned above.

1   DO THE STRATEGIES PROPOSED RELATE REALISTICALLY TO FUTURE
    LEVELS OF HOUSING NEED?

Housing need, as has been stressed before, is a difficult concept to evaluate. Nevertheless there is reason for concern that these proposals would not be sufficient to accommodate future need. Indeed it is implicit in the South Oxfordshire statement that, unless some 300 to 350 units are built each year for five years (a requirement needing between twenty to thirty acres of land each year) then the strategy will fail to deal with all but 'the most needy cases' (para. 2.3). Taken together with the second question raised by these strategies (see below), the proposal looks at best only a partial answer to future problems. The more so, in fact, when it is realised that the past record for new local authority construction has generally fallen well below this level of growth (Table 11.1).

Table 11.1   *Local authority house completions : South Oxfordshire District, 1971–8*

Years	No. of local authority completions
1971–2	55
1972–3	82
1973–4	347
1974–5	187
1975–6	140
1976–7	15
1977–8	93

Source: Oxfordshire Joint District Housing Group (1978).

The only statistical guide to levels of need is the local authority waiting list which, with some justification, is frequently condemned as a crude indicator. There are differing views on the value of the waiting list. On the one hand, the housing manager in one district was of the opinion that only some 10 per cent of waiting list applicants were in real need, that is, whose existing living conditions amounted to actual hardship by any reasonable standards. On the other hand, Larkin (in Shaw, 1979) has argued that in rural areas residential and other qualifying criteria are applied so strictly that many cases of real need are omitted from the lists.

For all their deficiencies, it is significant to consider the evidence of waiting lists in rural areas as part of the assessment of proposed strategies. Larkin (op. cit.) and others (for example, Penfold, 1974) have shown that waiting lists in rural areas are often as large if not larger than in some cities. In 1977 the waiting list in Cotswold District stood at 1,361, some 5·6 per cent of all households, while in South Oxfordshire the list numbered 3,122 – a proportion of 6·9 per cent of all households. Expressed as a ratio of housing completions to waiting list applicants, the figure for Cotswold

District in 1977 was 1:9, while that for South Oxfordshire for the period 1977/8 was 1:26 (though ratios in previous years had been significantly lower than this, though not below 1:10).

These very crude analyses are inevitably open to much criticism, but they do give some real cause to question the likely effectiveness of future strategies. They lead on to a consideration of a second important question:

2   ARE LOCAL AUTHORITY RESOURCES SUFFICIENT TO COPE WITH EXPRESSED HOUSING NEEDS?

There are major doubts here about the likely success of strategies, particularly in the light of restrictions upon local authority spending in the next few years.

In the first place, as has already been seen, the cutbacks in local authority spending in the recent past have already resulted in many rural areas receiving very low future public housing allocations. With perhaps only one-third to a half of all housing units actually receiving central government approval (Larkin, op. cit.) it is likely that some districts are left with only one major scheme and that, inevitably, in a town where economies of scale allow for some savings. With this pattern in mind, and the probability of more stringent cutbacks in public expenditure in the future, it seems most unlikely that policies for public housing development in villages, as suggested in the Cotswold strategy for example, will ever be realised.

Similarly, it would seem probable that resources for the improvement of the private housing sector will also suffer from financial cutbacks. Under the Housing Act 1974, local authorities may pay four types of grant for private house improvement – improvement grants, intermediate (formerly standard) grants, special grants and repairs grants. In practice only the first two are of major concern and the last type is only available in housing action areas and is therefore largely irrelevant to rural areas.

Local authorities make substantial use of these grant-awarding powers and there can be no doubt that a significant amount of the improvement in rural housing in the private sector (recorded in Chapter 3) has been helped by this financial aid. However, financial stringency coupled with inflation of housing costs must inevitably reduce this aid in the future. Table 11.2 gives the improvement record in South Oxfordshire District over the period 1974/5–1977/8. It is clear that intermediate grants, which are available as of right and are for the provision of basic amenities, where these are lacking, are relatively unimportant and affect only a few properties. Improvement grants, however, which are available at the discretion of the local authority and which are used to improve properties to a high all-round standard (DoE Circular 160/74), are much more important. The inflation in improvement costs in recent years is clear from Table 11.2 – a doubling of the average cost of grants per dwelling in just three years. This rise coupled

Table 11.2 *Improvement and intermediate grants for private housing: South Oxfordshire District, 1974/5–1977/8*

	Improvement grants							Intermediate grants					
	For dwellings			Grants approved (£)				For dwellings			Grants approved (£)		
Year	*Owner-occupied*	*Private rented*	*Total*	*Total*	*Average per dwelling*			*Owner-occupied*	*Private rented*	*Total*	*Total*	*Average per dwelling*	
1974/5*	67	45	112	84,252	752			5	6	11	3,201	291	
1975/6	80	26	106	131,978	1,245			14	5	19	6,093	320	
1976/7	54	23	77	101,593	1,319			10	1	11	4,698	427	
1977/8	71	20	91	141,770	1,558			8	2	10	4,443	444	

* Figures given for intermediate grants for 1974/5 refer to standard grants, which were replaced under the Housing Act 1974.
Source: Oxfordshire Joint District Housing Group (1975–8).

with financial stringency must put this sector of local authority housing policy in some jeopardy.

A third area where local authority resources may prove inadequate is regarding availability of land, particularly in rural areas where planning restrictions are especially severe. Moreover the demise of the Community Land Act from 1979 means that even if they had the financial resources many local authorities would have reduced opportunities to acquire sufficient land for their projected developments. Any land that is available and which the local authority can afford to buy is likely to be either in existing urban areas or on their fringes rather than in villages where it could contribute towards the local stock of rented housing. In the case of South Oxfordshire District, the continuation of a policy of new construction was estimated to require the acquisition of between 100 and 150 acres of land for building in the period to 1983. Stocks of local authority land obviously vary over time as land is purchased and sold by the authority. However, the amounts of land recorded as being available for housing revenue account purposes – barely more than sixty acres in the latter half of the 1970s – do not suggest that this goal is a certain one, particularly in circumstances of reduced finances and continued inflation of land prices.

A final area where local authority resources are involved is the actual stock of council houses. Despite the rural safeguards accorded to the sale of council houses in some parts of the countryside, there must be justifiable fears that the already limited stock of rented property in rural areas will be further diminished. Moreover it is certain that once such housing has passed into owner-occupation, there will be no effective way of controlling its future occupancy, for example, by local people who might otherwise be unable to get access to housing. The loss would further handicap the local authority in its housing policies and responsibilities by reducing the stock of rural properties and leaving the least attractive properties for rent by those who cannot afford to buy.

3   WHAT DO THE HOUSING STRATEGIES OFFER TO THE RURAL AREAS?

The third and final question relates essentially to the location not just of the existing council stock but also that of new development. The point is simple and has been made before. For all the concern expressed about the particular problems of smaller villages in the countryside (for example, the concern by Cotswold District Council to 'strengthen the community life'), it seems more than likely that if development does take place it will be in the larger villages and towns. Even in Cotswold District, where these conflicts are clearly recognised, the housing strategy specifies the towns of Moreton-in-Marsh, Northleach and Tetbury for the provision of new council dwellings. The policy to concentrate future housing developments in larger towns and urban fringes in South Oxfordshire District has been mentioned earlier in this chapter. The expected programme of housing projects given in the 1978 HIP submission re-emphasises this point, with virtually all schemes located in the main towns of this district (Didcot, Wallingford, Thame, and so on) or the larger villages, particularly where local authority involvement is already high, as in Berinsfield.

The significance of this point lies in the restricted choice of rented housing which local villagers are given and in the consequent drift away from villages where rented property is not available. Larkin (in Shaw, 1979) has documented evidence for this effect from West Oxfordshire. While the waiting list for council accommodation was often as high or higher in the villages as in the towns, only half of village applicants in 1975/6 were rehoused in their own village (compared with over 70 per cent of urban applicants) and 20 per cent were rehoused in nearby towns. Clearly this reflected in part the wishes of some people to move to urban areas and, equally, there was a counter-flow of town dwellers to the villages. None the less there must over time be a trend away from the smaller villages due to the location of public rented housing, which acts to reinforce the tendency to concentration from other causes.

The social consequences of policies of housing concentration cause general concern, but they are particularly serious for some sectors of the population. In the light of increasing mobility problems and the continual loss of services in small settlements, which have been emphasised elsewhere, the South Oxfordshire policy of new developments in villages, aimed essentially at local elderly and younger families, seems particularly unsatisfactory. These are precisely the groups which have mobility (and also often economic) problems. If public housing allocation is restricted to these groups then their lifestyles will inevitably suffer and village communities will become unbalanced in age and social structure.

THE SYSTEM OF HOUSING ACCESS

The relative strengths and weaknesses of different groups in competition for the limited supply of rural housing were considered in detail in Part Two. Here the theme is the system with which these groups have to contend. Two main aspects of this system are given consideration. In the public sector the main significance lies in the allocation procedures which are adopted by housing authorities to decide on eligibility for council property. In the private sector eligibility is decided by the availability of financial resources, their relationship to house prices and the way in which institutions such as building societies control these resources.

THE ALLOCATION OF PUBLIC HOUSING

It is not the intention of this section to review housing allocation procedures in a comprehensive way. That task has been ably carried out by a number of other researchers, notably Niner (1975) and in summary form in Murie, Niner and Watson (1976). The results of Niner's research indicated that, for all the seeming variation in allocation methods adopted by local authorities, there was little real difference between them. With regard to allocation *policy* all authorities concentrate on the relief of fairly strictly defined housing needs and as for actual *practice* 'the detailed differences of procedure have surprisingly little effect on the end results' (Murie, Niner and Watson, 1976, pp. 135–6). This does not mean, however, that there are no characteristics of local authority allocation systems which are particular to rural areas. In a number of areas there is no doubt that these systems have important consequences for people in the countryside.

Larkin (in Shaw, 1979) has maintained that restrictions on the eligibility of waiting list applicants are 'more common and more draconian' in rural areas than in towns. This applies particularly to residential qualifications, which must be relatively more difficult to fulfil in rural areas if only because of the shortage of housing and the lesser availability of employment. An informed opinion given off the record by a housing manager from the east of England confirmed Larkin's view that strict residential qualifications were generally more common in rural housing housing authorities. Authorities with such restrictions are, however, likely to argue that the requirements exist to protect local people who might otherwise have greater difficulty in gaining accommodation. Certainly there is great variation between authorities on this point – in the case of South Oxfordshire District the normal residential or employment period required is five or more years, whereas in Cotswold District (where housing demand is lower) only one year is needed. The implication is, perhaps, not that rural areas are necessarily harsher in their procedures than urban areas, but rather that pressure for housing is more significant in tightening the qualifications.

A second point on qualifications has already been raised earlier in this study. This concerns the way in which some tenants may not be able to qualify even though their circumstances are unsatisfactory. The clearest instance is in the case of the tied tenant who may find it impossible to transfer out of a system which he finds unsatisfactory largely because he cannot prove need in terms of, for example, overcrowding or ill health.

A third issue relates to the point made earlier about the location of council housing. It has been argued that the scarcity of council accommodation in many villages results in a drift to the towns and, moreover, causes applicants to specify locations where they feel their chances of gaining a tenancy are higher rather than specifying where they would like to live.

This may well happen, but it does not follow that the local housing authority is insensitive to it. In Cotswold District, for example, the points system specifically states that 'with a view to maintaining the quality of village life, reasonable preference shall be given to applicants wishing to continue to reside in their home parish, or an adjoining parish where

Council housing is located'. An additional three 'parochial points' can be awarded in such a case. Again in South Oxfordshire, the points system allows for up to a maximum of five points to be given for an 'established connection in a particular village ... for rehousing in that village'. Local ties and a concern for rural communities can, therefore, be taken into account in allocation procedures – at least in villages where local authority housing exists or is to be provided.

The drawbacks of local authority waiting lists have already been referred to, but they often provide the only evidence of housing need. Using waiting list statistics for Cotswold District it is possible to shed light on some of the points which have been raised. There were 1,361 applicants on the housing waiting list at the end of 1977. Some 488 had no points under the system operated by the authority while a further 514 applicants had only the three parochial points from stating a preference for housing in their existing town or village. The remainder (359) scored four or more points and it was only in these cases that household circumstances (overcrowding, sharing, health, and so on) were considered to be involved.

Conclusions from these limited data (Table 11.3), although tentative, do substantiate some of the points already made. A somewhat arbitrary distinction is created between towns in Cotswold District, where at least 400 households were recorded in the 1971 Census, and villages where household numbers were much smaller.

The numbers of applicants measured relative to the totals in each of the two categories scoring four or more points suggests that village housing and household circumstances are about as good (or as bad) as in the towns. When judged by the total of applicants for Cotswold District as a whole, however, 78 per cent of these needier cases were to be found in the towns and it is to be expected that this would be where the main thrust of local authorities housing authority would be focused.

There is, however, a notable difference in the proportion of applicants preferring to be rehoused in their own village or town. Some 45 per cent of village applicants made this preference, compared with only 35 per cent in the towns. This strongly confirms the point made before that people wish to remain in their own villages. Indeed the figure could arguably be higher since some of those village applicants who do not specify their own village may have felt that they stood a better chance of obtaining accommodation in a town.

One final point relating to housing allocation policies needs to be mentioned. All systems, however formally they may be phrased and however quantitative they might appear, retain a distinct element of personal judgement in the choice of tenants. Moreover the influence of elected members may also be significant in deciding on the validity and priority of an application. It has been argued that rural housing authorities are particularly prone to such personal influence – a study by Leicester Shelter Group (1976) reported that some rural authorities in Leicestershire

Table 11.3   Cotswold District: analysis of housing waiting list, December 1977

	Nil points		3 parochial points only		4 or more points		Total applicants	
	No.	%	No.	%	No.	%	No.	%
Towns*	393	38	372	35	280	27	1,045	100
Villages	95	30	142	45	79	25	316	100
TOTAL	488	36	514	38	359	26	1,361	100

* Towns defined as Tetbury, South Cerney, Fairford, Lechlade, Cirencester, Northleach, Bourton-on-the-Water, Stow-on-the-Wold, Moreton-in-Marsh, Blockley and Chipping Campden.
Source: Cotswold District Council Housing Department.

allowed individual councillors to choose tenants for vacancies occurring in their wards. These charges of favouritism, coupled with the general political backgrounds of many rural councillors, have led some people to be highly critical of the operation of any allocation system in rural areas, (for example, Larkin in Walker, 1978). The excessive personal influence of local councillors has also been condemned in recent statements by the DoE Housing Services Advisory Group.

These hypotheses are difficult if not impossible to test, even by an examination of allocations case by case. On the basis of the discussions held with officers in the two districts used as case studies, it was clear that local councillors were recognised as having a role to play in advising the housing manager, particularly in Cotswold District. It must be remembered that there are relatively few areas in which a local councillor can indicate his concern and commitment to the electorate, and that the allocation of public housing must inevitably be a prime area where success can be judged.

This role as 'advisor' is justified by those who see no real problem of conflict of ideas on at least two grounds. First, they argue, it is the responsibility of each elected member to represent his constituents and to further their interests. Secondly, the rigidity of a formal allocation system may mean that problem cases are not perceived by the housing manager sitting in the council offices. It is inevitable that waiting lists, as well as containing applicants whose true need is in doubt, leave out households which are truly in need. By a combination of ignorance, fear of authority, or whatever, their circumstances do not become known to the local authority. The role of the local councillor who knows his ward well can here be a positive one.

It would seem likely that this 'principle of local discretion', as Murie *et al.* (1976) have called it, can take many forms, some beneficial and some less so. Moreover on the basis of the limited evidence available, it seems probable that such influence is more likely to occur in rural areas than in towns. Personal relationships are closer (though not necessarily more harmonious), patronage has a longer tradition and the local political structures of rural areas make it more likely that 'who you know' is more important than 'what you know'.

HOUSE PRICES AND THE ROLE OF BUILDING SOCIETIES

This section deals with access to the private sector and in particular with two aspects of control, namely the price of rural housing, especially in relation to rural wages, and the role played by building societies.

Rural house prices

Information on rural house prices is notoriously difficult to obtain. In part this relates to the fact that the established price surveys rarely if ever disaggregate their data into rural categories. The one national survey where data are collected at a local authority level (the DoE/Inland Revenue Five per cent survey of mortgages) is generally only available at an aggregate level. Though data from this source referring specifically to rural house prices have been published in the past, permission to reproduce information specifically for Cotswold and South Oxfordshire Districts was refused on the grounds that the data would be misleading because of the small size of samples.

Information from the DoE/Inland Revenue sample which relates to rural areas has, however, been published by the Standing Conference of Rural Community Councils in its response to a discussion paper by the Countryside Commission on designated areas of outstanding natural beauty (Standing Conference of Rural Community Councils, 1979). The concern here was essentially with housing prices in AONBs and national parks in 1974/5, and examples from northern England and the South West were quoted (Table 11.4).

Table 11.4   *House prices in national parks and AONBs, 1974/5*

District or area	Average price (£)	As index of regional average
Alnwick	12,060	161
Tynedale	11,597	155
South Lakeland	10,555	141
Eden	9,767	130
Berwick	7,727	103
Northern Region	7,491	100
East Devon	15,282	135
South Hams	13,869	123
West Devon	12,588	111
Carrick	12,194	108
North Devon	11,594	103
North Cornwall	10,374	92
Devon and Cornwall	11,298	100

Source: Standing Conference of Rural Community Councils (1979), from DoE/Inland Revenue survey.

In all but one case in these examples prices in rural areas were above the regional average, in several instances substantially so. The location of these examples in areas of high landscape value where strict development control operates may be a significant factor in bidding up prices. It should be remembered, however, that at least 20 per cent of England and Wales is covered by national park and AONB controls and so the restrictions on building and the use of specific materials which can influence prices is far more widespread than is commonly realised. Information on house prices from other sources such as Penfold's (1974) study in the Peak District,

Bennett's (1976) study in the Lake District and Clark's (1980) study in East Hampshire confirm these data.

Data on rural house prices, though sparse, can be assembled from certain other sources, two of which are of particular relevance to the present study:

(1) a survey of the residential market in Oxfordshire and parts of Buckinghamshire and Berkshire conducted since January 1974 by the Department of Land Management and Development at the University of Reading (Byrne and Mackmin, 1974 *et seq.*). This continuing study is based on data abstracted from the records of one large estate agent, Messrs Buckell & Ballard.

(2) a survey conducted by the authors in the two study areas during the period July to October 1978 involving thirty-one estate agents. A total of 266 properties in South Oxfordshire District and 201 in Cotswold District are taken as indicative of price levels at that time.

In addition there is a variety of other sources where piecemeal information can be obtained, including informed opinion from, for example, estate agents and building society managers.

Data from the Reading University survey relate, of course, to urban as well as rural properties and the area to which they refer is defined only by the location of branch offices of the firm of estate agents. In the Berkshire offices (Newbury, Reading, Wallingford, Raybourne and Wantage) covering an area coincident with or adjacent to part of the South Oxfordshire survey area, the mean selling prices for particular house types recorded in the latter half of 1978 were as shown in Table 11.5.

Table 11.5 *House prices in Berkshire, July–December 1978*

House type	Mean selling price (£)
Detached	26,981
Semi-detached	20,453
Bungalow	29,816
Flat	17,890
Terrace	15,295
Other	36,455

Source: Byrne and Mackmin (1979).

Data from the survey conducted in Cotswold and South Oxfordshire Districts only represent a snapshot view at one point in time but they nevertheless give a clear indication of the general trend. Details of prices are given in Tables 11.6–8, both for rural properties within district boundaries elsewhere in the county and in adjacent counties that can be considered to fall within the same private market. The data for properties within the two districts have been aggregated in relation to the location within the rural

Table 11.6   *House prices in Cotswold District and environs, 1978*

Profile name or area	No. in sample	Price (£)		
		Mean	Median	Minimum
Agricultural	37	36,150	26,750	9,500
Retirement	43	30,069	26,850	8,500
Poor housing	1	15,000	15,000	15,000
Local authority	14	30,868	23,575	13,950
Armed forces	4	34,725	34,250	17,950
Cirencester	28	16,273	14,025	6,000
Moreton-in-Marsh	2	27,750	27,750	22,500
Tetbury	6	15,442	11,575	7,000
Gloucestershire	43	31,960	32,488	8,950
Wiltshire	12	37,450	29,975	22,500
Worcestershire	4	26,875	27,000	18,500
Oxfordshire	5	32,500	35,000	18,000
Warwickshire	2	42,500	42,500	35,000
All areas	201	29,846	26,500	6,000

Source: Survey of estate agents.

Table 11.7   *House prices in South Oxfordshire District and environs, 1978*

Profile name* or area	No. in sample	Price (£)		
		Mean	Median	Minimum
Traditional rural	23	45,465	40,000	15,500
Established professional	79	37,806	33,513	14,500
Local authority	2	19,300	19,300	16,150
Younger owner-occupier	39	26,264	22,513	14,250
Henley	45	34,108	30,000	11,500
Thame	12	23,129	22,050	13,500
Wallingford	9	27,794	18,500	9,750
Didcot	11	18,504	18,489	15,750
Oxfordshire	8	22,362	20,428	11,000
Berkshire	18	51,969	39,867	18,995
Buckinghamshire	20	40,098	31,775	12,500
All areas	266	34,878	29,951	9,750

* No properties were reported for sale within areas defined by the armed forces and poor housing profiles.
Source: Survey of estate agents.

Table 11.8 *The distribution of rural house prices in Cotswold and South Oxfordshire Districts, 1978*

Price range (£)	Cotswold District		South Oxfordshire District	
	No.	%	No.	%
<5,000	0	0	0	0
5,001–10,000	8	4·0	1	0·4
10,001–15,000	34	16·9	10	3·8
15,001–20,000	28	13·9	55	20·7
20,001–25,000	29	14·4	32	12·0
25,001–30,000	33	16·4	41	15·4
30,001–35,000	25	12·4	35	13·1
>35,000	44	22·0	92	34·6
TOTAL	201	100·0	266	100·0

Source: Survey of estate agents.

housing profiles which were considered in detail in Chapter 6, and also to the main market towns of the district. In this way it is possible to relate prices to the nature of rural households in the neighbourhood and in so doing to assess more clearly the position of local households relative to the private housing market.

Table 11.8 gives details of the distribution of house prices in the two study districts and emphasises the extent to which the prices of rural houses were clearly skewed towards the upper price brackets.

The relationship with rural wages
These data on house prices must be seen in relation to the level of incomes of those who might wish to purchase rural houses. The availability of private mortgage funds to the individual varies slightly between different lending agencies but on the whole is calculated on the basis of about 2·5–2·75 times the annual salary of the main earner in the household. Some building societies may be more generous by taking into account second salaries or, particularly in the case of small, local societies (see later), by lending on a higher proportion of the purchase price.

Table 11.9 attempts a simple analysis of the relationship between income and prices in the two study areas and the calculation of necessary income has been made on the basis of 2·75 times the salary and a 95 per cent mortgage advance. If anything, therefore, this figure somewhat understates the necessary income, and many households would have to find more finance to qualify.

Two main conclusions from these simple analyses are clear, even though the data is partial and in no sense a statistically derived sample. In the first instance there are obviously many rural households now in rented accommodation which, although preferring owner-occupation, can never aspire to it and must in consequence remain entirely dependent on the

Table 11.9   A comparison of rural house prices and incomes, 1977/8

Profile	Minimum house price (£)	Necessary income* (£)	Households reporting gross annual income: below £3,000 (%)	below £5,000 (%)
Cotswold District				
Agricultural	9,500	3,282	65·7	86·8
Retirement	8,500	2,936	42·7	72·1
Poor housing	15,000	5,182	56·6	78·9
Local authority	13,950	4,819	34·4	60·9
Armed forces	17,950	6,201	61·8	91·2
South Oxfordshire District				
Traditional rural	15,500	5,355	41·3	66·3
Established professional	14,500	5,009	29·7	50·8
Local authority	16,150	5,579	32·5	66·2
Younger owner-occupiers	14,250	4,923	21·6	45·9

* Necessary income calculated on the basis of a 95 per cent mortgage involving an advance of 2·75 × income.
Source: Surveys of estate agents.

rented sector. This must be the case particularly for households whose main earner is employed in agriculture where, as Winyard (in Walker, 1978) and others have shown, earnings are well below the average for manual workers, but other groups in the manual sector, the armed services and the retired are also affected. To illustrate this point further: in 1977 mean annual earnings without overtime in agriculture and horticulture in England were £2,929 (Ministry of Agriculture, Fisheries and Food data, 1978). Without other financial resources, therefore, the most that the average agricultural worker could hope to pay for a house would be c. £8,000. This price level was found on only three out of 201 occasions in the 1978 survey in Cotswold District and no price lower than £9,750 was recorded in South Oxfordshire. In all cases these minimum prices related to small properties in towns rather than villages. It is scarcely surprising that 30 per cent of respondents in Cotswold District to the survey conducted by Gloucestershire County Council for the structure plan (Freeman Fox & Associates, 1976) considered that most of the new houses which were built in this district should be council houses.

A second conclusion leading directly from this concerns the general availability of property. Although only a view at one point in time, the data in Table 11.8 show that few properties below £10,000 were to be found in 1978. Only one in five properties in the Cotswold area were priced at or below £15,000, while in South Oxfordshire this price limit included less than one in twenty properties. Moreover these cheaper properties were more likely to be found in towns rather than in villages, were generally smaller and therefore less suitable for family occupation and frequently required capital expenditure for improvement.

The role of building societies
The part played by financial institutions, particularly building societies, in housing access in urban areas has been documented by a number of researchers (for example, P. R. Williams, 1976). While the investigations made of building societies' operations in the two study areas were on too small a scale to represent a comprehensive assessment of their role in rural housing access, some broad conclusions are possible.

A total of eight building society branches (four in each study district) were contacted and interviews conducted with the respective managers. As well as branch offices of national societies, the sample included societies which operated only locally – in one case the society operated just two branch offices.

All building societies maintain a close link through their branches with the local area. Indeed it was clear from the interviews that managerial staff often consciously played an important local social role, for example through the membership of organisations like the local Rotary Club and Lions Club. In rural areas, particularly in small market towns, the position of such people perhaps takes on an additional importance to that of their counterparts in urban areas. The social responsibility of the professional was particularly stressed by a number of informants.

This appreciation of a local social role was especially evident in the case of the smaller societies that only operated within the area. It was argued that such societies were better able to perceive local needs for mortgage finance and there was some evidence that such societies were prepared to lend more to local people. In the past these local societies probably had a further advantage in that they were often prepared to lend on older properties which the national societies would not consider. However, in recent years most national societies have relaxed their rules on lending on older properties and there is probably now little difference in practice.

Local societies, partly because of their scale of operations and partly perhaps because of their willingness to lend in circumstances where national societies would refuse, tend to have higher rates for lending — usually about 1 per cent above the current national rate. In return these societies might be prepared to lend on perhaps three times a salary and be more appreciative of a second income. Equally they may have a more liberal policy with regard to modernisation of old rural houses.

While these societies stressed their close links with the local population and argued that their scale of operations allowed for greater flexibility in responding to local needs, the growth of national societies in recent years has probably meant that the contrasts between the two are now much less distinct. In particular the numbers of branches of the national societies, as opposed to franchised agencies, have increased and the personal role played by a local manager has now extended to even the smallest market town. National societies also tend to be recognised for participation in schemes whereby the local authority can nominate individuals for mortgage allocations, whereas local societies are generally not party to such schemes. In practice, however, this distinction is probably of little significance since housing authorities in predominantly rural areas have rarely participated in nomination schemes, and hence nominations tend to relate to mortgages in urban areas.

A further aspect of the social role played by building societies in rural areas also deserves mention. Although societies obviously exist for the prime purpose of lending on property, they also perform a substantial function as a savings agency. The very smallest societies are obviously used by many local people as an alternative to a bank or post office account — indeed one such society reported an increase in the level of small savings when banks stopped opening on Saturdays. For the larger branch office, its function as a depository for savings is quite significant. One manager of a branch office of a larger society in a Cotswold market town reported very substantial savings received across the counter each month. A good part of this came from older, often retired, people who were not saving for a mortgage, but who wanted a secure place for their savings and the feeling that they were helping young people towards home-ownership. If this practice is at all general then it means that very large sums of money might be received annually by building societies in a market town of perhaps 10,000 people serving a rural area. Of course while these sums do obviously increase the gross availability of mortgage capital it does not necessarily follow that the impact is felt in the local rural area. The whole question of local savings in relation to house purchase probably deserves further attention.

There is no evidence from these limited investigations that the restrictions to housing access which have been found in some building society practices in urban areas (for example, 'red lining') have an equivalent in the countryside. Indeed there is probably no such thing as an undesirable rural area within which societies would not lend. However, despite the apparent openness of access to rural housing finance, the major constraints of income and availability which have already been emphasised undoubtedly remain. Society managers when questioned in 1978 put the lower salary limit of prospective owners probably rather optimistically at £2,500–£3,000 in the Cotswolds, but were forced to admit that in their experience there were few properties which would be available at this level.

THE INFLUENCE OF LOCAL PLANNING

The final section of this chapter reviews the interaction of local planning and housing policies in terms of the context set by local and village plans. In doing so it has to contend with the patchy and very incomplete coverage so far achieved by local plans prepared under the Town and Country Planning Act 1971, and with the equally partial coverage of non-statutory village plans. Within the two case study areas, Cotswold and South Oxfordshire Districts, no local plans had been formally adopted by the end of 1979, so that direct comparison with other aspects of local planning and housing policy is not feasible.

The four main functions of a local plan, which may take the form of a district plan, a subject plan, or an action area plan, are stated to be (Department of the Environment, 1979b):

(a) to develop the policies and general proposals of the structure plan and to relate them to precise areas of land;
(b) to provide a detailed basis for development control;
(c) to provide a detailed basis for co-ordinating the development and other use of land;
(d) to bring local and detailed planning issues before the public.

An examination of the development plan schemes prepared by county planning authorities suggests that some 1,650 local plans will eventually be forthcoming; by the end of 1979, however, a mere sixty-nine plans had been placed on deposit and only twenty-nine had been adopted, largely because of the slow progress of submission and approval of structure plans which should set the strategic context for local planning. Few of the deposited local plans deal with rural areas, although the Fladbury District plan (Hereford and Worcester) relates to one village with a population of about 650, and the Porthmadog/Ffestiniog plan is attempting to consider the problems of industrial dereliction and rural isolation in part of Gwynedd.

The first function of the local plan, to elaborate and make specific the general proposals of the structure plan, is comparatively straightforward, as an example in the field of housing from Leicestershire illustrates. The structure plan identified Glenfield as one of a number of growth areas west of Leicester and allocated new housing to accommodate 'about 2,550' people in Glenfield by 1985 (Leicestershire County Council, 1976). The Glenfield District plan specifies an area of about seventy-seven acres in West Glenfield which will accommodate 940 dwellings with a population of approximately 2,400. It is envisaged in the local plan that development will be substantially completed by the early 1980s. The ability of the local plan to develop general policies into site-specific proposals with explicit detailing of implementation and phasing is clear.

Possibly the most crucial aspect of local plans in respect of rural housing, given that strategic allocation policies are the preserve of structure plans as discussed in the previous chapter, is the precise guide to development control which they can be expected to provide. Development control, increasingly viewed as the cutting edge of the post-1971 planning system, requires the determination of specific applications within a strategic and local policy framework. Local plans may therefore consist almost entirely of development control policies, as is the case with, for example, the Solihull Green Belt subject plan, but even where this is not the case they should consider strategic proposals in terms of their implementation, whether this involves location, density or even (somewhat dubiously) occupancy proposals.

This last point, the question of occupancy of new housing, has been a recurrent theme of Part Four of this study, but it deserves further mention because of attempts to translate local needs housing policies into specific action. The Coleorton District plan (Leicestershire) for example, states that 'land for approximately two, ten and fourteen local needs plots will be safeguarded'. But the plan contains no indication of methods by which new houses on these plots will be reserved for local households, however defined, and it is equally imprecise in respect of the grounds on which proposals for development on these plots which are not directed towards local needs could be refused, since it is implicit that the plots in question are acceptable for housing development on all other grounds. Local plans may justifiably specify locations and target densities for new housing, but districts may be exceeding the limits of their powers of planning control in introducing other considerations.

In many respects housing-related policies in local plans are so circumscribed by national guidance and by the overall context of the structure plan for the area that scope for local interpretation is negligible. One instance is the Kempsey District plan, prepared for a Worcestershire village which has undergone considerable expansion (Radford, 1970), which decrees that 'new development will not normally be permitted in the countryside'. Given the positive stance taken in *Development Control Policy Note 4* (Ministry of Housing and Local Government, 1969) against any further development in the open countryside unless an overriding agricultural or forestry need can be proved, it would be surprising if any local plan shaped a significantly different policy.

Clearly local plans, given the comparatively restrictive role of interpreting and further defining existing policies, have a limited influence upon the location and availability, and thereby indirectly on the price, of rural housing. Such influence as the planning system possesses has to a large degree already been exercised in other documents, although through their discharge of the development control function local planners have the ability to discriminate spatially. This discrimination has had uneven and not entirely predictable effects, with designation as green belt failing to stop rapid development in the Hertfordshire countryside (Pahl, 1966) and little difference observed between decisions on planning applications within, and adjacent to, the East Devon Area of Outstanding Natural Beauty (Blacksell and Gilg, 1977). In this latter case there was only a minimal difference between the ratio of permissions to refusals on either side of the AONB boundary (34 per cent of all applications were refused inside the AONB, 32 per cent outside the designated area) but there was a far greater tendency to attach conditions relating to siting, design and materials to permissions within the AONB.

All this suggests that the major role of local planning may lie in determining applications for development within a given framework rather than in formulating broad policies. Certainly this seems to be the case in Cotswold District, where attention to the details of development – and in particular to the use of local materials, thereby generating a healthy demand for reconstituted stone – is of crucial importance. A further feature of local planning in Cotswold District is the considerable emphasis upon local consultation: parish councils provide comment upon development proposals and, significantly, act as watchdogs for unauthorised developments, initiating over half of the 700 enforcement complaints dealt with by Cotswold District Council in 1974/5 (I. Jones, 1976).

Local consultation is by no means universal, however, particularly at the interface between different departments and committees with different priorities. One Cotswold example was the proposal in 1979 to close the village school at Quenington, east of Cirencester, and bus the children to the nearby school at Hatherop. Yet Quenington is a large village with a good deal of recent private and public housing development, and is designated as a 'main village' in the Gloucestershire structure plan (see Chapter 5), while Hatherop is little more than a hamlet and will receive no new development. Indeed, families in Hatherop 'are on the re-housing list for the very village whose school is to be closed' (*Daily Telegraph*, 1979).

The role of the parish council, despite its limited executive powers, is far from negligible in such cases, given the necessary commitment to effective consultation by all the agencies concerned in rural planning. In South Oxfordshire contravention of planning restrictions is, as in Cotswold, generally recognised as one of the central problems facing parish councils (Odd, 1976). A further dimension in this area, however, is the concern of rural communities at the suburbanisation of villages within commuting distance of Reading, Oxford and London, and the development of unplanned dormitory estates which, despite the designation of the Chilterns as an area of outstanding natural beauty, have been permitted in and around key settlements such as Goring and Woodcote, and also in Sonning Common.

Nevertheless the impression remains that, however the concern of local communities is expressed, it is unlikely to be fruitfully directed at local planners. Their role in respect of housing development, the particular concern of the present study, is distinctly limited to the consideration of applications within a highly constrained decision-making environment. These constraints are largely dictated by standard national guidelines on good planning practice and by the strategic thinking of county authorities which are able to set, within close limits, allocations for future development, together with controls upon both existing and planned development. Structure plans and Housing Investment Programmes, rather than local plans, are compulsory reading for those concerned with the location and availability of rural housing.

Chapter 12

Housing in the Countryside – towards the Future Imperfect?

This study has concerned itself with a view of the many issues which surround housing in the countryside. The compass has been broad, ranging from the physical conditions of rural dwellings to population movement through the stock of rural housing, with special emphasis upon the political and administrative framework which surrounds the access to rural housing. There has, however, been a central objective which has linked all the strands of the study – the recognition of the various groups which compete unequally for houses in the countryside.

The recognition of these groups has centred primarily on the designation of the rural housing profiles which were outlined in Chapters 4 and 6. In Chapter 4 a simple sevenfold division was proposed which recognised the transition from the old-established housing types based on the agricultural economy, through the retired sector to the urban-oriented owner-occupiers who have progressively invaded the accessible countryside. In between there were the important renting groups represented by the tenants of local authorities and the armed services.

The extension of this model of housing profiles to the level of the case studies enables a more detailed picture to emerge. The basic categories remain but their internal distributions are made clearer. Thus the transitional group is seen to include established owner-occupiers and younger, more recent owners on the one hand and the mobile home dweller on the other. The importance of the two other tenant groups, council house and armed services tenants, is emphasised again at the local level. A third extension of the profile analysis was seen in Chapters 7 and 8 which gave the evidence for the range of deprivation and advantage which can still be found in rural housing.

The examination of the character of these various housing profiles has underlined the great diversity of housing environments which exist in the English countryside. There is still to be found a variety of housing types, from mobile homes to stately country houses, and a variety also of ownership and letting patterns. A concurrent conclusion is, however, that this variety is threatened. The decline in privately rented property at a national level – from over 7 million dwellings before the First World War to under 3 million by the mid-1970s – has hit hard at what was always a major sector of the rural housing scene. To some extent this part of the private sector has been replaced by public housing but, as has been indicated, rural local authorities have in general been far less willing to invest in housing than have their urban counterparts. This relative decline in the rented sector has coupled with a post-1945 invasion by an affluent middle class, and the result has been the increasing dominance of the owner-occupier sector. The limited intrusion over the last sixty years of the rural council house into this picture of change from private renting to private owning is now increasingly endangered by council house sales.

A further conclusion is also related to the variety of housing environments. The assumption is often made that owner-occupation of a house is an ideal to which everyone aspires. Yet the results reported here back up previous studies which show clearly that this is not so. While owner-occupation may be utopia for many, its attractions are not universal. For some young couples, for example, the rented house still has its advantages, while the mobile home is clearly recognised by others as a good investment in their particular circumstances. More important, it is undeniably evident that for many rural people rented property remains the only realistic possibility when low incomes are matched against escalating house prices. Thus, from the viewpoint both of necessity and of choice, the decline in the range of rural housing should be considered with alarm.

THE ROLES OF RURAL HOUSING

This final chapter aims to consolidate the picture of competition and choice which has been at the centre of this book and to make a tentative assessment of future developments. Any such drawing together of arguments must be seen within a framework of the varied roles which rural housing plays in our society. Essentially this study has pointed to three such roles and it is only by appreciating these that a realistic perspective can be given to those elements of social, economic and environmental policy which influence the match between people and houses in the countryside.

The most basic of these roles is that of house as *home* – that is, the needs of rural households for shelter and a roof over their heads and for accommodation of a standard judged by society to be adequate. Yet this most obvious of roles for rural housing is frequently forgotten when some other characteristics of rural housing are considered. A second role is that of housing as *wealth*, the visible evidence of a family's investment and commitment to the future. The blandishments of building societies to save and prosper through owner-occupation have fallen on receptive ears in postwar Britain and the wisdom of their advice seems evident to every middle-class house-owner as he views the seemingly inexorable rise in the value of his property. No amount of dismissing the rise in the value of such investment as 'paper money' can hide the evident contentment which capital appreciation brings.

Related to the role of housing as wealth there is a third role which, though also proper to urban housing, is particularly characteristic of housing in the countryside. This is the role of rural housing as a *positional good*. Hirsch (1977) recognised the value of the good which, because of its scarcity and because of restrictions on increasing its supply, attains a greatly enhanced status. He cited the second home as an example of a positional good, but his arguments hold true for much non-recreation housing in rural areas. For centuries comfortable rural living was the prerogative of the few, a prerogative ensured by limitations on wealth and landownership. In more recent years those limitations on wealth have been eased somewhat and the middle classes have been quick to purchase their position in the countryside. But wealth still remains a powerful brake upon rural living for many who would wish it and, moreover, the supply of rural housing has been most effectively constrained in another direction by the strict controls on building in the countryside imposed by town and country planning. The objectives of postwar planning may have been phrased in terms of urban containment, of saving land for agriculture and, latterly, of safeguarding rural landscapes, but a crucial by-product has been to enhance the positional status of many rural houses. The house in the country has now become a key symbol of success for our acquisitive society.

These three roles must be borne in mind when any consideration is given to differential access to rural housing. For some households the achievement of the first role is a difficult enough goal; for others the motivation has long involved more than merely the need for shelter.

HOUSING COMPETITION AND HOUSING CHOICE

The recognition at the outset of the roles of rural housing as wealth and status over and above the more prosaic role as shelter forces an immediate distinction to be made between owners and tenants. It is no coincidence that the spectrum of housing opportunity which was put forward in Chapter 8 stressed the relative deprivation of the rural tenant against the advantage of the owner-occupier. The evidence of this and other studies is overwhelming on this point. From whatever viewpoint the position is assessed (housing quality, accessibility, household circumstances, capital asset) the dominant position of the owner-occupier is clear.

This basic distinction between the owner and the tenant should not, however, obscure some important exceptions to this general rule. The position of one tenant group, farmers, provides such an exception. Even here, though, the quality of housing (as seen in Chapters 3 and 6) at times leaves something to be desired. Nevertheless the security of tenure which this group is able to command puts them on a par with their colleagues in owner-occupation, and in the control which many tenant farmers have over their own workers through the tied cottage system they take on the effective status of landlords as well as owners. The fact that, as nominal tenants, they are unable to realise the capital value of their house and land on sale is irrelevant to many since a primary objective is succession. By virtue of exceptional treatment in the matter of capital taxation which has been won by farmers from successive governments, both Conservative and Labour, and because of virtually guaranteed tenancy succession, tenant farmers are in as fortunate a position as the owner-occupier. The third issue, of positional status, is again an exception. As a safeguarded occupier, the tenant farmer has in his house and land a positional good of the highest value. True, he may never have appreciated its worth in this respect, but this does not lessen the envy with which he is regarded by those who have bought their house and place in the rural community more recently and with considerably greater difficulty.

A second set of exceptions to this owner/tenant dichotomy relates to those owner-occupiers who share with tenants the essential concern for housing as shelter and for whom the other advantages of ownership are unimportant. A clear instance of this exception is the mobile home owner. Whatever the advantages which have been attributed to mobile home ownership, they cannot compare with those offered by permanent housing. As this study and official surveys have shown, mobile homes are frequently in poor condition and lacking essential amenities. They therefore fulfil the first role of housing as shelter inadequately; their fulfilment of the other two is generally even more limited. Their relatively short life means that they have little value as wealth and their positional status in society is marginal. Moreover, most owners of mobile homes are owner-occupiers in only the most tenuous of senses. They generally lease their pitch from the local authority or a private owner who retains all the essential elements of control of a landlord.

The position of mobile home owners has received significant publicity in recent years and their disadvantages have become better appreciated. Another owner group, however, has in general been forgotten in most discussions of rural housing disadvantage. The relatively poor owner-occupier, almost invariably an outright owner, has been shown in this study to have few of the advantages of his more affluent fellow owners. National surveys (Chapter 3) show clearly that some owner-occupiers, particularly the older outright owner, live in poorer housing conditions which need relatively high expenditure to bring them up to a reasonable standard. The surveys in Gloucestershire and Oxfordshire reported in this study emphasise the same point. Such owners may have a nominal advantage in so far as their property represents capital, but their low incomes make adequate repair impossible and their asset is, relative to other properties, a wasting one. Finally, the positional status of their house is irrelevant to them, unless they are able to realise it in the market. This they can only do at the expense of moving perhaps to an urban area where cheaper and smaller housing may be available away from their roots and when old age makes such a move particularly difficult.

The combination of older households with lower incomes and deeper roots has been shown (Chapter 9) to result in a low likelihood of household movement despite the incentive of better housing conditions. Indeed, the existence of a strong differentiation in respect of housing between the two groups of movers and stayers – older, low-income households tending to form part of the latter group – emerged as one of the principal links between housing and household movement. Neither group, of course, was homogeneous: the stayers included both low-income households renting privately and established professionals in owner-occupied commuter houses, while movers included households whose stay in mobile homes was very temporary and also spiralist households whose concern was to improve further their housing status. The common thread, however, was more psychological than related to house condition or other physical factors since movers were less satisfied with housing which was already of a higher overall standard than that occupied by stayers, and consequently were far more likely to move again to achieve still greater improvement.

During the twentieth century, and more particularly since the Second World War, the relative importance of the rural owner-occupier has increased substantially. At the same time there has been a notable improvement in the condition of rural housing in England. But the tenant groups remain and their relative position has worsened essentially because the advantages of rural housing as wealth and as status have accrued only to the owner. Tenants have become a residual minority and the gulf between them and house-owners has increased as rural wages have declined relative to urban and professional salaries and as house prices have spiralled ever upward. All groups have found themselves increasingly in an environment of competition for rural houses, but only for some has there been also a substantial element of housing choice.

THE RECORD OF POLICY

Housing policy, it has been argued, is only one strand in the complex web of state intervention which surrounds housing in the countryside. Town and country planning policies make up an element of at least equal weighting and there are other elements which should be considered, notably a postwar agricultural policy which has successfully boosted farmers' incomes and maintained their privileged position in the countryside.

Judged in the context of the owner/tenant dichotomy, government policy which has influenced rural housing often appears unhelpful and misguided. With the probable exception of housing conditions, the position of the rural tenant has been little advanced by housing and planning legislation. The only piece of postwar legislation which has been addressed specifically to the rural tenant, the Rent (Agriculture) Act 1976, has done relatively little to improve the real lot of the tied cottager. The security offered simply elevated him to the status of other protected tenants and did nothing to remove the dependency which characterises the link between job and house. Land-use planning policy has in general been negative in its approach to rural housing problems, whatever its other merits. In the first place it has concerned itself largely with matters of physical form and thus remains very much a blunt instrument in its effect upon social policy in housing. The limitations of the system were highlighted in Chapters 10 and 11 with specific regard to structure planning. The system can be credited in part with a general improvement in the physical fabric of the built countryside but the improvement has done little to solve the essential problems of housing access in rural areas.

The central tenet of postwar planning has been urban containment and in this it has been remarkably successful. Whether through strict development control, especially in the open countryside, through the designation of conservation areas, the listing of buildings and the control of building materials, or through the restriction of permitted development to key villages, planners have forestalled the growth of the urban countryside with commendable success. The benefits have been measured in terms of farmland saved and vernacular architecture preserved. The price has been all but forgotten, and it has been paid by those rural dwellers who have been outpaced by the restriction of supply. Rural housing has been controlled as a matter of land-use policy and those who cannot keep pace have been given the artificial choice of either accepting second-best in the form of the rented house or moving to the towns.

The record of housing, as opposed to planning, policy has in its own way been equally negative, particularly with regard to the rural tenant. The catalogue of housing policy noted in Chapters 10 and 11 emphasises the relative impoverishment of housing opportunity which misguided policy has provoked. Successive Rent Acts have reduced the pool of private tenancies outside agriculture to the point where those remaining are either the province of the rich or, in the less accessible countryside, the very poor who have been forced into often substandard accommodation. The decline in the private tenancy has inevitably put greater pressure upon housing let by the local authority. Yet here, too, the record is poor. Chapter 3 showed how there have always been far fewer council houses in rural areas than in the towns, and the building record of rural local authorities continues at a low level. An unwillingness in the past to spend money on public housing has been compounded in more recent years by inflation and the high costs of construction, and the low level of finance available from central government. Allocations for housing construction and improvement made under the Housing Investment Programmes since 1977 have consistently told against rural areas.

The growing importance of the limited pool of rural council housing brings into sharp relief the policy enshrined in the Housing Act 1980 to encourage the sale by local authorities of council houses to sitting tenants. From the viewpoint of the rural worker, the council house is often his only hope of remaining in the countryside, given the level of rural wages in relation to rural house prices. From the viewpoint of the local housing authority, the council house is the main tool with which it can carry out its responsibilities to ensure the reasonable housing of the population it serves. If within a decade substantial numbers of rural council houses have disappeared, then the tied house will remain as the only major exception to a general rule of owner-occupation. The English countryside will, with the exception of the tied housing needed for the agricultural industry, have become a prime example of a property-owning democracy. The result may appeal to some, but the cost will have been borne by the sons and daughters of rural workers who have been forced to the town.

Faced with the destructive influence of legislation upon the rented housing sector, the attempts by some local housing authorities to protect local people from unequal competition seem inadequate and even misguided. The suggestions made in some structure plans that local need should be specifically favoured have been followed up by active policies in several counties. The policies have generally attempted a definition of 'local' which relates to employment or, even more tenuously, to local connections, and the mechanism has generally been restrictions on the occupation of new houses under section 52 of the Town and Country Planning Act 1971.

The difficulties and drawbacks with such policies are obvious. They refer only to new housing which is in any case limited by development plan and development control policies. The attempted definitions of 'local' are often artificial in the extreme and, even if they could be enforced, are of uncertain strength in the long term. Even if new housing is thus limited there is no assurance at all that local people can afford it, whatever their eligibility.

Behind this well-meaning attempt to grapple with recognised housing problems in rural areas, there is a basic miscalculation of the real nature of rural housing deprivation. Housing need and the restriction of housing choice are often the lot of the local rural dweller, but they are not simply a function of his rural connections. There is a danger that because policies are defined in the context of local people the real reasons behind housing deprivation – poor wages, low status and poor bargaining power – will be forgotten. Indeed there is a further danger that, when some people in rural areas are elevated to a special status for housing allocation simply on a questionable definition of local need, others with equal housing need will effectively be demoted. Roots, and rural roots in particular, may well be a highly prized commodity in a materialistic and transitory society. Such roots, however, are as much positional goods as are the rural houses of the middle-class elite and, as such, they make a poor foundation for social policy.

SOME POLICY OPTIONS

This generally depressing picture of past policy is slightly relieved by genuine attempts on the part of some rural housing authorities to develop humane and workable policies and to experiment with new ideas and policy options. Indeed in its own way the strong opposition, often from Conservative councils, to government proposals in 1979/80 to sell rural council houses is an indication of a willingness to provide solutions.

The record of rural housing authorities with regard to rural housing initiatives is, however, generally poor and patchy. The much-valued 'third arm' of housing policy, the housing association, has had relatively little success in rural areas. The small size of rural schemes has made them less than attractive to the Housing Corporation and there have been inevitable problems of under-capitalisation. None the less there have been sufficient successes for this option to remain viable. While in general, as Chapter 10 showed, housing associations have tended to respond to special needs (such as retired farmworkers) rather than general needs, initiatives such as that of the Development Commission and the Housing Corporation in trying to link housing with new industrial investment in rural areas are to be welcomed. Although the success rate has so far been disappointing, schemes in Devon, Shropshire and Cumbria have already shown the relevance of this important linking of rural development and rural housing.

While there are certainly problems for housing associations in rural areas, they are probably not much greater than many of those already faced by small rural authorities. Given sufficient government encouragement and funding, the potential of housing associations and similar options such as co-ownership and equity sharing schemes is probably substantial. In effect the schemes use government support to help bridge the gap between the lower-income household and the private mortgage barrier which is naturally weighted towards the rising price of rural houses. Two further ways in which this gap might be bridged are by special allocation policies for mortgage finance by building societies and council building or purchase for sale.

Links between building societies and local authorities have been encouraged in recent years and the local authority now has the right to nominate people for mortgage funds from a separate pool. In practice it has been the urban areas which have tended to benefit most but there is no reason why the system could not be more successful in rural areas.

Building for sale could equally be more effectively employed, providing that sufficient finance was made available. Schemes such as those which have operated in Suffolk, Cornwall and Northumberland whereby council tenants and those on the waiting list are able to buy new houses from the local authority at a reasonable price while the council retains a right to repurchase within, say, five years, provide an obvious example. Where new-build schemes are unlikely because of the constraints of planning and sewerage and water restrictions, purchase by the local authority of houses in private ownership is a further possible solution, whether for further sale to existing council tenants or to add to the stock of council housing for letting. Indeed the mismatch between the size of housing and many private (often elderly) households which this study has indicated, suggests that this course of action would be particularly fruitful, given the availability of public funds.

Local authority activity in the rental market has not been restricted to council housing. A scheme pioneered in North Wiltshire (Shelburne, 1976, 1978) attempted to circumvent the restrictions of the Rent Acts with regard to tenant security. In this case the local housing authority, which was not subject to the same restrictions as a private landlord, was able to sublet property, often on a short-term basis, which it had leased from private owners. Property which might otherwise have lain vacant was thus made available to tenants, while owners were able to reclaim their property should they need to with more certainty than if they had agreed a private tenancy.

Many of these options involve an attempt to secure for those with limited resources an element of the capital appreciation which is so attractive for the owner-occupier. However earnestly such options are followed in the future (and the recent past has seen relatively little movement due largely to controls on public spending), there will remain for a long time an element of the rural population which cannot be reached by such schemes. Even if owner-occupation were to become possible for many more rural people now, many of their children would find themselves in the same position as their parents a generation later. Caught between the upper millstone of spiralling housing prices and a limited housing stock and the nether millstone of low rural wages, they have recourse only to rented housing. In an ideal world it might be considered desirable that everyone would own their house and no one would own another's but that ideal is far in the future. In the meantime the demise of the rented rural house, whether by legislation which frightens landlords into sales or by selling off the local authority housing stock, can only serve to harm those elements in rural society who are least able to help themselves.

The privately rented housing stock has now been decimated and that which remains still exhibits aspects of patronage and poor standards. The future, then, for those groups for whom ownership remains but a dream lies only with the rural council house. The allocation policies of some local authorities may justly be criticised: there has been far too little investment in rural council housing, particularly in the recent past, and council estates may well often be characterless and barren in their appearance. Yet despite these criticisms, the stock of housing built by rural local authorities ever since the Addison Act of 1919 has made a massive contribution to rural social welfare and rural economic well-being. Moreover the evidence of this study clearly confirms the extent to which this contribution has been fully appreciated by rural people. For some it has meant a first step towards a dream of owner-occupation. For others, where ownership remains impossible or is not regarded as a desirable goal, it continues as a popular and much-needed resource and a worthy investment of public money over the years. If society wishes to continue that investment in the interests of agriculture and other rural industries and more especially in the interests of a commitment to housing welfare for rural as well as urban people, then it must safeguard the future of the rural council house rather than put it in jeopardy.

RURAL HOUSING IN A POST-INDUSTRIAL SOCIETY

This chapter started with an examination of the three roles of rural housing – as house, as wealth and as status – and the ensuing discussion has emphasised the results of the different objectives which flow from each of these roles. All that has been said has stressed the unequal contest between those groups which can easily view housing in all three roles and those households which must concentrate upon the first alone.

Developments in society are likely to exacerbate the conflicts between these differing views. In the shorter term the issues of economic recession and energy crises are likely to dominate the scene. Here it is certain that the groups in the countryside which have already proved their material success will continue to gain relative to those who have lost out in the past. Escalating prices and shortages of fuel will certainly restrict the easy accessibility to the countryside which has characterised the postwar years, but the more damaging effects will be felt by the low-paid rural worker and the private tenant in the isolated hamlet rather than by the commuting professional man.

One possible future, particularly if energy problems continue well into the twenty-first century, is of a repopulated countryside where both society and economy have taken on an essentially local orientation. Some people have argued for a programme of resettlement as an attractive and viable future when energy shortages have enforced a change away from large-scale commuting and a petrol-based agriculture. For many people this represents a more environmentally satisfying approach to rural society.

A second possible future postulates not a retreat to the countryside in the face of material shortages, but rather a post-industrial invasion on the strength of a micro-electronic revolution. The advantages which this technological revolution will bring have been well advertised. A massive decline in the need for direct manual labour coupled with the ability to control industrial, administrative and creative processes from afar will, it is argued, break for ever the restrictions implicit in the link between home and workplace. In their more futuristic scenarios, advocates of these advantages stress the enhanced role of the countryside in the lifestyles of post-industrial man. Remoteness will no longer be a handicap to be overcome by costly transport systems, the long rural weekend of the favoured few will have become the permanent abode of the masses in a pastoral idyll every bit as exaggerated as the romantic views of the historic countryside which some present writers have.

There seems little doubt that a combination of these various pastoral idylls will come about – indeed for some they have already arrived. It is equally conceivable that the numbers for whom such a future becomes a happy reality will increase substantially. Yet it is even more certain that this progress will leave behind many who will not benefit. The haves will increase, but the plight of the have-nots will appear all the more parlous. Those who doubt this result and who see nothing but advantage in new revolutions, whether technical or ecological, should remember that the English countryside has seen many such revolutions before. The agricultural revolutions of the last two hundred years and the transport revolution of the twentieth century are two obvious examples. Whatever their other characteristics, they both had one thing in common: along with their successes and their advantages they brought their social refugees, those who lost out to the new advances and whom history passed by. A cardinal feature of the social limits to growth is the fact that those who are in the vanguard of social change gain most and those who come late gain least. In the realm of rural housing this study has shown that the pecking order has already been clearly drawn. It is the essential role of social policy to ensure that those who come late are at least assured of a reasonable deal.

References

ABEL-SMITH, B., and TOWNSEND, P. (1965), *The Poor and the Poorest* (London: Bell).

AMBROSE, P. (1974), *The Quiet Revolution* (London: Chatto & Windus).

ARONSON, H. (1913), *Our Village Homes: Present Conditions and Suggested Remedies* (London: Munby).

ARTHUR RANK CENTRE (1976), *Housing the Retired Rural Worker* (Kenilworth: Arthur Rank Centre).

ASSOCIATION OF COUNTY COUNCILS (1979), *Rural Deprivation* (London: Association of County Councils).

ASSOCIATION OF DISTRICT COUNCILS (1978), *Rural Recovery: Strategy for Survival* (London: Association of District Councils).

BANKS, S. (1978), private communication, University of Reading, Reading.

BATES, M., and CUDMORE, B. V. (1975), *Country Planning: A Restudy* (Oxford: Institute of Agricultural Economics, University of Oxford).

BENNETT, S. (1976), *Rural Housing in the Lake District* (Lancaster: University of Lancaster).

BERESFORD, M. W. (1954), *The Lost Villages of England* (Guildford, Surrey: Lutterworth Press).

BEST, R. H. (1976), 'The extent and growth of urban land', *The Planner*, vol. 62, no. 1, pp. 8–11.

BIELCKUS, C. L., ROGERS, A. W., and WIBBERLEY, G. P. (1972), *Second Homes in England and Wales*, Studies in Rural Land Use No. 11 (Wye: Wye College).

BINDER, B. (1978), 'The importance of political decisions', *Local Government Chronicle*, no. 5809, pp. 872–4.

BLACKSELL, A. M. Y., and GILG, A. W. (1977), 'Planning control in an area of outstanding natural beauty', *Social and Economic Administration*, vol. 11, pp. 206–15.

BLOWERS, A. (1972), 'The declining villages of County Durham', in *New Trends in Geography, IV: Social Geography* (Milton Keynes: Open University).

BLUMEN, I., KOGAN, M., and MCCARTHY, P. J. (1955), *The Industrial Mobility of Labour as a Probability Process* (Ithaca, New York: Cornell University Press).

BRACEY, H. E. (1952), *Social Provision in Rural Wiltshire* (London: Methuen).

BRETT, L. (1965), *Landscape in Distress* (London: Architectural Press).

BUCKLER, P. (1978), 'Rural housing today and tomorrow', unpublished paper presented to Farmers' Club Seminar, London.

BYRNE, P., and MACKMIN, D. H. (1974 *et seq.*) *The Residential Market in Oxfordshire and Parts of Berkshire and Buckinghamshire* (Reading: Department of Applied Land Management, University of Reading).

CAIRD, J. B. (1972), 'Population problems of the Islands of Scotland with special reference to the Uists', unpublished paper presented to Institute of British Geographers' Annual Conference, Aberdeen.

CENTRAL HOUSING ADVISORY COMMITTEE (1944), *Rural Housing: 3rd Report* (London: HMSO).

CHERRY, G. E. (ed.) (1976), *Rural Planning Problems* (London: Leonard Hill).

CHESHIRE COUNTY COUNCIL (1977), *County Structure Plan: Written Statement* (Chester: County Planning Department).

CHILDS, G., and MINAY, C. (1977), *The North Pennines Rural Development Board: A Rural Development Agency in Theory and Practice* (Oxford: Oxford Polytechnic).

CLARK, D. (1980), *Rural Housing in East Hampshire* (London: National Council of Social Service).

CLOKE, P. J. (1977), 'An index of rurality for England and Wales', *Regional Studies*, vol. 11, no. 1, pp. 31–46.

CLOKE, P. J. (1979), *Key Settlements in Rural Areas* (London: Methuen).

CONNELL, J. (1974), 'The metropolitan village: spatial and social processes in discontinuous suburbs', in J. Johnson (ed.), *Suburban Growth* (London: Wiley), pp. 77–100.

CONNELL, J. (1978), *The End of Tradition – Country Life in Central Surrey* (London: Routledge & Kegan Paul).

CONSTANDSE, A. K. (1962), 'Planning in agricultural regions', *Sociologia Ruralis*, vol. 11, pp. 79–104.

COUNTRY LANDOWNERS' ASSOCIATION (1976), 'Views of the Country Landowners' Association on the government consultative document – the abolition of the tied cottage system in agriculture', *Housing Monthly* (Feb./Mar.), pp. 27–9.

COUNTRYSIDE REVIEW COMMITTEE (1976), *The Countryside – Problems and Policies: A Discussion Paper* (London: HMSO).

COUNTRYSIDE REVIEW COMMITTEE (1977), *Rural Communities: Discussion Paper No. 2* (London: HMSO).

COWIE, W., and GILES, A. (1957), 'An enquiry into the reasons for the "drift from the land"', *Selected Papers in Agricultural Economics*, vol. 5, pp. 70–113.

CRICHTON, R. (1964), *Commuters' Village: A Study of Community and Commuting in a Berkshire Village* (London: Macmillan).

CROFTON, R., and WEBSTER, D. (1974), 'Improving housing allocation', *The Planner*, vol. 60, no. 8, pp. 839–42.

CROTHERS, R. J. (1970), 'Factors related to the community index of satisfactoriness', *Ekistics*, vol. 30, no. 177, pp. 107–9.

CULLINGWORTH, J. B. (1968), *A Profile of Glasgow Housing, 1965*, University of Glasgow Social and Economic Studies Occasional Papers, No. 8 (Edinburgh: Oliver & Boyd).

Daily Telegraph (1979), 'The village school', *Daily Telegraph* (9 July).

DARLEY, G. (1978), 'Rural settlement – rural resettlement: the future', *Built Environment Quarterly*, vol. 4, no. 4, pp. 299–310.

DAVIDSON, J., and WIBBERLEY, G. P. (1977), *Planning and the Rural Environment* (Oxford: Pergamon).

DEPARTMENT OF ECONOMIC AFFAIRS (1965), *The West Midlands: A Regional Study* (London: HMSO).

DEPARTMENT OF THE ENVIRONMENT (1973), *Development for Agricultural Purposes*, Circular 24/73 (London: HMSO).

DEPARTMENT OF THE ENVIRONMENT (1974), *Structure Plans*, Circular 98/74 (London: HMSO).

DEPARTMENT OF THE ENVIRONMENT (1977), *Mobile Homes in England and Wales, 1975* (London: HMSO).

DEPARTMENT OF THE ENVIRONMENT (1978), *English House Condition Survey, 1976: Part 1, Report of the Physical Condition Survey* (London: HMSO).

DEPARTMENT OF THE ENVIRONMENT (1979a), *National Dwelling and Housing Survey* (London: HMSO).

DEPARTMENT OF THE ENVIRONMENT (1979b), *Memorandum on Structure and Local Plans*, Circular 4/79 (London: HMSO).

DEROUNIAN, J. (1979), *Structure Plans and Rural Communities* (London: National Council of Social Service).

DICKINSON, G. C. (1958), 'The nature of rural population movement – an analysis of seven Yorkshire parishes based on electoral returns from 1931–1954', *Yorkshire Bulletin of Economic and Social Research*, vol. 10, pp. 95–108.

DOLING, J. (1976), 'The family life cycle and housing choice', *Urban Studies*, vol. 13, pp. 55–8.

DONNISON, D. V. (1967), *The Government of Housing* (Harmondsworth: Penguin).

DOWNING, P., and DOWER, M. (1973), *Second Homes in England and Wales* (London: HMSO).

DRUDY, P. J. (1978), 'Depopulation in a prosperous agricultural subregion', *Regional Studies*, vol. 12, pp. 49–60.

DUERDOTH, N. (1980), statement made in a paper at a rural housing seminar, National Council of Social Service.

DUNN, M. C. (1973), 'Patterns of population movement in Herefordshire: implications for rural planning', paper presented to Institute of British Geographers' Annual Conference, Birmingham.

DUNN, M. C. (1979), 'Patterns of population change and movement in Herefordshire 1951–71 and their implications for rural planning', unpublished PhD thesis, University of Birmingham, Birmingham.

DUNN, M. C., RAWSON, M. J. C., and ROGERS, A. W. (1980a), 'Housing and population movement in English rural areas', unpublished report to the Social Science Research Council.

DUNN, M. C., RAWSON, M. J. C., and ROGERS, A. W. (1980b), *The Derivation of Rural Housing Profiles*, Centre for Urban and Regional Studies, Research Memorandum No. 76 (Birmingham: University of Birmingham).

EDWARDS, J. A. (1971), 'The viability of lower-order settlements in rural areas: the case of north-east England', *Sociologia Ruralis*, vol. 11, pp. 247–76.

EDWARDS, J. A. (1973), 'Rural migration in England and Wales: an appraisal of major sources of information', *The Planner*, vol. 59, pp. 450–3.

EDWARDS, S. L., and PENDER, M. (1976), 'Indicators of local prosperity data bank', *Statistical News*, no. 32, pp. 3–7.

EMERY, F. (1974), *The Oxfordshire Landscape* (London: Hodder & Stoughton).

FLETCHER, P. (1969), 'The control of housing standards in a rural district: a case study', *Social and Economic Administration*, vol. 3, no. 2, pp. 106–20.

FORESTER, T. (1976), 'A Cotswold ghost', *New Society*, vol. 38, no. 740, p. 501.

FRANKENBERG, R. (1966), *Communities in Britain* (Harmondsworth: Penguin).

FREEMAN FOX & ASSOCIATES (1976), *Gloucestershire: A Survey of Public Attitudes* (London: Freeman Fox).

GASKIN, M. (1971), *Freight Rates and Prices in the Islands* (Inverness: Highlands and Islands Development Board).

GASSON, R. (1975), *Provision of Tied Cottages*, Department of Land Economy, Occasional Paper No. 4 (Cambridge: University of Cambridge).

GILDER, I. M. (1979), 'Rural planning policies: an economic appraisal', *Progress in Planning*, vol. 11, pt 3, pp. 213–71.

GILG, A. W. (1978), *Countryside Planning: The First Three Decades 1945–1976* (Newton Abbot: David & Charles).

GLOUCESTERSHIRE COUNTY COUNCIL (1978), *The Draft Structure Plan for Gloucestershire* (Cheltenham: Gloucestershire County Council).

GOLANT, S. M. (1972), *The Residential Location and Spatial Behaviour of the Elderly*, Research Paper 143 (Chicago: Department of Geography, University of Chicago).

GORDON, L, and WHITTAKER, R. M. (1972), 'Indicators of local prosperity in the South West Region', *Regional Studies*, vol. 6, pp. 299–313.

GREEN, R. J. (1971), *Country Planning: The Future of the Rural Regions* (Manchester: University of Manchester Press).

GREEN, R. J. and AYTON, J. (1967), 'Changes in the pattern of rural settlement', in *Planning for the Changing Countryside*, proceedings of a Town Planning Institute Conference (London: Town Planning Institute).

GREGORY, D. (1972), *Green Belts and Development Control*, Centre for Urban and Regional Studies, Occasional Paper No. 12 (Birmingham: University of Birmingham).

GRIEVE, R. (1972), 'Problems and objectives of the Highlands and Islands', in J. Ashton and W. H. Long (eds), *The Remoter Rural Areas of Britain* (Edinburgh: Oliver & Boyd), pp. 130–45.

Guardian (1976), 'The cesspits', *Guardian* (28 April).

GWYNEDD COUNTY COUNCIL (1978), *Second Homes in Gwynedd*, Monitoring Working Paper 2 (Caernarfon: County Planning Department).

HADDON, R. F. (1970), 'A minority in a welfare state society: the location of West Indians in the London housing market', *New Atlantis*, vol. 2, pp. 80–133.

HAKIM, C. (1976), *Census-Derived Indicators for Small Areas*, Office of Population Censuses and Surveys (London: HMSO).

HALL, P., THOMAS, R., GRACEY, H., and DREWETT, R. (1973), *The Containment of Urban England* (London: Allen & Unwin).

HARVEY, G. (1978), 'Tied cottages and the law', *Farmers' Weekly*, vol. 89, no. 26, pp. 44–7.

HAVINDEN, M. A. (1966), *Estate Villages* (London: Lund Humphries).

HEREFORD AND WORCESTER COUNTY COUNCIL (1978), *Rural Community Development Project* (Worcester: Hereford and Worcester County Council).

HEREFORDSHIRE COUNTY COUNCIL (1969), *Application to the Board of Trade for the Area Comprised in the Administrative County to be Specified as a Development Area* (Hereford: Herefordshire County Council).

HEREFORDSHIRE COUNTY COUNCIL (1973), *County Structure Plan Water Study Report* (Hereford: County Planning Department).

HERTFORDSHIRE COUNTY COUNCIL (1976), *Hertfordshire County Structure Plan*

Written Statement (Hertford: Hertfordshire County Council).

HIGHLANDS AND ISLANDS DEVELOPMENT BOARD (1974), *Rural Housing in the Highlands and Islands*, Occasional Bulletin 5 (Inverness: HIDB).

HIRSCH, F. (1977), *Social Limits to Growth* (London: Routledge & Kegan Paul).

HM TREASURY (1976), *Rural Depopulation: Report of an Inter-Departmental Working Group* (London: HM Treasury).

HOSKINS, W. G. (1955), *The Making of the English Landscape* (London: Hodder & Stoughton).

HOUSE, J. W. (1965), *Rural North-East England, 1951–61* (Newcastle: University of Newcastle upon Tyne).

HOUSE, J. W., and KNIGHT, E. M. (1965), *Migrants of North-East England, 1951–1961: Character, Age and Sex* (Newcastle: University of Newcastle upon Tyne).

HOWARD, E. (1902), *Garden Cities of Tomorrow* (London: Faber; reprinted 1946).

IRVING, B. L., and HILGENDORF, E. L. (1975), *Tied Cottages in British Agriculture* (London: Tavistock Institute for Human Relations).

JACKSON, V. J. (1968), *Population in the Countryside: Growth and Stagnation in the Cotswolds* (Birmingham: West Midlands Social and Political Research Unit, University of Birmingham).

JACOBS, C. A. (1974), *Rural Housing in Denbighshire* (Wrexham: Denbighshire County Council).

JENNINGS, P. (1968), *The Living Village: A Picture of Rural Life Drawn from Village Scrapbooks* (London: Hodder & Stoughton).

JOHNSTON, R. J. (1966), 'Components of rural population change', *Town Planning Review*, vol. 36, pp. 279–94.

JOHNSTON, R. J. (1967), 'A reconnaissance study of population change in Nidderdale, 1951–61', *Transactions of the Institute of British Geographers*, vol. 41, pp. 113–23.

JOINT OXFORDSHIRE COUNTY AND DISTRICTS GENERAL COMMITTEE (1975), *Housing in Oxfordshire* (Oxford: Oxfordshire County Council).

JONES, C., GUDJONSSON, S., and PARRY LEWIS, J. (1976), *Movers and Non-Movers: A Study Commissioned by the DoE into Household Mobility* (Manchester: Centre for Urban and Regional Research, University of Manchester).

JONES, H. R. (1965), 'Rural migration in central Wales', *Transactions of the Institute of British Geographers*, vol. 37, pp. 31–45.

JONES, I. (1976), 'Planning and the parishes – 4. Asset or liability?' *Local Government Chronicle*, no. 5690, pp. 358–9.

KARN, V. A. (1977), *Retiring to the Seaside* (London: Routledge & Kegan Paul).

KNOX, P. L. (1978), 'Territorial social indicators and area profiles – some cautionary observations', *Town Planning Review*, vol. 49, no. 1, pp. 75–83.

LARKIN, A. (1978a), 'Ghettos of rural poverty', *New Society*, vol. 44, no. 815, pp. 362–4.

LARKIN, A. (1978b), 'Rural Housing – too dear, too few and too far', *Roof*, vol. 3, no. 1, pp. 15–17.

LARKIN, A. (1978c), 'Second homes – their position in rural housing provision', in M. Talbot and R. W. Vickerman (eds), *Social and Economic Costs and Benefits of Leisure* (Leisure Studies Association).

LAW, C. M., and WARNES, A. M. (1976), 'The changing geography of the elderly in England and Wales', *Transactions of the Institute of British Geographers*, n.s. vol. 1, no. 4, pp. 453–71.

LEATHER, P. (1979), 'HIPs – room for improvement', *Housing and Planning Review*, vol. 35, no. 1, pp. 5–7.

LEE, T. (1960), 'A test of the hypothesis that school reorganisation is a cause of rural depopulation', *Durham Research Review*, vol. 3, pp. 64–73.

LEICESTER SHELTER GROUP (1976), *Housing Allocation Policies in Leicestershire* (Leicester: Leicester Shelter Group).

LEICESTERSHIRE COUNTY COUNCIL (1976), *Coleorton District Plan* (Leicester: The County Council).

LEWIS, G. J. (1967), 'Commuting and the village in mid-Wales: a study in social geography', *Geography*, vol. 52, pp. 294–304.

LITTLEJOHN, J. (1964), *Westrigg: The Sociology of a Cheviot Parish* (London: Routledge & Kegan Paul).

LONG, J. R. (ed.) (1962), *The Wythall Enquiry: A Planning Test Case* (London: Estates Gazette Press).

MARSHALL, J. L. (1968), 'The pattern of house-building in the inter-war period in England and Wales', *Scottish Journal of Political Economy*, vol. 15, no. 2, pp. 184–205.

MARTIN, W. T. (1957), 'Ecological change in satellite rural areas', *American Sociological Review*, vol. 22, pp. 175–85.

MARTIN, I. (1976), 'Rural communities', in G. Cherry (ed.), *Rural Planning Problems* (London: Leonard Hill), pp. 49–84.

MASS OBSERVATION (1966), *Village Life in Hampshire* (Winchester: Hampshire County Council).

MASTERMAN, C. F. G. (1909), *The Condition of England* (London: Methuen).

MELLOR, B. (1966), 'Cambridgeshire: a rural planning policy and its implementation', *Official Architecture and Planning*, vol. 29, pp. 1126–41.

MERSEYSIDE COUNTY COUNCIL (1979), *Merseyside Structure Plan: Draft Written Statement* (Liverpool: County Planning Department).

MID-WALES INDUSTRIAL DEVELOPMENT ASSOCIATION (1973), *Sixteenth and Final Annual Report* (Newtown: Mid-Wales Industrial Development Association).

MILLER, T. (1973), 'Military airfields and rural planning', *Town Planning Review*, vol. 44, no. 1, pp. 31–48.

MILNER-HOLLAND (1965), *Report of the Committee on Housing in Greater London* (London: HMSO).

MINISTRY OF HOUSING AND LOCAL GOVERNMENT (1967), *Housing Standards, Costs and Subsidies*, Circular 36/67 (London: HMSO).

MINISTRY OF HOUSING AND LOCAL GOVERNMENT (1969), *Development in Rural Areas*, Development Control Policy Note 4 (London: HMSO).

MORRIS, R. N., and MOGEY, J. (1965), *The Sociology of Housing* (London: Routledge & Kegan Paul).

MOSELEY, M. J. (1971), 'The use of factor analysis in the identification of "growth centres" in East Anglia', *Reading Geographer*, vol. 2, pp. 50–8.

MOSELEY, M. J. (1978), *Social Issues in Rural Norfolk* (Norwich: Centre of East Anglian Studies).

MOSELEY, M. J. (1979), *Accessibility: The Rural Challenge* (London: Methuen).

MOSS, L., and PARKER, S. (1967), *The Local Government Councillor* (London: HMSO).

MURIE, A., NINER, P., and WATSON, C. (1976), *Housing Policy and the Housing System* (London: Allen & Unwin).

MUSGROVE, F. (1963), *The Migratory Elite* (London: Heinemann).

MYRDAL, G. (1957), *Economic Theory and Underdeveloped Regions* (London: Duckworth).

NATIONAL FARMERS' UNION (1975), *Service Houses* (London: National Farmers' Union).

NATIONWIDE BUILDING SOCIETY (1970), *Why Do People Move?*, Occasional Bulletin 99 (London: Nationwide Building Society).

NEEDLEMAN, L. (1965), *The Economics of Housing* (London: Staples).

NEWBY, H. (1977), *The Deferential Worker* (Harmondsworth: Penguin).

NEWBY, H. (1979), *Green and Pleasant Land?* (London: Hutchinson).

NEWBY, H., BELL, C., ROSE, D., and SAUNDERS, P. (1978), *Property, Paternalism and Power* (London: Hutchinson).

NEWMAN, J. (1964), *Limerick Rural Survey, 1958–1964* (Tipperary: Muintir Na Tire).

NICHOLSON, R. J., TOPHAM, N., and WATT, P. A. (1975), 'Housing investment by different types of local authority', *Bulletin of Economic Research*, vol. 27, pp. 65–86.

NINER, P. (1975), *Local Authority Housing Policy and Practice: A Case Study Approach*, Centre for Urban and Regional Studies, Occasional Paper No. 31 (Birmingham: University of Birmingham).

NORFOLK COUNTY COUNCIL (1975), *North Walsham Area Study* (Norwich: Norfolk County Planning Department).

NOTTINGHAMSHIRE COUNTY COUNCIL (1978), *County Structure Plan Written Statement* (Nottingham: County Planning Department).

ODD, N. (1976), 'Current aspects of rural planning', *Built Environment Quarterly*, vol. 2, no. 2, pp. 167–9.

O'DONOVAN, P. (1977), 'Mystery of the dying village and the silent squire', *Observer* (30 January), p. 11.

OFFICE OF POPULATION CENSUSES AND SURVEYS (1973), *1971 Census Small Area Statistics Explanatory Note* (London: HMSO).

OPENSHAW, S., and CULLINGFORD, D. (1979), 'Some comments on methods available for measuring rural deprivation', unpublished paper to Royal Town Planning Institute/Regional Studies Association Conference on Rural Deprivation, Anglian Regional Management Centre.

O'RIAGAIN, P. (1972), 'Planning in the Irish Republic: 1. Rural planning', *Journal of the Royal Town Planning Institute*, vol. 58, pp. 443–9.

OXFORD AGRICULTURAL ECONOMICS RESEARCH INSTITUTE (1944), *Country Planning: A Study of Rural Problems* (London: OUP).

OXFORDSHIRE COUNTY COUNCIL (1976), *First Structure Plan for Oxfordshire* (Oxford: Oxfordshire County Council).

OXFORDSHIRE JOINT DISTRICT HOUSING GROUP (1975–8), *Oxfordshire Housing Statistics* (Oxford, annual).

PAHL, R. E. (1965), *Urbs in Rure: The Metropolitan Fringe in Hertfordshire*, Geographical Papers, No. 2 (London: London School of Economics).

PAHL, R. E. (1966), 'The social objectives of village planning', *Official Architecture and Planning*, vol. 29, no. 8, pp. 1146–50.

PAHL, R. E. (1975), 'Urban processes and social structure', ch. 12 of *Whose City?* (Harmondsworth: Penguin).

PARIS, C. (1979), 'HIPs and housing need – the Oxford experience', *CES Review*, no. 5, pp. 19–27.

PARK, R. E., BURGESS, E. W., and MCKENZIE, R. D. (1925), *The City* (Chicago: University of Chicago Press).

PENFOLD, S. F. (1974), *Housing Problems of Local People in Rural Pressure Areas: The Peak District Experience and Discussion of Policy Options* (Sheffield: Department of Town and Regional Planning, University of Sheffield).

PLANNING ADVISORY GROUP (1965), *The Future of Development Plans* (London: HMSO).

RADFORD, C. (1970), *The New Villagers: Urban Pressure on Rural Areas in Worcestershire* (London: Frank Cass).

RAVENSTEIN, E. G. (1885), 'The laws of migration', *Journal of the Royal Statistical Society*, vol. 48, pp. 167–235.

RAWSON, M. J. C. (1978a), *Rural Housing and Population in Cotswold District: A Statistical Appraisal from Census Data*, Working Paper No. 5 (Wye: Wye College, University of London).

RAWSON, M. J. C. (1978b), *Rural Housing and Population in South Oxfordshire District: A Statistical Appraisal from Census Data*, Working Paper No. 6 (Wye: Wye College, University of London).

RAWSON, M. J. C., and ROGERS, A. W. (1976), *Rural Housing and Structure Plans*, Working Paper No. 1 (Wye: Wye College, University of London).

REES, T. L. (1978), 'Population and industrial decline in the South Wales coalfield', *Regional Studies*, vol. 12, pp. 69–77.

REX, J., and MOORE, R. (1967), *Race, Community and Conflict* (London: OUP).

ROCCA, A. (1978), 'The kindness that killed Great Tew', *Observer Colour Magazine* (5 November), pp. 30–40.

ROSSI, H. (1977), *Shaw's Guide to the Rent (Agriculture) Act 1976* (London: Shaw).

ROWNTREE, B. S. (1901), *Poverty: A Study of Town Life* (London: Macmillan).

RUTTER, M. L., and MADGE, N. (1976), *Cycles of Disadvantage: A Review of Research* (London: Heinemann).

SAUNDERS, P. (1978), 'Domestic property and social class', *International Journal of Urban and Regional Research*, vol. 2, no. 2, pp. 233–51.

SAUNDERS, P. R. (1977), *Housing Tenure and Class Interests*, Urban and Regional Studies Working Paper 6 (Brighton: University of Sussex).

SCOTT REPORT (1942), *Report of the Committee on Land Utilisation in Rural Areas*, Cmnd 6378 (London: HMSO).

SHAW, J. M. (1976), 'Can we afford villages?' *Built Environment Quarterly*, vol. 2, no. 2, pp. 135–7.

SHAW, J. M. (ed.) (1979), *Rural Deprivation and Planning* (Norwich: Geo. Abstracts).

SHELBURNE, LORD (1976), 'The problems of the private landowner', in Arthur Rank Centre (1976).

SHELBURNE, LORD (1978), 'Rural Housing Today and Tomorrow', unpublished paper presented to Farmers' Club Seminar, London.

SHELTER (1974), *Tied Accommodation* (London: Shelter).

SHELTER (1980), *Survey of Second Homes* (London: Shelter).

SHORT, J. (1978), 'The regional distribution of public expenditure in Great Britain', *Regional Studies*, vol. 12, no. 5, pp. 499–510.

SHROPSHIRE COUNTY COUNCIL (1977), *Villages and the Countryside*, Structure Plan Discussion Paper No. 5 (Shrewsbury: Shropshire County Council).

SHROPSHIRE COUNTY COUNCIL (1978), *Salop County Structure Plan Written Statement*, (Shrewsbury: County Planning Department).

SIMMIE, J. M. (1972), *The Sociology of Internal Migration*, Working Paper No. 15 (London: Centre for Environmental Studies).

SIMPSON, R. (1977), 'For richer, for poorer', *New Society*, vol. 42, no. 788, pp. 299–301.

SOUTH WEST ECONOMIC PLANNING COUNCIL (1975), *A Survey of Second Homes in the South West* (London: HMSO).

STANDING CONFERENCE OF RURAL COMMUNITY COUNCILS (1978), *The Decline of Rural Services* (London: National Council of Social Service).

STANDING CONFERENCE OF RURAL COMMUNITY COUNCILS (1979), *Whose Countryside?* (London: National Council of Social Service).

STOCKFORD, D., and DORRELL, P. (1978), 'Social services provision in rural Norfolk', in M. J. Moseley (ed.), *Social Issues in Rural Norfolk* (Norwich: Centre of East Anglian Studies, University of East Anglia), pp. 59–76.

STONE, P. A. (1970), *Urban Development in Britain: Standards, Costs and Resources 1964–2004* (Cambridge: CUP).

SUFFOLK COUNTY COUNCIL (1976), *Rural Settlement*, Structure Plan Policy Paper 5 (Ipswich: County Planning Department).

THORBURN, A. (1971), *Planning Villages* (London: Estates Gazette Press).

THORNS, D. C. (1968), 'The changing system of rural social stratification', *Sociologia Ruralis*, vol. 8, pp. 161–78.

TOWNSEND, P. (1979), *Poverty in the United Kingdom* (Harmondsworth: Penguin).

WALKER, A. (ed.) (1978), *Rural Poverty: Poverty, Deprivation and Planning in Rural Areas* (London: Child Poverty Action Group).

WARFORD, J. (1969), *The South Atcham Scheme* (London: HMSO).

WEBBER, R. (1977a), *Cumbria Social Area Analysis*, Technical Paper 22 (London: Planning Research Advisory Group).

WEBBER, R. (1977b), 'Area typologies and local housing strategies: the Haringey example', *CES Review*, no. 2, pp. 104–8.

WEBBER, R., and CRAIG, J. (1976), 'Which local authorities are alike', *Population Trends*, no. 5, pp. 13–19.

WELSH OFFICE (1964), *Depopulation in Mid-Wales* (London and Cardiff: HMSO).

WEST MIDLAND REGIONAL STUDY TEAM (1971), *A Developing Strategy for the West Midlands* (Birmingham: West Midland Planning Authorities Conference).

WEST MIDLANDS ECONOMIC PLANNING COUNCIL (1970), *Note on the Western Counties* (Birmingham: West Midlands Economic Planning Council).

WHITE, J., and DUNN, M. C. (1975), *Countryside Recreation Planning: Problems and Prospects for the West Midlands*, Centre for Urban and Regional Studies, Occasional Paper No. 33 (Birmingham: University of Birmingham).

WILLIAMS, P. R. (1976), 'The role of institutions in the inner London housing market: the case of Islington', *Transactions of the Institute of British Geographers*, n.s. vol. 1, no. 1, pp. 72–82.

WILLIAMS, R. (1973), *The Country and the City* (London: Chatto & Windus).

WILLIAMS, W. M. (1956), *The Sociology of an English Village: Gosforth* (London: Routledge & Kegan Paul).

WISSINK, G. A. (1962), *American Cities in Perspective, with Special Reference to the Development of their Fringe Areas* (New York: Van Gorcum).

YOUNG, M., and WILLMOTT, P. (1973), *The Symmetrical Family: A Study of Work and Leisure in the London Region* (London: Routledge & Kegan Paul).

Appendix I

Interview survey – location of survey areas

Locations for the major interview survey were chosen from the enumeration districts which made up the rural housing profiles recognised by the cluster analysis (see Chapter 6). The table below gives the locations by parish in which interviews took place, together with the relevant housing profile and number of interviews conducted. The sample was chosen randomly from the 1977 Electoral Register, ensuring a representation of one-third as movers, judged as those households not found on the 1975 Electoral Register. In practice, of course, generally rather more than one-third representation was achieved owing to households which had moved between the compilation of the Register and the time of survey. The sampling procedure and the questionnaire were tested in a pilot survey in Kent.

Location	*Profile*	*No. of interviews*
South Oxfordshire District		
Marsh Baldon		
Lewknor	traditional rural	150
Pishill with Stonor		
Warborough		
Rotherfield Peppard	established professional	150
Stoke Row		
Berinsfield		
Long Wittenham	local authority housing	100
Chinnor		
Sonning Common	younger owner-occupiers	100
Benson	armed forces	50
Wheatley		
Marston	poor housing	100

Location	Profile	No. of interviews
Cotswold District		
Bourton on the Hill		
Shipton	agricultural	150
Hazleton		
Tetbury Upton		
Chipping Campden		
Evenlode	retirement	100
Oddington		
Aldsworth		
Sherborne	poor housing	100
Windrush		
Down Ampney		
Kempsford	local authority housing	100
Little Rissington	armed forces	50

Variables used in the national correlation, regression and cluster analyses

This appendix lists the variables used in Chapter 3 for the national correlation and regression analyses and for the cluster analysis in Chapter 4. The origin of most variables is the 1971 Population Census, but most of the data were obtained through the DoE Local Indicators Project.

Variable no.	*Variable description*
1	total number of private households
2	average number of persons per private household
3	percentage of population in households, aged 0–14 years
4	percentage of population of working age in private households (males 15–64, females 15–59)
5	percentage of population of pensionable age in private households (males 65 + , females 60 +)
6	percentage of households with no car
7	percentage of households with 2 or more cars
8	percentage of owner-occupier households
9	percentage of households renting local authority accommodation
10	percentage of households renting private unfurnished accommodation
11	percentage of households renting private furnished accommodation
12	percentage of households in non-permanent buildings
13	percentage of households in shared dwellings
14	percentage of households with more than one person per room
15	percentage of households with less than 0·5 persons per room
16	average number of rooms per dwelling
17	percentage of households lacking exclusive use of one or more basic amenities
18	percentage of all males present aged 15 or over who are economically active
19	percentage of all females present aged 15 or over who are economically active
20	percentage of all married females present (aged 15–39) who are economically active
21	percentage of all economically active males who are unemployed (seeking work)

Variable no.	*Variable description*
22	percentage of all economically active females who are unemployed (seeking work)
23	percentage of total population with higher education (Higher National Certificate or degree)
24	percentage of households with heads in SEGs 1, 2, 3, 4
25	percentage of households with heads in SEGs 13, 14
26	percentage of households with heads in SEGs 5, 6
27	percentage of households with heads in SEGs 8, 9, 12
28	percentage of households with heads in SEGs 7, 10, 11
29	percentage of households with heads in SEG 15
30	percentage of households with heads in SEG 16
31	percentage of domestic properties with rateable values of less than £30
32	percentage of domestic properties with rateable values greater than £100
33	postwar housing as a percentage of total housing stock
34	index of accessibility to service centres (as defined in Gordon and Whittaker, 1972)
35	percentage of population in private households who are married females aged 16–29
36	percentage of population in private households who are married females aged 30–44
37	percentage of population in private households who are married females aged 45–59

Notes:

(1) Socio-economic group (SEG) classification is as follows:

  1 employers and managers in central and local government, industry, commerce, and so on – large establishments
  2 employers and managers in industry, commerce, and so on – small establishments
  3 professional workers – self-employed
  4 professional workers – employees
  5 intermediate non-manual workers
  6 junior non-manual workers
  7 personal service workers
  8 foremen and supervisors – manual
  9 skilled manual workers
  10 semi-skilled manual workers
  11 unskilled manual workers
  12 own account workers (other than professional)
  13 farmers – employers and managers
  14 farmers – own account
  15 agricultural workers
  16 members of armed forces
  17 indefinite.

(2) The SEG base has been recalculated to omit group 17 (indefinite).
(3) In variables 24 to 30 heads of households include both economically active and retired persons.
(4) Variables 1 to 30 only were used in the cluster analysis reported in Chapter 4.

Variables used in the district correlation, regression and cluster analyses

Data from the 1971 Census were analysed for 178 enumeration districts in Cotswold District and 233 enumeration districts in South Oxfordshire District, excluding special enumeration districts, which cover such establishments as prisons and hospitals, and excluding enumeration districts with a minimum population of less than twenty-five persons. Where necessary specific variables were derived from the Small Area Statistics by computation. Further details are given in Dunn, Rawson and Rogers (1980a), appendix VI and a more comprehensive review of census variable definition can be found in Hakim (1976).

Variable no.	Variable description	Variable code name used in Figures 6.3 and 6.4
Population and household		
1	total number of private households	HHOLD
2	average number of persons per private household	AVPERS
3	percentage of population not in private households	
4	sex ratio (females per 100 males)	
5	percentage of population (in households) aged 0–14 years	YOUNGPOP
6	percentage of population of working age in private households (males 15–64, females 15–59)	
7	percentage of population of pensionable age in private households (males 65 + , females 60 +)	
8	married persons per 1,000 population aged 15–24 years	YOUNGWED
9	fertility ratio of married women (children 0–4 per 1,000 married women aged 15–44)	
10	percentage of households with no car	NOCAR
11	percentage of households with 2 or more cars	2CAR
12	percentage of owner-occupier households with no car	

Variable no.	Variable description	Variable code name used in Figures 6.3 and 6.4
13	percentage of households renting local authority accommodation with no car	NOCAR/LA
14	percentage of households renting private accommodation with no car	
15	percentage of one-person households	
16	percentage of households with six or more persons	6HHOLD
17	percentage of households with children	KIDS
18	percentage of households with one pensioner living alone	
19	one- or two-person households with one or two persons of pensionable age as a percentage of all private households	
20	single parent families with one or more dependent children as a percentage of all private households	

Housing

21	percentage of owner-occupier households	OWNOCC
22	percentage of households renting local authority accommodation	LARENT
23	percentage of households renting private unfurnished accommodation	RENTUNF
24	percentage of households renting private furnished accommodation	RENTFUR
25	percentage of vacant dwellings	VACANT
26	percentage of households in non-permanent buildings	
27	percentage of households in shared dwellings	
28	percentage of households with more than 1·5 persons per room	
29	percentage of households with more than one person per room	$>1\cdot0$ p.p.r.
30	percentage of households with less than 0·5 persons per room	$<0\cdot5$ p.p.r.
31	percentage of households in shared dwellings with over 1·5 persons per room	
32	percentage of owner-occupier households with more than one person per room	
33	percentage of households renting from a local authority with more than one person per room	
34	percentage of households renting private accommodation with more than one person per room	
35	average number of rooms per dwelling	
36	percentage of one-person households with one or two rooms	
37	percentage of one-person households with five or more rooms	

Variable no.	Variable description	Variable code name used in Figures 6.3 and 6.4
38	percentage of two-person households with five or more rooms	
39	owner-occupier households with one or two rooms as a percentage of all households with one or two rooms	
40	households renting local authority accommodation with one or two rooms as percentage of all households with one or two rooms	1/2RM/LA
41	households in privately rented accommodation with one or two rooms as a percentage of all households with one or two rooms	
42	owner-occupier households with seven or more rooms as percentage of all households with seven or more rooms	7RM/OO
43	households renting local authority accommodation with seven or more rooms as percentage of all households with seven or more rooms	7RM/LA
44	households in privately rented accommodation with seven or more rooms as percentage of all households with seven or more rooms	7RM/PR
45	percentage of households lacking exclusive use of one or more basic amenities	
46	percentage of households which share or lack bath	
47	percentage of households which share or lack hot water	
48	percentage of households which share or lack inside toilet	
49	percentage of owner-occupier households which share or lack bath	
50	percentage of households renting local authority accommodation which share or lack bath	
51	percentage of households in privately rented accommodation which share or lack bath	
52	percentage of owner-occupier households which share or lack hot water	
53	percentage of households renting local authority accommodation which share or lack hot water	
54	percentage of households in privately rented accommodation which share or lack hot water	
55	percentage of owner-occupier households which share or lack inside toilet	
56	percentage of households renting local authority accommodation which share or lack inside toilet	
57	percentage of households in privately rented accommodation which share or lack inside toilet	

Variable no.	Variable description	Variable code name used in Figures 6.3 and 6.4
Employment		
58	percentage of all males present aged 15 or over who are economically active	
59	percentage of all females present aged 15 or over who are economically active	WORK(F)
60	percentage of all married females present aged 15–59 who are economically active	
61	percentage of all economically active males who are unemployed but seeking work or sick	
62	percentage of all economically active females who are unemployed but seeking work or sick	
63	percentage of total population with higher education (Higher National Certificate or degree)	
64	percentage of households with head in SEGs 1, 2, 3, 4	
65	percentage of households with head in SEGs 13, 14	FARMER
66	percentage of households with head in SEGs 5, 6	
67	percentage of households with head in SEGs 8, 9, 12	SKILWORK
68	percentage of households with head in SEGs 7, 10, 11	MANWORK
69	percentage of households with head in SEG 15	AGRICWORK
70	percentage of households with head in SEG 16	FORCES
Migration		
71	percentage of population who are 5-year migrants within local authority area	
72	percentage of population who are 5-year migrants into local authority area	
73	percentage of population changing address within 5 years previous to census	
74	percentage of 5-year migrants into local authority area who are schoolchildren	
75	percentage of 5-year migrants into local authority area who are pensioners	

Notes:
(1) For variables 64 to 70 heads of households include economically active and retired persons.
(2) Socio-economic group (SEG) base was recalculated to omit group 17 (occupation inadequately described).
(3) SEG classification as in Appendix II.

Appendix IV

Structure plans

Thirty structure plans were consulted in connection with Chapter 10:

District or county	Date submitted
Approved plans	
Buckinghamshire	1977
Cheshire	1977
East Cleveland	1975
East Sussex	1975
Herefordshire	1974
Hertfordshire	1976
Isle of Wight	1976
Leicestershire	1974
Leicestershire (Rutland)	1977
Norfolk	1977
North East Lancashire	1978
Oxfordshire	1976
Peak District	1976
South Hampshire	1974
Staffordshire	1973
Suffolk	1977
Warwickshire	1973
West Berkshire	1977
Worcestershire	1973
Submitted plans	
Bedfordshire	1977
Central Berkshire	1978
Derbyshire	1977
East Berkshire	1978
Kent	1977
Mid Hampshire	1978
Northamptonshire	1977
North East Hampshire	1978
Salop	1978
Surrey	1978
West Sussex	1978

Index

For Product Safety Concerns and Information please contact our EU
representative GPSR@taylorandfrancis.com
Taylor & Francis Verlag GmbH, Kaufingerstraße 24, 80331 München, Germany

9 780367 678180